PHILOSOPHERS
BEHAVING BADLY

PHILOSOPHERS
BEHAVING BADLY

NIGEL RODGERS
AND
MEL THOMPSON

Peter Owen Publishers
London and Chester Springs

PETER OWEN PUBLISHERS
73 Kenway Road, London SW5 0RE

Peter Owen books are distributed in the USA by
Dufour Editions Inc., Chester Springs, PA 19425-0007

First published in Great Britain 2005 by
Peter Owen Publishers

ISBN 0 7206 1219 5

Printed and bound in Spain by Graficás Diaz Tuduri

CONTENTS

A *Cautionary Note* . . . 7

Introduction 9

1. Jean-Jacques Rousseau: The Philosopher as Victim 15

2. Arthur Schopenhauer: The Rebarbative Bodhisattva 41

3. Friedrich Nietzsche: A Sickly *Übermensch* 63

 Feature: Nietzsche and Nazism 91

4. Bertrand Russell: The Mathematics of Human Behaviour 93

5. Ludwig Wittgenstein: Anger and Asceticism 125

6. Martin Heidegger: Magician, Predator, Peasant and Nazi 151

 Feature: The Héloïse Complex 179

7. Jean-Paul Sartre: Intellectual Tyranny, Charm and Bad Faith 181

 Feature: Women Philosophers Behaving Badly 203

8. Michel Foucault: Madness, Sex and Punishment 205

 Feature: Demetrius, Philosopher King of Athens 225

Postscript 227

Further Reading 229

Index 235

A CAUTIONARY NOTE...

The authors wish to assure the reader that they have used their best endeavours to be scrupulously and equally unfair to all the philosophers included and highly selective in the material that they have sought to examine. Neither should the fact that a philosopher has not been mentioned in this volume be taken to imply that he or she may be considered to be of good character.

Further we have resisted the temptation to distinguish carefully between bad behaviour, foolishness and plain moral turpitude. Such distinctions are relevant only to the moralistic evaluation of behaviour, whereas our intention is merely to introduce the follies of the wise, thereby presenting them anew from the embarrassment of sanctification.

However, in doing so, we recognize that integrity is frequently preserved as a key feature of the morally used life. Hence it has been necessary to modulate in order to both the life and principle contributions to thought of each of the metaphysicians whose follies here we examine, since we consider the wiser form of behaviour to be that which goes counter to those things that one professes to be just and true. Thus we present an introduction to eight thinkers of the modern period, with their thought set in the context of their lives. Modern is the term generally taken to refer to philosophy produced since the time of Kant (1724-1804). There were, of course, many ancient iniquities and medieval misdemeanours, but these are beyond the scope of our present enquiry.

A CAUTIONARY NOTE . . .

The authors wish to assure the reader that they have used their best endeavours to be scrupulously and equally unfair to all the philosophers included and highly selective in the material that they have sought to examine. Neither should the fact that a philosopher has not been mentioned in this volume be taken to imply that he or she may be considered to be of good character.

Further, we have resisted the temptation to distinguish carefully between bad behaviour, foolishness and plain social ineptitude. Such distinctions are relevant only to the moralistic evaluation of behaviour, whereas our intention is merely to introduce the follies of the wise, thereby preserving their memory from the embarrassment of sanctification.

However, in doing so, we recognize that integrity is frequently presented as a key feature of the morally good life. Hence it has been necessary to include an outline of both the life and principle contributions to thought of each of the philosophers whose behaviour we examine, since we consider the worst form of behaviour to be that which goes counter to those things that one professes to be just and true. Thus we present an introduction to eight thinkers of the modern period, with their thought set in the context of their lives. Modern is the term generally taken to refer to philosophy produced since the time of René Descartes. There were, of course, many ancient iniquities and medieval misdemeanours, but these are beyond the scope of our present enquiry.

INTRODUCTION

INTRODUCTION

*Every great philosophy is the confession of its founder, a kind of secret
and unacknowledged personal memoir.* — Friedrich Nietzsche
Why does there exist something rather... — Martin Heidegger

For 2,500 years philosophers have faced the recurrent question: what
relevance does their reasoned thinking have to life outside the lecture
hall? Socrates — who might thereby realistically be considered the founder
of Western philosophy — claimed that true intellectuality consisted in
the act of moral living, and spent his life following this precept. In
Meno, to cite one example, Socrates is seen trying to educate the boys,
and accelerate their logical faculty in a more rigorous example. The
Athenians finally tired of his constant questioning and forced him to an
untimely death in 399 B.C.

Spurned by Socrates, but prolonged by Plato, permeated into
posterity, Plato's idealism was to be closely followed by Aristotle —
who later characterized as pure reason to the wiser rational mind ...
[remaining text too faint / reversed to read reliably]

INTRODUCTION

'Every great philosophy is the confession of its founder, a kind of secret
and involuntary set of personal memoirs.' – Friedrich Nietzsche
'Who thinks greatly must err greatly.' – Martin Heidegger

For 2,500 years philosophers have faced the recurrent question: what
relevance does their reasoned thinking have to life outside the lecture
hall? Socrates – who taught Plato, traditionally considered the great-
est Western philosopher – claimed that the intellectually 'unexam-
ined life is not worth living' and spent his life roaming the streets of
Athens trying to persuade fellow Athenians to examine their lives
and so change them. But his is hardly an encouraging example. The
Athenians finally tired of his constant questioning and voted to put
him to death in 399 BC.

Scarred by Socrates' fate, philosophers, led by Plato, retreated into
academe – Plato founded the very first academy deliberately *outside*
the city – determined to have nothing to do with contemporary
politics. In *The Republic*, his blueprint for the good society, Plato
argued that *only* philosophers were really fit to rule, since they alone
were fully rational, capable of repressing their baser passions and per-
ceiving the true good. *The Republic* was intended as an ideal, not to
be realized on earth, but Plato could not resist returning to politics.
He made no fewer than three visits to the court of the tyrant Dionysius
of Syracuse in Sicily, hoping to awaken the spark of philosophy in
Dionysius' son, Dionysius II. The results were disastrous. The
younger Dionysius became simply a tyrant with philosophical pre-
tensions and lost his throne, partly because he could not control his
sexual appetites. (His father had perceptively warned him off other
men's wives – in vain.) Plato barely escaped with his life, while

Syracuse itself was engulfed in recurrent civil war. After that, most philosophers kept clear of politics for a long time – such farcical exceptions as Demetrius of Phalerum, briefly dictator of Athens, only reinforcing the point that philosophy and politics almost never mix.

Philosophers are not and have never claimed to be sages or saints, leading lives of impeccable virtue. Their arguments are intellectual and their individual foibles do not automatically invalidate their conclusions. But if philosophers are not priests neither are they artists of any type who can claim a complete dissociation between their lives and their work – and such a claim by any philosopher may be disputed. Artists, musicians and poets can behave outrageously badly and still be accepted as great poets, musicians, painters, etc. – indeed, bad behaviour often enhances their posthumous reputations. Lord Byron's fame would be far less if he had remained happily married, going to bed early and sober, instead of leading the picaresque life he did. If Picasso had remained faithful to his first wife, his reputation and arguably his art could have suffered. As for Wagner . . . Wagner seduced friends' and benefactors' wives, sponging off anyone who would support him in his life of sybaritic luxury. This included Jewish admirers, although he himself was a pioneer of rabid anti-Semitism. Yet he wrote music that makes him 'perhaps the greatest genius that has ever lived', according to W.H. Auden, music that has, despite all subsequent history, been loved and performed even by Jewish musicians from Mahler to Daniel Barenboim.

From philosophers, however, we expect, not unreasonably, nobler, wiser behaviour, demonstrating at least some attempt to live up to their ideals. The word philosopher means lover of wisdom, which suggests high-browed, disinterested pursuit of virtue or truth, no matter how defined. Many have lived up to this ideal. In Ancient Greece, Zeno of Citium, the first Stoic, and Epicurus, founder of Epicureanism, were poles apart intellectually but lived lives of similarly resounding virtue. Spinoza in seventeenth-century Holland and Kant in eighteenth-century Germany were both notably upright, private men. If Spinoza

was something of a hermit, solitude was effectively forced upon him by his daringly heretical views that outraged all shades of contemporary opinion. Kant, living in an easier age, was a supremely social being, entertaining a small circle of friends and colleagues regularly. Both men wisely eschewed the temptations to enter public life. Although both were offered prestigious university posts, both preferred praise or criticism from a few peers and students to the flattery of the mighty – or, in today's terms, the adulation of the media.

But others – at times the most celebrated – have succumbed. Fame, sex and power – and sometimes all three, although money, refreshingly, has seldom figured – have lured them from their ivory towers to try to employ their intellectual brilliance in a world which has had little regard for anything academic. Sometimes they have behaved badly, sometimes just sadly, for philosophers, while godlike in the intellectual sphere, can be the sorriest children in the world of power and money. The saddest, or worst, case may be Martin Heidegger, who left his hermitage in the Black Forest in 1933 to become a notorious propagandist for the new Nazi regime. His philotyrannical ardour did him no good even with the Nazis, who, like most dictatorships, wanted acquiescent mediocrity not towering but eccentric genius. Heidegger, in fact, suffered professionally from his brief post as rector of Marburg University in 1933, but he never, in the thirty-one years that he lived after the fall of the Third Reich, acknowledged his fault. At the other political extreme, Jean-Paul Sartre, the existentialist guide to so many in the mid twentieth century, became for some years an apologist for Soviet Communism, long after the evils of the Gulag had been exposed.

Politics is not the only area of life often incompatible with philosophy. Bertrand Russell, after completing his monumental *Principia Mathematica* in collaboration with Alfred North Whitehead in 1913, felt entitled to pronounce authoritatively on all lesser human problems, especially marriage, bringing up children and sexual relations. He wrote copiously – an estimated 2,000 words a day – laying down the

law as interpreted by a progressive man of the early twentieth century. But his own marital life was anything but exemplary. Three acrimonious divorces had left broken hearts and households and affected some of his descendants so disastrously that their lives were literally wrecked. His wider philanderings earned him the nicknames the Philosophical Rake or Dirty Bertie. Even his political views could be erratic. Famous for leading the campaigns against nuclear weapons, and much earlier as a conscientious objector in the First World War, he is less well known for urging pre-emptive nuclear war against the Soviet Union in the 1940s, a time when the USSR did not have its own nuclear weapons.

Others, with no interest in politics or public life, have propounded beliefs that sound exhilaratingly convincing on paper, seemingly offering new visions of the world. Their half-mesmerized followers tend to revere them as infallible prophets or gurus. Ludwig Wittgenstein dominated philosophical life at Cambridge in the 1930s and 1940s with charismatic authority, his followers being so influenced by him that they even copied his style of dress. Wittgenstein's own life was deliberately austere. He rejected his immense inherited wealth, eschewing even the modest comforts of an academic for a life of quasi-monastic asceticism. Such an attitude is defensible – many mystics and saints have rejected personal ties and wealth to concentrate on their visions, and Wittgenstein, by temperament, clearly should be numbered among the great ascetics of history. But in a real monastic order, such self-flagellating exhibitionism is controlled and channelled *ad majorem gloriam Dei* – to the greater glory of God, not of the monk. For Wittgenstein – who once applied to enter a monastery but was rejected as unsuitable – such asceticism resulted in many ways in an arid and sterile personal life. The fanaticism, at times physical violence, with which he expounded his vastly subtle and profound thought sprang in part from his crippled inner life. Far from 'showing the fly the way out of the bottle', as he claimed in one of his incomparable metaphors, he wrecked the lives of many of his disciples,

surprisingly few of whom actually became philosophers after being browbeaten and bullied by their idol.

Philosophers prefer to ignore if possible – and to deplore when impossible – any connection at all being made between the life and the work. As long as philosophy concentrated on epistemological problems (concerning what we know and how we know it), logic and linguistics, it could remain safely academic. But, with the recent new focus on ethics, it has again been emerging from the cloister. At the same time books and television series are appearing that present philosophy in the form of self-help guides, almost as variants of the Pilates Technique or the Eat Yourself Thin Diet. But philosophy is not comparable with these, being an ambiguous, potentially perilous field for the unwary and not a form of chicken soup for the soul or mind.

Probably no philosopher is more perilous for the unwary than Friedrich Nietzsche. Certainly no philosopher today is more popular, even trendy. His reputation now eclipses that of Marx and all other thinkers as books about his life and work cascade from the presses. As much psychologist as philosopher, emphatically not a system builder but an aphorist, this intellectual tightrope walker (to borrow a favourite image) boasted of overturning the tables of the law. Above all, he insisted on being a *Ja-sagender*, saying yes to life, denying the life-deniers of not just the Judaeo-Christian tradition but of the Platonist, Buddhist and most other traditions. Often he did so in the most brutal way imaginable, praising despots like Cesare Borgia, who embodied his aristocratic, *übermenschlich* (superhuman) ideal. Nietzsche was deliberately outraging his ancestral Christianity, an attack he carried further in rubbishing Christianity's disastrously negative views on sex.

Nietzsche has been accused of many things, including being the 'godfather of Fascism', an accusation that intermittently resurfaces. Nietzsche can scarcely be accused of promiscuity, however, for his own sex life was almost non-existent. His one remotely serious affair,

13

with Lou Salomé – which got no further physically than a kiss on the cheek – ended in his humiliating rejection. If he had not very probably died of syphilis, he could have been presumed to have died a virgin.

'The greatest souls are capable of the greatest vices as well as the greatest virtues,' observed Descartes. Those seeking in philosophy a guide for the perplexed should be aware that while philosophy can enlighten it can also mislead and delude. Philosophers' own behaviour, sometimes bad, sometimes sad, occasionally downright mad, may not be exactly an 'involuntary set of personal memoirs' but it is seldom *entirely* unconnected with their thinking. At times their lives affect or shape their thoughts directly.

So we should look at how some of the greatest philosophers – and they *were* great philosophers – lived their own lives, and how their choices in life confirmed or negated their thinking, before taking their advice on how to lead our own.

1
JEAN-JACQUES ROUSSEAU (1712–78):
THE PHILOSOPHER AS VICTIM

'God made all things perfect, man meddles with them and they are ruined.'

– Jean-Jacques Rousseau, *Emile*

'Man was born free and everywhere he is in chains!' With this call for revolution – political, cultural and social – Rousseau became a patron saint both of the French and Romantic Revolutions. Revered by extreme Jacobins such as Robespierre for his rejection of a corrupt society and his concept of the General Will mystically manifesting itself in huge gatherings, Rousseau's influence since his death has been immense. For those who rejoice in radical dictatorships of the Left or Right, he is an indisputable hero; for others, be they liberal, conservative or merely sceptical, he is anathema. Even more significant, if sometimes less contentious, has been his insistence on the natural goodness of humanity before its corruption by civilization. This has had an overwhelming impact, especially on attitudes to children's education and upbringing, as well as on wider ideas of individual responsibility. Every teacher today who is exhorted to let children express themselves freely rather than try to transmit existing knowledge or ideas to them is experiencing indirectly the lasting impact of Rousseau's thought. Similarly, every criminal who pleads that he is the victim of society, rather than responsible for his own crime, is echoing unconsciously Rousseau's own views that an individual, with his *amour de soi* (self-love), is inherently virtuous and that it is only wrong environments that lead to wrong doing.

But Rousseau the man, the nature-loving revolutionary who rejected most of the eighteenth and earlier centuries' civilization and longed to return to a state of nature, led a life often far removed from

simple, heroic naturalness. There is no need to dig for the dirt in Rousseau's life, for he left much of it exposed in his *Confessions*, a self-justifying and self-pitying literary masterpiece, unprecedented in its apparent candour. It is less truthful than he claimed, however. For someone who outspokenly rejected the inequality of his age, Rousseau proved adept at living off the rich and powerful, although he repeatedly bit the aristocratic, often female, hands that fed and pampered him. Worse – for some things might be excused a man who started life with few advantages – the philosopher who preached the vital importance of good parenting showed himself callously ready to abandon all five of his children to an orphanage where, as was often the case then, most of them soon died. Even by eighteenth-century standards, this was outstandingly heartless, hypocritical behaviour.

Soon after Rousseau's death he became almost universally revered, even among aristocrats, less for his contributions to formal philosophy than for his hugely influential novels. In their breathless, often lurid pages he mingled philosophy, sensationalism and sentimentality in a newly 'romantic' way that the age adored. His fame as a political and social visionary continued to spread in the nineteenth century. An early prophet of the return to nature and the rejection of civilization's restraints and hypocrisies, Rousseau was a father of the Romantic Movement, still among the most influential artistic and intellectual movements today. Anyone moved to buy a bottle by a label saying 'Natural Mineral Water' is paying unwitting homage to Rousseau's belief that the natural is always preferable to the artificial – and also to his often muddled thinking, which can amount to little more than the higher sentimentality. (What might constitute *unnatural* water? a sceptic might ask.) But perhaps his greatest impact has been on the way we have come to canonize the plight of the totally innocent, if often surprisingly articulate, victim. This was a role Rousseau played superbly throughout his life. The revolution in sentiment that he thus engendered is still very much with us.

Jean-Jacques Rousseau was born on 28 June 1712 in the city state

of Geneva. Although tiny, with a population of less than 10,000, Geneva was an independent city state linked to the Swiss Confederation, very proud of its austerely republican Calvinist traditions, a pride Rousseau inherited. Although by the eighteenth century Geneva was actually ruled by a small clique of its richest citizens, it was still a relatively free city compared with its neighbours, the absolutist monarchies of France and Sardinia (Piedmont-Savoy). Rousseau always remained essentially an outsider in France, distrusting its large cities and cosmopolitan society, and sharing Plato's longing for near autarkical simplicity.

Rousseau's mother came from quite a smart family socially, but she died soon after his birth, and in his infancy he was cared for by an aunt. His father, a profligate watchmaker who supplemented his income with dancing lessons, fled the city rather than face the courts after a fight. He left his son, then aged ten, in the care of an uncle who handed him over to be educated by a local clergyman, Pastor Lambercier, and his sister. There, Rousseau discovered the pleasure of being spanked by Mlle Lambercier, an attractive thirty-year-old. He admitted that this experience shaped his sexual tastes all his life. 'Even after having attained marriageable age this odd taste still continued and drove me nearly to depravity and madness . . . To fall at the feet of an imperious mistress, obey her mandates or implore pardon, were for me the most exquisite enjoyments, and the more my blood was inflamed by the efforts of a lively imagination the more I acquired the appearance of a whining lover,' he later confessed.

Rousseau's lifelong masochism seems to have found its outlet almost exclusively in masturbatory fantasies. It probably expressed an infantile craving for total attention and reassurance, originating in his loveless childhood. As he admitted, 'Although born a man in some respects, I long remained and still am a child in many others.' While he always enjoyed having imperious, preferably aristocratic, women boss him around, he was never a practising flagellant and certainly no rival to the Marquis de Sade, whose views on humanity's

17

real nature – which Sade thought inherently depraved and vicious – would later invert and subvert his. Outside the bedroom, however, Rousseau always believed that women should be kept firmly subordinate, as they had been in Ancient Rome or Greece. One accusation he never had to face was that of treating women as political or social equals.

Rousseau had read about the ancient Romans and Greeks as a child in Plutarch's *Parallel Lives*, one of the books that had belonged to his mother. 'I was a Roman at the age of twelve,' he boasted, although it was Sparta, that primitive and archetypal 'closed society', that he later revered. His period of studies ended when he was apprenticed to an engraver at the age of thirteen. Such a plebeian life lacked appeal, and after three years he fled Geneva. According to his *Confessions*, his exile began more or less by chance. One Sunday, returning late after a day spent rambling in the country, he found the city gates closed to him, so he simply wandered off. Just across the Genevan frontier lay the more glamorous Catholic monarchy of Piedmont. Rousseau painlessly converted to Catholicism, hoping to obtain a post with the Savoyard nobility. He found instead the support of Madame de Warens, an aristocratic former Swiss Protestant herself, who made a point of 'encouraging' young male converts. In Turin, the Piedmontese capital, Rousseau worked as a lackey in a nobleman's household. There he stole a pink silk ribbon, a trifling crime but one which he blamed on Marion, another servant. She steadfastly denied it and appealed to his better nature – in vain, as he stuck to his accusation. Finally, their baffled employer dismissed them both. 'Never was wickedness further from my thoughts than in that cruel moment when I accused the unhappy girl,' Rousseau later declared, going on to say that his friendship with her was the cause of the trouble, for he simply blamed the first person who came into his mind to escape embarrassment. Such pilferings, and his accompanying refusal to acknowledge, let alone express regret for, even indisputable faults, persisted throughout his life.

Rousseau then toyed with the idea of becoming a priest, briefly entering a seminary before leaving to enrol in a choir school, something far closer to his real gifts. Other odd jobs included becoming the secretary of a bogus archimandrite who claimed to be collecting alms to restore the Holy Sepulchre in Jerusalem; later he became the gigolo of a rich lady by posing as a Scottish Jacobite noble. But it was at Madame de Warens' house among the mountains at Chambéry, which he made his home, that he enjoyed the happiest moments of his life with the woman he always called *maman*. Eventually, when he reached twenty-one, she let him into her bed, following which he lived contentedly with this rather plump mother-substitute, avidly reading and further developing his genuine musical talents when not servicing his patroness. Rousseau was even willing to share Madame de Warens' favours with her elderly odd-jobman, contentedly inheriting his rival's clothes after he died.

The end of this extended idyll came in 1742, when the thirty-year-old Rousseau finally set off for Paris to make his name. A year later, thanks to another aristocratic lady, he found himself in Venice as secretary to the French Ambassador, a drunk who neglected to pay Rousseau his salary but who *did* supply him with high-class prostitutes, who floated into his life in gondolas. Venice was then famed for its courtesans and general *douceur de vie*, but neither for long captivated Rousseau, who was mainly terrified of catching syphilis. One of the whores, Zulietta, caused him to burst into tears when she revealed that she had only one nipple. Annoyed, she replied, oddly perceptively, 'Gianni, stop chasing women and go and study maths instead!'

Rousseau finally decided to demand his back salary from the government in Paris in 1744. He hoped also to get an opera he had written produced there and to publish a novel form of musical annotation, using numbers to mark notes, which he had just invented. He had no success with any of these projects – although much later he finally got some of his salary – which soured his feelings towards France and especially towards Paris. But, in the capital in 1745, he

met Thérèse Levasseur, the one woman with whom he established a long-lasting, if intermittent, relationship. Then a girl of eighteen working in his hotel laundry, Thérèse seems to have been unusually lacking in almost all obvious charms. Undeniably ugly – according to extant portraits – she was also hopelessly illiterate, unable even to tell the time by the clock, ill-mannered and stupid, except when it came to fleecing Rousseau of whatever money he had, in which she was abetted by her equally repellent, if somewhat brighter, mother.

What attracted Rousseau to her – apart from her reputed skills as a cook – is hard to say. Possibly her very charmlessness appealed to his masochistic psyche, although there is no evidence to suggest that she ever spanked him. Far more probably she assuaged his deep-rooted sense of social inferiority. No matter what happened to him in the wider world, he could always rely on feeling superior to Thérèse, whom he so consistently treated as his servant that his guests often regarded her as one – but a servant whom he repeatedly ridiculed in company. Although they never were married legally, they quickly had five children, all of whom Rousseau insisted on abandoning. 'From these liaisons were born five children, all of whom were placed in the Foundling Hospital with so little thought of their later identification that I did not even keep a record of their dates of birth,' he admitted in a letter years later. He justified his actions by claiming that, as he could not give them the paternal care they deserved, they were better off elsewhere. But he also turned down the offer of foster homes from rich admirers such as Madame d'Epinay and the Duchess of Luxembourg, declaring with true paranoia, 'I am sure they [his children] would have been brought up to hate, perhaps to betray, their parents.'

Over the next few years Rousseau earned a meagre living copying music and writing articles on music and political economy (both subjects in which he was self-taught) for the new *Encyclopédie*. This great project was edited by Denis Diderot, like Rousseau a provincial outsider making his way in Paris. Originally no more than a translation

of *Ephraim Chambers' Cyclopedia*, the *Encyclopédie* grew into one of the intellectual landmarks of the eighteenth century, propagating in its thirty-four volumes the Enlightenment's chief ideas about the sciences, society, politics, indeed all human life. Its radicalism finally made it so unpopular with the French government that it was banned, some later volumes being printed secretly. Contributors faced intermittent threats of imprisonment – Diderot himself was locked up in 1749 for attacking traditional arguments for the existence of God – although these threats were tempered by secret sympathizers within the heart of the *ancien régime*. Through Diderot Rousseau came to know other *philosophes* – a term implying not formal philosophers but politically active intellectuals – such as Voltaire and Jean d'Alembert, also contributors to the *Encyclopédie*. But Rousseau was seldom fully at ease in such circles. He never shared their central belief that humanity was on the broad road to perfectibility if only ancient superstitions and restraints – especially religious and political ones – were abolished in a spirit of rational enquiry. He also was aware of his intellectual limits in such highbrow circles, although he could charm and impress the most sophisticated audiences when he wished.

Fame came unexpectedly in 1750. Rousseau had entered a competition set by the Academy at Dijon that asked, 'Has the restoration of the arts and sciences had a purifying effect upon morals?' The expected answer was 'Yes', perhaps with qualifications. With audacious, shocking originality, Rousseau said 'No!' His *Discourse on the Sciences and Arts: The First Discourse* (*Discourse sur les sciences et les arts*) won the first prize, as much for its beautiful prose – Rousseau was a superb writer – as for its iconoclastic content. Rousseau maintained that the advance of civilization had ruined original human virtue. By creating artificial wants (such as printing, sugar, furniture), 'progress' had enslaved, not liberated, humanity. Far from endorsing the Enlightenment's core belief in reason, he saw cultural development destroying our primal innocence. Rousseau's arguments for natural innocence were not wholly original. Others, notably Diderot, had

21

already suggested that, in a truly natural state, men would feel unforced love for their neighbours. They had attacked traditional Christianity, where humanity is regarded as tainted by original sin and redeemable only through God's grace. In contrast, the *philosophes* saw human beings as essentially good and potentially free. Modern man's *amour propre* – Rousseau's term for self-love, pride or self-promotion encouraged by a society where each competes with the other, judging others by social position and wealth rather than by their inherent worth – was contrasted with *amour de soi* (care for oneself), the basic and natural sense of self-preservation that can go with *pitié* or compassion for others. Civilization's cardinal fault, for Rousseau, was that it had transformed innocent, self-limiting *amour de soi* into viciously competitive and socially divisive *amour propre*.

Rousseau passionately shared, and helped to propagate, the eighteenth century's growing admiration for the Noble Savage, that paragon of primal virtue to be found somewhere far removed in space and time from the corrupt present. 'I dare not speak of those happy nations who do not even know the names of many vices which we find difficult to repress: the savages of America, whose simple, natural government Montaigne preferred . . . not only to the laws of Plato but to the most perfect vision of government philosophy can ever suggest!' he wrote in an ecstatic footnote in the *Discourse*. But, with vestigial realism, he never suggested that eighteenth-century Europeans should return *en masse* to the virgin forest. Instead, he looked back to the city states of the ancient world, especially to Sparta, that 'republic of demi-gods rather than of men . . . the eternal proof of the vanity of science while the vices, under the guise of the fine arts, were being introduced to Athens'. Rousseau also praised early Rome, before its corruption by the 'seductive and subtle Greeks'. The heroic republics that Rousseau held up for approbation would later inspire the French Revolution.

Despite his professed admiration for such ascetic republics, Rousseau was still hoping for official recognition and a post at the

notoriously luxurious, indeed debauched, rococo court of Louis XV, then ruled by Madame de Pompadour, that most glamorous and intelligent of royal mistresses. In 1752 Rousseau's opera *The Village Soothsayer* (*Le Devin du village*) was performed with vast success at Fontainebleau in front of the king. At the time the so called Querelle des Bouffons, a war of musical ideas, was raging between the advocates of traditional stately French opera, led by the elderly Jean-Philippe Rameau, and those of Italian opera, who urged a more naturalistic, livelier approach. Rousseau sided with the Italians, savagely attacking Rameau in an open letter in 1753. Louis XV, although he could not disown the French national school, personally preferred Rousseau's Italian style and offered him a pension. For some reason Rousseau, out of pride or social awkwardness, declined to turn up and accept it. He later said it was not the royal presence but the haughty footmen who put him off, but he suffered from recurrent bladder problems, which meant he had to hurry to the lavatory every half-hour – not ideal for a courtier in Europe's grandest palaces. Although he abandoned all attempts to become a court composer, Christoph Gluck, the great eighteenth-century opera reformer, later said, 'All I have tried to accomplish . . . is the kind of work Rousseau would have produced if he had not forsaken composition to write books.'

Rousseau's career as a revolutionary intellectual was, in contrast, taking off in the country that has always revered intellectuals. While he declared that he preferred to live off what he made by his writings to being maintained in courtly luxury, his one play (that he also turned into an opera), *Narcisse* – which contained further attacks on the arts, sciences and literature, although he himself was currently contributing to all three – proved a costly flop. He made little money copying sheet music at ten sous a sheet or writing on music for the *Encyclopédie*. In practice he soon found wealthy patrons among the French *grande bourgeoisie* and nobility. As he always considered gratitude as being incompatible with real friendship, he took care never to show any. His views on friendship were also unusual, for he regarded

each relationship solely in terms of the pleasant sensations it gave him, ignoring any claims of mutual obligation that might be expected from him. If he spurned overt support – except for free accommodation – Thérèse happily pocketed the money that admirers often gave them secretly. While Rousseau, Thérèse and her mother shared a tiny garret flat, Rousseau revelled in being lionized in the Paris salons, then among the most exciting centres of literary, artistic and scientific discussion in the world.

In 1755 Rousseau published a long article, A Discourse on Political Economy (Le Citoyen: ou Discours sur l'économie politique), in the Encyclopédie, as well as his Discourse on Inequality, called the Second Discourse (Discours sur l'origine et les fondemontals de l'inégalité parmi les hommes), another attempt to win a prize. In this he envisaged the first humans leading solitary lives – although not ones that were, in the words of the seventeenth-century English philosopher Thomas Hobbes, 'solitary, poor, nasty, brutish and short'. Instead Rousseau implausibly argued that early humans were originally asocial beings, men and women meeting casually in the woods to mate, with women then giving birth and looking after their children alone. As he reviewed human progress from its earliest egalitarian innocence to his own extremely unequal age, he moderated his earlier primitivist arguments a little, conceding that the arts and sciences need not always corrupt but do so now because of the age's depraved inequality. This itself stemmed from the invention of private property. 'The first man who enclosed a piece of land and said to himself, This is mine, was the real founder of civil society. What crimes, wars, murders, miseries and horrors would humanity have been spared if someone had pulled up the stakes, filled in the ditch and cried out, Do not listen to this impostor!' he wrote in terrible indictment.

Rousseau also regarded the invention of farming and metalworking as damnable. And he had no time for reason, either. 'Reason engenders egocentrism . . . Reason is what turns man in upon himself. Reason is what separates him from all that troubles and afflicts

him,' he proclaimed. He ended the *Second Discourse* on a note of high egalitarian rhetoric, 'As there is hardly any inequality in nature, all the now prevalent inequality derives from the advance of the human mind, finally growing permanent and legitimate by establishing property and laws . . . Moral inequality, authorized by positive right alone, clashes with natural justice . . . The privileged few gorge themselves with luxuries while the starving multitudes want the bare necessities of life.' He now began to see himself as embodying all these primeval virtues, as he, uniquely among human beings, had shed all the vices of society to regain his 'natural goodness'.

This *Second Discourse*, far more shocking than the rather Arcadian first, won no prizes, to his disappointment. He seems to have been expecting still to be fed by the hands he had bitten, for the Dijon Academy was part of the Establishment. He sent a copy of the *Discourse* to Voltaire, hoping for his support, but the latter replied, with typically scathing wit, 'I have received your new book against the human race and thank you for it. Never was so much effort deployed in an effort to make us stupid. One longs on reading your book to walk on all fours. But as I lost that habit more than sixty years ago, I fear that it is impossible to resume it.'

This marked the beginning of what became, after further exchanges of icy courtesies, a notorious enmity, cemented when Rousseau read Voltaire's reactions to the great Lisbon earthquake of 1755. It had struck on a Sunday morning, killing tens of thousands of worshippers assembled in churches around the city. For Voltaire, this particular aspect of a natural catastrophe suggested there was no benign god or providence behind the universe. Although most *philosophes* were nominally Catholics, in practice they were usually Deists, believing in a creator god detached from, but overseeing, his creation, as a watchmaker keeps an eye on his ticking watches. Rousseau rejected such a superficial, if optimistic, view. Far more abhorrent to him, however, was Voltaire's pessimism. 'Voltaire, in pretending always to believe in God, never really believed in anybody

25

but the devil, since his pretended God is a malevolent being who, according to him, finds all his delight in doing harm,' he wrote, adding that if the people of Lisbon had remained properly dispersed in the fields and woods far fewer would have died from the earth-quake – a novel argument for the country life. (Voltaire's indirect response to this was *Candide*, his famous novel.) So started the feud between the sceptical, cynical Voltaire, with his belief in civilization and reason, and Rousseau, high priest of the new cult of unrestrained feeling and unspoilt nature.

Rousseau always considered himself a Christian, although his was a personalized, pick-and-mix version of Christianity, freed from all ethical considerations. It centred on seeing Christ as an early victim, in fact a forerunner of himself. Rejecting original sin, Rousseau had no need of redemption, viewing Christ's sacrifice on the cross as an irrel-evance. Understandably, he was never fussy about denominations. Wanting to return to his native city as a celebrity, he had to recon-vert to Calvinism to reclaim his citizenship. This he duly did in 1754, but he did not find Geneva sympathetic. His new enemy, Voltaire, who had just settled there in illustrious exile from persecution in France, was giving grand parties at which solid Genevan burghers rubbed shoulders with dissolute French nobles, to mutual amazement.

Voltaire also tried to start a theatre in Geneva to perform his own plays, but theatre was banned in the puritanical republic. D'Alembert supported Voltaire in an article in the *Encylopédie*. Rousseau, now conveniently forgetting his own earlier dramatic efforts, vociferously supported the ban, mainly out of enmity of Voltaire. He attacked all theatre for its inherent frivolity, licentiousness and especially the shocking way it gave women 'the same power over their audiences as they have over their lovers', leading to universal moral corruption. 'In general women like and appreciate no art and have no genius,' he declared. By contrast, the ever-sage Ancient Greeks and Romans had barred women from performing in theatres. (Rousseau was not com-pletely starry-eyed about the ancient world, however, admitting that

its leisured classes had depended heavily on slaves, something then often overlooked.)

To ingratiate himself further with his native city, Rousseau had dedicated the *Discourse on Inequality* to it, praising Geneva as a model of a 'well-tempered democracy'. This proved a mistake. The city fathers were not remotely egalitarian and gave the book such a chilly reception that the author grew annoyed. Instead of returning permanently to Geneva, in 1756 Rousseau moved to near Montmorency, a mere twelve miles outside Paris – although, as the roads were abominably muddy, it seemed much further for visitors. Here, as the pampered if touchy guest of Madame d'Epinay, the cultured wife of the Receiver General, he was given use of the Hermitage. This was a spacious, recently renovated house of some size and comfort – it even had a rudimentary form of central heating – within the vast Epinay estate, where Rousseau settled down with his two *gouvernantes* (housekeepers), Thérèse and her mother, now aged eighty, who cadged money off Madame d'Epinay. Madame d'Epinay, however, was strictly forbidden to call on her illustrious guest without a specific invitation. In the following years of rural retreat Rousseau produced his greatest works.

The first was a romantic, indeed sentimentally melodramatic, novel *Julie: ou la nouvelle Héloïse* (the title intentionally recalls Abelard and Héloïse) that he began writing that summer, reading out sections to admiring friends in the forests near by. In it, virtuous, idealistic but aristocratic young Julie, brought up (inevitably) among the Swiss lakes and mountains, falls in love with her tutor, young, idealistic, virtuous but bourgeois Saint-Preux. 'Heaven has made us for each other!' exclaims Julie. 'Never was there such a perfect union. Our souls, too closely intermingled, can be no longer separated.' Saint-Preux finally seduces an ecstatically willing Julie. But her father, snobbish Baron d'Etange, forbids her to marry a commoner, insisting she marry atheistic, cynical but aristocratic Wolmar instead. Paradoxically, Julie ends up obeying her father and social conventions by marrying

Wolmar, despite her real love for Saint-Preux, the admirable man later joining the Wolmar household to tutor Julie's sons. This, as some readers commented, was hypocritical or dishonest behaviour, with Julie abandoning the man she truly loved for a richer rival. But the whole book makes little sense, incongruously mingling, in Rousseau's words, 'voluptuous imaginings' with 'the gentle colours of innocence'. Julie's vicissitudes (pregnancy, miscarriage), melodramatically described, mingle with lyrical descriptions of Alpine scenery and general philosophical reflections to make the book something more – or less – than a true novel.

Although *La Nouvelle Héloïse* now seems ludicrously mawkish, it became an international bestseller on its eventual publication in 1761. It won Rousseau international fame – although at first he claimed only to be its editor – and changed lives and fashions across Europe. Julie herself was hailed as an ideal woman and role model, quivering with the truest, unfettered passions. Rousseau, perhaps belatedly half realizing what he had written, later appended a preface saying it should not be read by the young and innocent, which, of course, attracted precisely such readers.

Nature had copied art before the publication of *La Nouvelle Héloïse*. In 1757 Rousseau fell hopelessly in love with the pretty and amiable Countess Sophie d'Houdetot, nineteen years his junior. She loathed her husband but already had a full-time lover, the Marquis de Saint-Lambert. She first won the philosopher's heart by calling on him wearing riding breeches and carrying a whip, which obviously appealed to him. If pleased by Rousseau's ardent attentions – and for once he was desperately in love – she seemingly felt more solicitude for this often ill, much older man than desire, at least at first. 'Immortal memory of innocence and bliss! In that grove, sitting on a grassy bank beneath an acacia tree in full blossom, I found words to match my heart's emotions. It was the first and only time in my life . . . What intoxicating tears I shed at her feet . . . I sighed. I kissed her. What a kiss – but that was all,' he wrote in his *Confessions* with his usual scant

regard for truth. At the time they made no secret of their liaison, walking around together arm in arm, even under Madame d'Epinay's window. Quite how much sex they had is questionable, for he describes himself arriving at their meetings 'weak, exhausted and scarcely able to stand up', indicating that he masturbated *en route* to their rendezvous, as was still his habit.

Rousseau communicated with Sophie via letters carried by the safely illiterate Thérèse, but one day Madame d'Epinay intercepted and read them. Rousseau was deceiving not just Thérèse, still his long-term partner, but his hostess, who herself had romantic feelings for him, with exactly the duplicity that he had openly attacked in aristocratic society. Further, in his *Moral Letters* (*Lettres Morales*) of 1757, he preached the importance of marital fidelity, so hoping to weaken Saint-Lambert's hold over Sophie and advance his own cause. Alas, when his rival returned gravely ill from the wars, Sophie turned all her attentions to him, leaving Rousseau out in the cold – and also out of favour with Madame d'Epinay. He then lost the friendship of Diderot, who considered his overall behaviour to his hostess unforgivable. However, Rousseau soon found other rich patrons, moving only a few miles to a cottage offered him by the Duke of Luxembourg. The Duke and Duchess soon became such good friends of the avowedly egalitarian philosopher that Rousseau had special rooms reserved for him in the Hôtel Luxembourg, their great house in Paris. When not hobnobbing with the nobility, Rousseau was absorbed in writing two major but dissimilar works, *Emile: Concerning Education* (*Emile: ou de l'éducation*) and *The Social Contract* (*Du contrat social*).

Emile, while supposedly a novel, is really about education. The young Emile is brought up in rustic isolation far from any city or even other children, with an omniscient tutor (Rousseau in thin disguise) to educate and look after him. His interests are observed as he develops; his practical skills, such as woodworking, are encouraged; books are long forbidden him (apart from *Robinson Crusoe*, that bible of

eighteenth-century primitivists); and he is only belatedly introduced to intellectual studies, the very last of which is religious philosophy. This inverted the age's normal educational process, in which children had the catechism, Bible and, if male, mathematics, Greek and Latin beaten into them at an early age. Emile escapes corporal punishment, but some of the 'instructive' humiliations the tutor inflicts on him are hardly less sadistic. The book aims to show how, kept free of society's corruption, human beings are both innocent and wise. It starts with the ringing declaration, 'God made all things perfect, man meddles with them and they are ruined.' However, since even Emile must ultimately deal with society, he is gradually introduced to it.

Emile is anathema to feminists, for at the appropriate age (twenty) Emile is allowed to meet his preselected mate, sweet young Sophie – a resonant name for the author, of course, but in the book she becomes just another of Rousseau's fantasy women. She, too, has been prepared for this moment, if in a very different way. While Emile's desires and impulses have seldom been thwarted, merely diverted, Sophie has had all her desires restricted. Such systematic, typically conservative constraint was, in Rousseau's view, essential to educating girls so that they would come to obey, care for and support their men. He considered abstract speculative thinking beyond the grasp of any woman – not an original view among Western philosophers. By contrast, Emile's radical educational views have proved among the most influential of Rousseau's writings. Few primary schools today do not in some way bear witness to his beliefs in letting children develop according to their own nature.

Emile also contains the famous, if dramatically irrelevant, passage known as 'The Creed of a Savoyard Priest'. In it Rousseau propounded his own view on the Supreme Being, as he often called God, rejecting all religious revelation in favour of a sublime contemplation of nature, in which the divinity becomes manifest. 'I immerse all faculties in God's divine essence . . . but I do not pray to him. What should I ask of him? To alter the course of nature and do miracles for

my sake? . . . Neither do I pray to God for the power to do right, for why should I ask for what he has given me already? . . . Men's revelations only degrade God by giving him human passions . . . To the ineffable mysteries surrounding God, men add absurd contradictions, and instead of bringing peace on earth they make men proud, intolerant and cruel.' Rousseau went on to describe Jesus as the wisest and most lovable of mortals, but Christians do not regard Jesus as mortal. Such a 'natural religion' – essentially pantheistic but appealing solely to the heart not the head, unlike Spinoza's – rejected Protestant and Catholic Churches alike, which landed its author in grave trouble.

The Social Contract, Rousseau's most serious attempt at political philosophy, was written at the same time. Starting with its famous trumpet call – 'Man is born free but is everywhere in chains. One man thinks himself the master of the others but remains more of a slave than they are' – it continues in pursuit of what have turned out to be incompatible goals: liberty, equality, fraternity. The idea of a social contract was not in itself original. (Seventeenth-century thinkers had elaborated on various theories about social contract: Hobbes, taking a typically dark view of the human condition, saw men in desperation forming covenants or contracts to save themselves from each other; while John Locke, more optimistically, saw humanity coming together voluntarily. All such theories derived from God's Covenant with the Hebrews, as described in the Old Testament, which was well known to Bible-reading Protestants such as the Pilgrim Fathers – who had drawn up their own contract on the *Mayflower* – and to Genevan Calvinists.) Rousseau, now moderating earlier beliefs in noble savagery, accepted that humanity had reached a point where it could no longer live according to nature. Instead, everyone should trade in their natural freedom for a superior republican freedom, making 'a total alienation of himself and all his rights to the whole community'. Rousseau envisaged that a society developing from this Social Contract would promote 'true laws' – as opposed to the false actual laws of the eighteenth century – which all must then obey.

31

While rejecting current absolute monarchies and the English parliamentary system – he said the English people enjoyed freedom only on election days – Rousseau did not advocate full democracy, even in small states like Geneva. 'If there were a nation of gods, it would govern itself democratically. A government so perfect is not suited to men,' he said, ignoring the example of classical Athens. When he proposed that (male) citizens could only vote on laws put to them by the executive, Rousseau was thinking again of Ancient Sparta, both his and Plato's ideal city, where an elective aristocracy, composed of paragons of rectitude and virtue, governed the imperfect masses. In the Spartan assembly ordinary Spartans could simply shout assent or dissent to proposals brought before them, those who shouted loudest winning the vote. This version of direct, if much restricted, democracy struck Rousseau as best, but he could be flexible. For a state as large as France he was even prepared to consider a monarchy of some sort. It would not, however, be a hereditary monarchy like the Bourbons (and all other kingdoms in eighteenth-century Europe) but one in which the sovereignty of the people was incarnated in an ideal ruler.

By accepting the Social Contract, which is renewed each day in some mystical manner, man loses his 'natural liberty and unqualified right to lay hands on all that tempts him', but in return he gains 'civil liberty and rightful ownership of what belongs to him'. He also acquires the moral liberty of self-mastery, for 'obedience to a law prescribed for oneself is liberty'. The obvious question arises: how can a group of disparate individuals have one will, obeying which makes all its members free? Rousseau answered by proposing an artificial *volonté générale*, or General Will, in which all would share and which would override any private will. The General Will would 'force men to be free' and, in consequence, virtuous. Legal penalties, including execution, would help individuals enslaved by their base passions to return to their original true virtue. This is among Rousseau's most controversial concepts and open to abuse, as the French Revolution demonstrated.

Many of Rousseau's phrases reappeared only marginally amended in *The Rights of Man* drawn up by French revolutionaries. Robespierre followed Rousseau in equating liberty with public virtue and believing that self-elected guardians of public virtue, such as the Committee of Public Safety, had a divine right to eliminate the unvirtuous with the aid of Docteur Guillotin's new machine.

When *Emile* and *The Social Contract* were published in 1762, thanks in part to the Luxembourgs' help, Rousseau suddenly faced persecution from the powerful vested interests, both religious and political, he had so blithely attacked. In both France and Geneva his books were banned, and a warrant was issued for his arrest. Rousseau had to flee France, finding refuge for a time in Moitiers in Neuchâtel, a semi-independent Swiss canton. His open letter to the Archbishop of Paris defending his religious views – asserting that he was 'a disciple of Jesus Christ, not of priests', rejecting the doctrine of original sin and reiterating his belief that man is naturally good – was also banned in Geneva. In disgust Rousseau renounced his Genevan citizenship for good. Even in Moitiers the villagers finally turned on him and stoned his house, in part because he looked bizarrely foreign, going around in an 'Armenian' gown of his own design that kept him warm and helped him deal with his worsening urinary problems. All this under-standably fuelled both his self-pity and paranoia – although Voltaire had endured worse persecution for his views, having been imprisoned twice.

Frederick II of Prussia, that model of enlightened despotism and religious scepticism (and erstwhile friend of Voltaire) who owned lands near by, had offered Rousseau asylum, but he finally accepted refuge in England in 1766 through the help of the Scottish philosopher David Hume. Hume, among the most magnanimous and affable of men, did everything he could to help the now increasingly paranoid Rousseau. Although theoretically risking arrest, Rousseau enjoyed a triumphant journey through France – *The Village Soothsayer* was performed in his honour in Strasbourg – and was lionized again in Paris. On arrival in

London, Rousseau, now a celebrity in Britain, too, received endless visitors and invitations. Soon Thérèse joined him – she had been seduced on her journey by the insatiable James Boswell, later Dr Johnson's biographer. Thanks to Hume, King George III offered the republican philosopher Rousseau a modest pension, which put him on the spot: he badly needed the money but did not want it known that he was being paid by a king. His prevarication lost him this royal stipend, but before then, again through Hume's good offices, he was offered Wootton, a magnificent country house in Derbyshire with a large estate. Its nominal rent (£30 per annum) included full board and a complement of servants.

Here Rousseau went for long walks 'botanizing' (plant collecting and nature worshipping), and the local gentry, including Erasmus Darwin (grandfather of Charles), paid him visits, intrigued by this curious foreigner. For a year Thérèse and he were happy at Wootton despite foul weather, and he began writing his *Confessions*. However, Thérèse managed to alienate all the servants there less by being his mistress – something Georgian England often accepted – than by her bad manners. Finally, the servants retaliated by putting cinders in Rousseau's soup – or so Rousseau said – and he abandoned Wootton, leaving only a long letter of accusation for his unfortunate host, listing all the horrors that he had endured as a guest.

Rousseau had earlier written an astonishingly hostile and remarkably long (7,500 words) letter to Hume, accusing his benefactor of betraying and mocking him. The accusation, although totally unfair to Hume, arose from a hoax letter concocted by Horace Walpole – but purportedly from the King of Prussia – that lampooned Rousseau. The philosopher had absolutely no sense of humour, making him acutely vulnerable to any ridicule. Amazed, Hume tried to calm his friend, but in vain; their friendship was at an end. Hume, to counter Rousseau's possible attacks, then published their correspondence, revealing Rousseau as dishonest and paranoid. This in turn led Rousseau to regard Hume as among the worst of his many enemies.

Hume *had* been annoyed to discover that Rousseau was not as poor as he had claimed to be, thanks to royalties from his bestselling books, yet he finally described Rousseau very generously, 'He has only *felt* during the whole course of his life, and in this respect his sensibility rises to a pitch beyond what I have seen any example of . . . He is like a man who was stripped not only of his clothes but of his skin and turned out in this situation to combat with the rude and boisterous elements.'

Rousseau perforce returned to France in May 1767, at times travelling under a pseudonym. Even now, although he had quarrelled with most of his intellectual friends, he was not without aristocratic support. The Prince de Conti sheltered him at his château in Normandy for a year, but Rousseau felt he was surrounded by spies and enemies among the prince's servants, all wanting to hand him over for imprisonment in the Bastille. On leaving the prince, he finally 'married' Thérèse, supposedly to make her position respectable. But it was an illegal, farcical ceremony that he himself conducted, marriages between Protestants and Catholics then being banned in France. Afterwards he harangued the guests at the wedding banquet, saying how lucky they were to know him, and then burst into tears. Poor Thérèse, who had been given only minutes to prepare for her nuptials, seems to have believed that she was truly married.

Rousseau's paranoia grew ever worse as he wandered from town to town, at times encountering difficulties with the authorities, although he was never arrested. In this over-excited condition he continued writing his longest masterpiece, his *Confessions*. The title deliberately echoes St Augustine's famous *Confessions* of AD 397, but Rousseau's aim was very different from the great theologian's. Augustine's *Confessions* were primarily addressed to God and recounted his many past sins and subsequent salvation, through God's grace, from a state of sin. Rousseau's outpourings, in contrast, were addressed to an entirely human audience. They do not recount his path to salvation, because he did not believe he needed saving.

Instead, they show him as an essentially innocent being – in every sense – more sinned against than sinning, making his way through a callous, hypocritical world in which he was invariably the innocent party, shockingly ill-treated by others. 'I have always thought and still think myself the best of men,' he declared straight-faced.

Rousseau had chosen as his motto Juvenal's *vitam impendere vero*, consecrate one's life to truth, and he spared no one's blushes – except perhaps those of Sophie d'Houdetot, for he implied that they had exchanged no more than a kiss. As he finished each part, he read sections aloud to admirers in Paris. By 1770 he had been allowed back into France provided he did not publish anything – a concession that enraged the still-exiled Voltaire, who longed to return home. One reading session lasted eighteen hours, and some listeners wept openly, moved by the accounts of his tribulations. However, other Parisians grew alarmed that the next sensational revelations might concern them, so further readings were eventually banned. The *Confessions*, a truly pioneering work, was only published in 1782. Its mix of sensationalism and self-pity, thinly disguised as candour, anticipates later confessions by its author's refusal ever to accept any responsibility or blame for anything. The whole world was guilty: Jean-Jacques was innocent!

Among his last works, written in 1776, was his *Dialogues: Rousseau, Judge of Jean-Jacques* (*Dialogues: Rousseau, juge de Jean-Jacques*), in which he expressed his now quite manic belief that his life exactly mirrored that of Jesus. Just as Jesus had failed to convert the Jews, so Rousseau had failed to convert the Swiss and French. Both men suffered persecution; both were guiltless. Modern humanity needed a saviour to return it to innocence and nature: that man was Jean-Jacques. Afraid that this work would never be published, Rousseau tried to gain God's protection by placing a copy on the high altar of the cathedral of Notre Dame in Paris but was frustrated on finding the altar gates locked. Instead, he gave a copy to Brooke Boothby, a former neighbour at Wootton who was passing through

Paris. (Boothby duly published it after Rousseau's death.) Growing ever more frantic, Rousseau made hand-written copies of a broadsheet, 'To All Frenchmen Who Still Love Justice and Truth', which he tried to hand out in the streets of Paris. Few people accepted it. That October he was knocked over in the street by a large dog. Strangely, the shock seems to have lessened his mania sufficiently for him to write his final work, *Reveries of the Solitary Walker* (*Reveries du promeneur solitaire*).

It starts with a stupendously egocentric declaration, 'Here I am then, left alone on earth without brothers, relations, friends or any society but myself.' This ignored Thérèse, his ever-faithful, much-abused partner of thirty years, and all the others – the Luxembourgs, the Prince de Conti and old friends like Paul Moutou of Geneva – who still supported him. But the *Reveries*, describing the beauties of nature and using the word *romantique* with its modern meaning for the first time in French, are among the finest works of someone who, whatever his faults, wrote with a lyricism rare in his age.

Rousseau died of a stroke on 2 July 1778 at Ermenonville, thirty miles east of Paris, where he had been living in a pavilion lent to him by yet another aristocratic supporter, the Marquis de Girardin. He was buried on the Isle des Peupliers, a suitably romantic lake island so-called because of its poplars. It quickly became a place of pilgrimage, as Rousseau's reputation, reviving after his death, rocketed him to even greater fame than he had enjoyed while living. The *beau monde* that he had ostentatiously despised was soon traipsing out from Paris to pay its respects at his tomb, among them Queen Marie-Antoinette. She was honouring, of course, not the prophet of revolution and equality but the writer of sentiment and natural feeling. A young man even committed suicide on the island, hoping to be buried beside his idol. Come the Revolution, the secular canonization of Rousseau accelerated. On 9 October 1794, as musicians played Rousseau's own music, his coffin was unearthed and carried in a solemn cortège to Paris. There, he was ceremoniously reburied in

the Panthéon – which had recently become the temple of the Supreme Being – ironically, opposite his old enemy Voltaire. Voltaire had got there first, in 1791, during the early liberal phase of the Revolution. The two adversaries' images were later carried side by side in revolutionary processions, something that might have amused neither. Robespierre proclaimed at Rousseau's interment, 'He attacked tyranny openly, he spoke of the divinity enthusiastically; his manly eloquence painted in flaming colours the appeal of virtue . . . his pure teaching, inspired by nature, was profoundly opposed to vice.'

Rousseau's posthumous reputation has been more mixed. In Shelley's last great poem, 'The Triumph of Life' (1822), Rousseau plays the same visionary role as a guide that Virgil had for Dante in *The Divine Comedy*, if rather more ambivalently. (The poem is unfinished.) Byron, the most famous Romantic poet of the nineteenth century, eulogized Rousseau in the third Canto of *Childe Harold* (1816):

> His love was passion's essence – as a tree
> On fire by lightning with ethereal flame
> Kindled he was, and blasted: for to be
> Thus, and enamoured, were in him the same.
> In him existence and o'erflowing teems
> Along his burning page.

About Rousseau's literary impact, there can be no dispute. *La Nouvelle Héloïse* is the first true piece of romantic fiction, with all that that implies.

Later philosophers have often condemned him as lacking the first essential of a true philosopher: the ability and desire to examine matters intellectually. In the twentieth century, as totalitarianism flourished, Rousseau's reputation plummeted. Isaiah Berlin called him the 'first militant lowbrow'. Bertrand Russell, thinking of Rousseau's tyrannical

General Will, went further, claiming that 'Hitler was the outcome of Rousseau'. But twentieth-century totalitarianism had many parents, and as a political prophet Rousseau was superseded by Marx, a much weightier figure intellectually. Rousseau's relevance for us today is as the prophet of nature, of naturalness, of unrestrained feeling, along with his belief, expressed in the *Confessions*, that to reveal all was somehow to excuse all. Here Rousseau lastingly changed attitudes, sometimes with indisputable benefits.

Few would deny that some of his educational ideas are positive. Mediated by reformers such as Johann Pestalozzi, Friedrich Froebel and Maria Montessori, they have helped move teaching from the centuries-old routines of soul-crushing rote learning to something at least potentially more joyful – although arguably the pendulum has swung now too far from transmitting tradition. Rousseau's mystical, pantheistic feelings among the woods, lakes and mountains, lyrically described in books such as *La Nouvelle Héloïse* and *Emile*, has influenced almost every subsequent generation. Wordsworth, when writing:

> One impulse from the vernal wood
> May teach you more of man,
> Of moral evil and of good,
> Than all the sages can.

was echoing Rousseau's creed that contemplating unspoilt nature improves people morally, a belief that became almost canonical in the nineteenth century across northern Europe and North America. But Rousseau's own life was a disastrous mass of contradictions and inconsistencies. Praising conjugal love, he never properly married but displayed callous neglect of Thérèse, his lifelong partner. Adoring children, he readily abandoned his own. Believing that intellectual hatreds were the worst, he engaged in endless battles of ideas. Deploring the advent of printing, he was a prolific writer. A hater of privilege and wealth, he always relied on the rich and great for support.

Damning the corruption of the theatre, he wrote many plays and operas himself.

Rousseau, the first great thinker to stress the primacy of feeling over thinking, remains a founding father of the Romantic Movement, of which we remain in many ways the nearly bankrupt heirs. The Green Movement, now perhaps the only true challenge to global industrialism, in part inherits Rousseau's belief in nature's pristine perfection and his consequent distrust of technology and large organizations. But the self-delusion, self-pity and paranoia dominating his life are hardly the qualities we might hope for in a green guru.

2
ARTHUR SCHOPENHAUER (1788–1860): THE REBARBATIVE BODHISATTVA

'Life is a wretched business. I have decided to spend it trying to understand it.' – Arthur Schopenhauer, letter to Christoph Wieland, 1809

Arthur Schopenhauer is a surprisingly relevant philosopher for the twenty-first century. Almost the first major Western thinker not to try to justify the ways of God to men – because he had no personal god – he was the very first to appreciate Hinduism and Buddhism and among the first to reject the dualism of mind and body axiomatic in Western philosophy since Plato. This led him, among other things, to recognize, with a startlingly modern honesty, the centrality of sex in human life. 'Sexual desire . . . is not only the strongest of desires but is even specifically of a more powerful kind than all the others,' he declared. He likewise opposed vivisection because he saw no absolute division between animals and humans, at that time taken generally for granted.

This makes Schopenhauer refreshingly different from most earlier Western philosophers, for whom the non-European world too often hardly exists. He has another rare merit: he writes lucidly, often wittily, usually free of philosophical jargon. Because of this, and the supreme importance he gives to art, he has been widely read outside academe by writers as diverse as Tolstoy, Hardy, Conrad, Proust, Thomas Mann, Beckett and Houellebecq. Mann even proclaimed that, 'Schopenhauer, as psychologist of the will, is the father of all modern psychology,' a claim Freud acknowledged. He surpasses even Freud, however, in his pessimism about the human predicament. For our present age, where angst is so entrenched that it is in perpetual danger of becoming the new black, Schopenhauer might appear the ideal apostle of an enlightened, humane pessimism.

Schopenhauer's bleak view of the world as a place of almost unrelieved sorrow dominates his *magnum opus*, *The World as Will and Representation* (*Die Welt als Wille und Vorstellung*), published in 1818 when he was only thirty.

> If that veil of Maya, the *principium individuationis*, is lifted from the eyes of a man so that he no longer makes the egotistical distinction between himself and the person of others . . . then it follows automatically that such a man, recognizing in all beings his own true and innermost self, must also regard the endless sufferings of all that lives as his own . . . No suffering is any longer strange to him . . . Wherever he looks, he sees suffering humanity and a suffering animal world and a world that passes away.

His essential view remained unchanged over his long life. 'Nothing is more useful than to accustom yourself to regarding this world as a . . . sort of penal colony . . . one might indeed consider that the appropriate form of address between man and man ought not to be sir or monsieur but fellow sufferer, *compagnon de misères*,' he wrote in *Parerga and Paralipomena*, his last work of 1851, which essentially restated earlier works more pithily.

Soon after publishing this, he finally began to win his rightful place as Germany's foremost living philosopher, indeed the greatest in all Europe. In the twentieth century his prestige suffered a partial eclipse, although the century's wars and other horrors might be said to justify his pessimism fully. Yet the blighting shadow cast by the man himself – who was not just philosophy's greatest misanthrope with no real friends or family but a misogynist without rival in the hardly feminist annals of Western thought and an unashamedly selfish reactionary, stingier and grumpier than any Scrooge – has always tended to obscure the brilliance of his philosophy.

For Schopenhauer, far from possessing the *mens aequa* (calm mind) of a philosopher, was by his own admission prone to 'mistrust,

irritability, violence and pride'. Unsurprisingly, given such a confession, he never married and lived completely alone almost all his adult life. Paranoid about being robbed, he distrusted everybody, starting with his own bank. He used to insist that a bank clerk should bring the interest on his (large) wealth to his lodgings every week to be counted. He hid piles of gold coins under his ink cellar and dividend vouchers in the pages of his diaries or books, swore dreadfully at his housekeeper if he thought she had moved or even dusted anything of value and 'walked trembling' each day to be shaved by his barber, fearful that the latter might suddenly decide to cut his throat.

As Schopenhauer was politically far to the right, his fears may not have been entirely groundless. During the abortive Liberal revolution of 1848 in Frankfurt, he welcomed government troops into his apartment so that they could shoot down on demonstrators – the *canaille* or rabble who potentially threatened his unearned income. He took a darkly Hobbesian view of society and government, thinking authoritarian government essential and that meliorist attempts to improve life politically and socially were futile considering the ineradicable evil of humankind. 'The chief source of the most serious evils affecting man is man himself: *homo homini lupus* (man is a wolf to man) . . . The conduct of men towards one another is characterized as a rule by injustice, extreme unfairness, hardness and even cruelty . . . the necessity for the State and for legislation rests on this fact.'

'In order to live in solitude, one must have the temperament of a god or a beast,' Montaigne had written, echoing Aristotle. For the hermit-like Schopenhauer, the beast predominated, as he admitted with typical candour:

> Nature has played its part in hardening my heart by endowing it with mistrust, irritability, violence and pride . . . I have inherited from my father that fear which I myself curse . . . and fight with all the will-power I possess, but which on the slightest occasions overwhelms me with such force that I see vividly before me misfortunes

which are merely possible or even scarcely imaginable . . . As a youngster I was tormented by imagined diseases and quarrels . . . From Naples I was driven by fear of smallpox, from Berlin by fear of cholera. In Verona I was seized by the *idée fixe* of having taken poisoned snuff . . . Whenever there was a noise at night, I would start from by bed and grab my sword and pistol, which I always kept loaded.

As his mother, in one of their rare later correspondences, pointed out, 'Two months in your rooms without seeing a single person, that is not good, my son.'

Even worse than his opinion of himself was his opinion of others, especially women:

Women are suited to being the nurses and teachers of our child-hood precisely because they themselves are childish, silly and short-sighted, in a word, big children their whole lives long; a kind of intermediate stage between the child and man, who is the actual human being 'man' . . . Only a male intellect clouded by the sexual urge could call the stunted, narrow-shouldered, broad-hipped and short-legged sex the fair sex . . . More fittingly . . . women should be called the unaesthetic sex. Neither for music, nor poetry, nor the plastic arts do they possess any real feeling for receptivity.

In his misogyny, at least, Schopenhauer practised what he preached. He never married, had no affairs with women on his social or intellectual level – difficult but hardly impossible for so intelligent a man – instead preferring the company of maids or actresses. Even these he treated badly. Such misanthropy and misogyny makes his relative neglect more understandable. But he remains among the greatest, most radical Western philosophers, who tried to give a unified metaphysical view of the world, something twentieth-century analytical logicians neglected to do.

Schopenhauer considered himself to be the direct (and sole) heir of the greatest Western philosopher since Plato, namely Kant, who died in 1804, but his thought and even language at times recall those of Buddhism. Crucially, he reached conclusions about the essential unity of the noumenal world (the unknowable ultimate reality) closer to Buddhism and Hinduism than Kant. For both Kant and Buddhism there are two levels of reality, only one of which we experience with the senses. Kant distinguished between phenomena, or the sensorially experienced world, and noumena, inherently unknowable. Kant held that what we experience is largely determined by our sensory apparatus – things are as they are, in space and time, because that is the only way we can see them. Buddhism similarly regards the ordinary, experienced world of *samsara*, of separate entities, as simply conventional reality, holding that at a deeper level individuality is illusory. Beneath everything there is nothingness, *shunyata*, the indivisible whole at the heart of everything.

Schopenhauer, unlike Kant but like much Eastern thought, recognized that the noumenal world must be a single, undifferentiated reality, for, when it takes on separate characteristics, it becomes part of the world of phenomena. This noumenal unity, which he called both *Ding an sich* (thing in itself), following Kant, and the Will, his own term, underlies the phenomenal world of daily life in which we exist. But it can, on very rare occasions, be experienced directly. This transcendently liberating yet indescribable experience can be summed up in the Sanskrit phrase *Tat twam asi*: 'You are that.'

Schopenhauer claimed to have reached his conclusions independently of Indian thought. However, he read the *Oupnekhat* – Friedrich Majer, an orientalist, had introduced him to this Latin translation of a Persian version of the *Upanishads* in 1813, so some way from the original – while completing his first major work, so Indian influences cannot be altogether ruled out. He called this first book *On the Fourfold Root of the Principal of Sufficient Reason (Über die vierfache Wurzel des Sotzes vom zureichenden Gründe)* – he always had

a knack for choosing unappealing titles. What Eastern spiritual thinkers claim to know through meditation and direct insight, however, Schopenhauer had reached through pure reason. If the routes leading to these conclusions were different, so were their responses. For the similarities in their views of the universe and diagnoses of the human condition cannot hide the huge gulf between Siddhartha Gautama, the Buddha, and Arthur Schopenhauer as men.

The Buddha, like all great sages, was noted for his benevolence and compassion. He encapsulated his teaching in his Four Noble Truths: all animate life is suffering (*dukkha*); suffering arises from insatiable individual cravings (*tanha*); suffering can be ended through annihilating individuality and cravings (*nirvana*); this is best attained through the Noble Eightfold Path, his 'Middle Way' (*magga*) between asceticism and self-indulgence. This can be followed by everyone, male and female, rich or poor, upper or lower class. By the caste-ridden standards of India in the fifth century BC, it was a very democratic path of liberation. The life and teachings of the Buddha still inspire millions. An important concept in Buddhism is the Bodhisattva, a saint-like being, who, moved by compassion, turns back on the threshold of nirvana to help suffering humanity towards enlightenment. Practical compassion is a cardinal Buddhist virtue.

It was never to be one of Schopenhauer's. Like the Buddha he saw our suffering as deriving from our mistaken belief in the separate existence of our individual selves. Like the Buddha he also rejected Hindu concepts of full reincarnation. To win release from suffering, which is caused by the strivings of our *individual will* (as distinct from the Universal Will, the *Ding an sich*), he, too, advocated transcending the egoistic will. This could be attained through disciplined asceticism, denying all worldly pleasures so that the illusory individual ego or will is extinguished, sometimes by literally starving to death, so permitting unity with the noumenal. So far, so (reasonably) conventional, although Schopenhauer did not specify the exact regime to be followed to reach this end. (The noumenal is, of course, called God

by many Western mystics but not by Schopenhauer.)

More original, and far more enticing for Schopenhauer and many of his readers, was the prospect of liberation through art. 'When an aesthetic perception occurs, the [individual] will completely vanishes from consciousness. But will is the source of all our troubles and sufferings,' he pointed out.

> Then all at once the peace, always sought but always escaping us . . .
> comes to us of its own accord, and all is well with us. It is the pain-
> less state, prized by Epicurus as the highest good, the godlike state;
> at that moment we are delivered from the miserable pressure of the
> will. We celebrate the Sabbath of the penal servitude of willing; the
> wheel of Ixion stands still.

Such epiphanies are not for everyone, however. 'The most excellent works of any art, the noblest production of genius, must eternally remain sealed books to the dull majority of men and are inaccessible to them. They are separated from them by a wide gulf, just as the society of princes is inaccessible to common people,' he went on with unabashed elitism. This was not just petty snobbery, however, for Schopenhauer revered artistic genius *literally* above everything. 'Always to see the universal in the particular is precisely the fundamental characteristic of genius, whereas the normal man recognizes in the particular only the particular as such . . . which alone interests him, is relevant to his will.' Further, the greater the genius, the greater the pain experienced. 'The person in whom genius is found suffers most of all,' he declared. The artistic genius, who perceives the noumenal for only a brief moment before he has to return to purgatorial existence, creates artworks that allow others the occasional consolations of aesthetic serenity. In this the true artist resembles a Bodhisattva, turning back to help humanity.

Schopenhauer, an exceptionally cultured man, appreciated all the arts from drama to painting. He considered architecture distinctly

inferior because it was partly utilitarian and at times also worried that the depiction of bowls of succulent fruit in, say, Dutch still lifes might be so sensually appealing that it would rouse the will, so negating the requisite detachment. Strangely, he was less worried about the obvious erotic appeal of so much Western art, with its recurrent obsession with the female nude.

Music, however, he regarded not just as the highest art form but as being effectively on another plane altogether. He saw in music – 'the true universal language which is understood everywhere' – the direct expression of the noumenal Will. Other arts imitate the world of Ideas, eternal forms intermediate between the noumenal and phenomenal spheres. (Schopenhauer here reiterated Plato's ideas about ideal forms, albeit in a highly unorthodox way.) But 'music, since it passes over the Ideas, is also quite independent of the phenomenal world, positively ignores it, and to a certain extent could still exist even if there were no world at all, which cannot be said of the other arts . . . Therefore music is by no means like the other arts, namely a copy of the Ideas, but a copy of the Will itself.' Schopenhauer, in fact, anticipated the quasi-sacramental role that art was to have for many of the most intelligent and sensitive people in the West over the next 150 years.

Salvation through art does not, however, ensure enlightenment or liberation, as Schopenhauer's miserable life reveals. While many philosophers' lives have been troubled, it is still surprising to discover that the author of such enlightened, honest books was a selfish, gloomy boor, whose treatment of others, not just of women, would disgrace any man, let alone a philosopher. This cannot be attributed to any obvious ill fortune or ill health. Wealthy, healthy, well connected, handsome enough when young, a brilliant conversationalist when he wished to be, Schopenhauer *chose* to lead a solitary life, without a family or even, most of the time, a mistress. He got on especially badly with his mother, whom he did not see for the last twenty years of her life, and had few real friends, especially in later life when he became a slave to his own timetable.

For his last twenty-seven years, the man who was such an intrepid intellectual pioneer followed a self-imposed routine as rigid as that of a prisoner. Every day he got up at seven, had a bath but no breakfast, worked at his (long-ignored) writings until noon, then played the flute – very well but solely for his own enjoyment – lunched lavishly and lengthily but usually alone at the Englischer Hof, Frankfurt's best hotel, occasionally talking to the smartest foreign guests or army officers. He then went to read the newspapers in the library, preferably *The Times* of London, took one of his series of beloved poodles – usually called Atman, from the Sanskrit – for a walk, once more alone, often muttering to himself. Later he might attend a play or concert, again usually alone, before returning home and, as if sated with so much company during the day, refused all uninvited callers before going to bed at ten. This fixed routine superficially resembles that of his hero Kant, whose daily walks around his native Königsberg were so punctual that citizens set their clocks by him. But Kant was a cheerful, sociable man whose regular habits allowed his thought to develop and mature over the course of his long life. By contrast, the inflexibility of Schopenhauer was the outward, visible form of an inflexible pessimism that ruled both his life and work and the product of his numerous neuroses.

The roots of Schopenhauer's misanthropy and pessimism should be sought in the traumas of his childhood and youth rather than his Kantian–Buddhist philosophy, whose conclusions simply served to confirm his pessimism. This pessimism may have been innate, however, and partly hereditary. Unlike many German philosophers Schopenhauer's father was no impoverished, high-minded clergyman but a wealthy, cosmopolitan, cultured, *very gloomy* merchant from Danzig – now Gdansk in Poland, then a German free mercantile city ruled by patrician merchants such as his father Heinrich Floris Schopenhauer. Danzig was, however, threatened by the growing power of Prussia, an aggressively militaristic state. In contrast, Heinrich Schopenhauer admired Britain's commercial and political

liberties. In late 1787 he took his pregnant young wife Johanna to England. Possibly he was thinking of settling there; perhaps he just intended to acquire British nationality for his unborn son. For some reason he changed his mind and the couple returned hastily across rough roads through a northern winter to Danzig, where Arthur was born on 22 February 1788.

Arthur was cursed with a mother who strongly disliked her own children. (A daughter called Adele, born nine years later, had a pathetic life.) This was not such a rarity at the time, for Johanna, like many women of her class, had not married for love but to please her family – Heinrich Schopenhauer was nineteen years older than her. However, she had reason to feel morose, being marooned most of the year on the isolated Schopenhauer country estate, visited only at the weekend by Heinrich. Johanna, naturally vivacious and sociable, grew depressed and bored, particularly with her baby. 'Like all young mothers I, too, played with my new doll,' she later wrote sardonically, but she never found much pleasure in her son at any age. This lack of spontaneous maternal affection – although he was never maltreated by his parents – may account for Schopenhauer's lifelong failure to give and receive any emotional warmth in human relationships. Later rejections or snubs, both personal – especially from his mother – and professional from German academe, can merely have deepened this childhood wound.

When Prussia annexed Danzig in 1793 the Schopenhauers moved to the larger port of Hamburg, also a free city, where Heinrich prospered even more, buying a large house. The future philosopher-recluse grew up in one of the grandest houses of one of Europe's wealthiest cities – it even boasted a ballroom where his mother entertained the city's high society (this included writers and artists, for she had literary ambitions). Meanwhile, her son attended school with the sons of other rich merchants, where they learned chiefly what was needed to become rich, worldly merchants themselves. Schopenhauer, although content enough at first, gradually discovered that he wanted

more from school than this, wanted to study Latin and Greek – the boys had a few token Latin lessons – essential for university but irrelevant for commerce. His father, however, intended his son to take over the family business, but first he decided to use a rare interlude of peace in the wars between France and Britain to travel in 1803.

With uncharitable cunning he offered Arthur a choice: either accompany his parents on a two-year grand tour of Britain and France and then settle down to becoming a merchant, or stay quietly behind studying for university. Inevitably, the fifteen-year-old Schopenhauer chose the former, despite feeling guilty about renouncing scholarship for the glamorous greater world. However, he enjoyed both seeing London society (although not his few weeks in an English boarding-school) and climbing mountains in southern France, the grandeur of which moved him to novel ecstasy. Seeing 6,000 captives in the galleys at Toulon moved him to new horror, however. 'In my seventeenth year . . . I was gripped by the misery of life as was the Buddha in his youth when he looked upon sickness, old age, pain and death . . . my conclusion was that this world could not be the work of an all-good being but rather that of a devil who had brought creatures into existence to delight in their suffering.' The miseries of life were already obsessing the adolescent.

In due course the family returned to northern Germany, where a dreary life learning commerce in a counting-house awaited the young Schopenhauer. He was saved from it by the sudden death – probably suicide – of his father, who jumped or fell from a warehouse window in 1805. Heinrich Schopenhauer had for some time been showing signs of physical and mental illness, so his death may not have been a complete surprise. Schopenhauer, who now began to admire his father dead more than he had living, never admitted that Heinrich's death was suicide. Significantly, he believed that we inherit character from our fathers and intelligence from our mothers – on the face of it a bizarre belief, considering how unlike his mother's his own intellect was, and one unsupported by genetics. But he despised his mother's

character, belittling her late-flowering literary talents while soon regarding his father as a model of sagacious nobility neglected by a frivolous wife. (Schopenhauer himself always rejected suicide, arguing it offered a false prospect of escape from life, although he showed his usual independence in rubbishing the conventional laws against it.)

Johanna, at last free of her much older husband, now determined to live the life she wanted. She sold up the family business and house and in 1806 moved with Adele to Weimar, a tiny independent duchy illuminated by the splendour of its Prime Minister Johann Wolfgang von Goethe. Goethe was Germany's greatest poet, greatest play-wright, greatest man of letters and greatest man of science. In fact, he was brilliant at almost everything *except* philosophy. Johanna soon made herself one of the great man's best female friends – but not his lover – and Weimar's smartest hostess. The Grimm brothers, authors of the fairy-tales, were among other distinguished visitors. Whatever her faults – she seems to have been snobbish and sillily 'artistic' – Johanna was certainly not dull. She became a successful writer of poems and novels, and Franz Schubert even set one of her poems to music. Such success was galling to her long-unrecognized son.

Perversely, Schopenhauer, although there *was* now no family busi-ness, at first tried to honour his dead father's wishes by continuing to work in a Hamburg counting house, a decision that deepened his depression further. A poem he wrote at around this time reveals both his gloom and his limitations as a poet:

> In the middle of a stormy night
> I woke in great fear
> Heard the storm howling outside . . .
> But no gleam, no faint glow
> Could pierce the deep night . . .
> Then a tremendous fear gripped me,
> I felt so anxious, alone and abandoned.

The lines are too typical of the romantic pessimism of the time, of adolescence at any time, to be taken seriously. Anyway, his mother, far from insisting that Schopenhauer continue his repugnant career, urged him to give it up. In March 1807 she wrote to him, 'I know only too well how little youthful cheer you enjoyed, how far you tend towards melancholy brooding inherited . . . from your father.' Encouraged by Johanna – without whom he might have remained moping in Hamburg – Schopenhauer quit his merchant's apprentice life in May 1807 and entered a gymnasium (grammar school) at Gotha, not far from, but not actually in, Weimar, to cram for university. Johanna, while not wanting her son to emulate his father, did not envisage him living with her. The last thing she needed, while establishing a salon to attract the *beau monde* of Weimar, was an awkward teenage son brooding in the background. Even Goethe initially fell silent when he spotted his hostess's angst-laden offspring.

Schopenhauer, for the first time at the age of nineteen fully applying his formidable intellectual powers, so impressed his tutors that he began to be seen as a budding genius. Moving to Weimar to continue his studies, he was offered accommodation not in his mother's house but in lodgings – another maternal rebuff that, even at the age of twenty, hurt. In 1809 he entered the university of Göttingen, first reading medicine, then philosophy. He devoured the works of Plato and Kant, becoming fascinated with philosophy. At about this time he wrote to a family friend, Christoph Wieland, who had warned him against studying so useless a subject, 'Life is a wretched business. I have decided to spend it trying to understand it.' He was to stick to this judgement and decision all his life. Meanwhile, he read widely in the seven languages he had already mastered – Latin, Greek, French, English, Spanish, Italian and German. When not studying, he played the flute, attended plays and concerts and talked with other students, impressing them with his eloquence. Although he was now of age, his mother still tried to control the income from his paternal inheritance, another cause of dispute between them. She also had doubts about

the wisdom of her son, whom she expected to marry, becoming a philosopher, a notoriously unprofitable profession. But Schopenhauer was determined on his career.

'Epicurus is the Kant of practical philosophy just as Kant is the Epicurus of speculative philosophy,' he wrote with precocious insight in a margin in 1810. Epicurus, seeing no order within the universe to guide us towards the good life, thought humanity must define its own good: happiness. Similarly Kant, who had died in 1804 but still towered over German philosophy, saw causality and value as being learned from human experience rather than as qualities discoverable in the outer world. Kant criticized speculation beyond the sphere of human knowledge; Epicurus saw a world dominated wholly by chance. In making the creative role of the human mind central, Kant made himself central to European philosophy.

But at the new university of Berlin, the Prussian capital, another generation of philosophers, led by Johann Fichte and Georg Friedrich Hegel, was propounding more exciting, if more contentious, ideas. Schopenhauer enrolled there in 1811 'in the expectation of meeting a genuine philosopher and a great spirit in Fichte'. He was deeply disappointed on both counts. 'What was senseless and meaningless took refuge in obscure exposition and language. Fichte was the first to grasp and make use of this privilege,' he cried, voicing an exasperation with Fichte's philosophical obscurity that many have since felt. And Hegel was even worse – 'that clumsy and nauseating charlatan, that pernicious person, who completely disorganized and ruined the minds of a whole generation'. Hegel, however, dominated German thought in the early nineteenth century.

Schopenhauer continued to attack these two thinkers throughout his life, damning what he saw as their wilful obscurity, their toadying to authority and their lack of intellectual honesty. 'Fichte . . . and Hegel are in my opinion not philosophers, for they lack the first requirement of a philosopher, namely a seriousness and honesty of enquiry.' Such language, startlingly outside the tones of normal scholarly dispute, hurt

his reputation and status far more than his actual views did. Even in 1840 the Royal Danish Society (then closely attuned to German cultural developments) declined to honour him because he had once abused such eminent thinkers of his age.

Suddenly it became a stirring age for Germany politically. In 1812 Napoleon marched his Grande Armée, 600,000 strong, right through Prussia to attack Russia. At the news of his immense defeat that winter in the Russian snows, Germany, for long prostrate and patient under French rule, began to ferment with nationalist ardour. Many young and not so young Germans, including the portly Fichte, flocked to the colours in patriotic euphoria. But not Schopenhauer. 'I was not born to serve mankind with my fist but with my head, and my fatherland is greater than Germany,' he wrote with fine independence, slipping away to Weimar in May 1813. He had more important things on his mind than wars of national liberation. 'In my mind there grows a work, a philosophy that would be ethics and metaphysics in *one*.'

Predictably, Schopenhauer quarrelled with his mother in Weimar, moving to a village inn where, remote from the sounds of battle, he wrote *On the Fourfold Root of the Principle of Sufficient Reason*. This gained him a doctorate from Jena University, and he presented a bound copy to his mother in November in Weimar. She commented that such an oddly named book must be intended for pharmacists. He retorted that his works would still be for sale when her trivia had been forgotten. She replied sweetly that indeed they would, the entire print run. While these literary rivals bickered, Schopenhauer began a brief, but for him vital, relationship with Goethe.

Goethe had also been unmoved by the eruption of German nationalism. He admired Napoleon even in defeat, continuing to wear the Légion d'honneur given him by the Emperor. Surrounded by the usual sycophants, Goethe now realized that the young doctor had an exceptionally powerful, independent mind. He particularly hoped that Schopenhauer would support his heterodox views on the subjective nature of colour, for the great polymath felt hurt by what he

saw as the malevolent neglect of his *Farbenlehre* (colour theory), which rebutted Isaac Newton's then standard theory of optics. Schopenhauer was sympathetic, as his own views on the subjectivity of experience coincided vaguely with Goethe's. Throughout the winter of 1813–14 the two men had long talks on this and other matters far removed from salon chatter. When Schopenhauer left Weimar in May, Goethe wrote him a discerning farewell couplet, 'If you wish to find joy in life / You must grant value to the world.' They continued to correspond for eighteen months, but their friendship cooled when Schopenhauer realized that Goethe saw him merely as a propagandist for his colour theory, while he had his own increasingly different ideas, outlined in an essay, 'On Vision and Colours' ('Über das Sehn und die Farben'). Goethe later called Schopenhauer 'a usually mis-judged, difficult-to-know . . . deserving young man' – a kinder judge-ment than most. This was the one intellectually equal friendship of Schopenhauer's life. From now on he would think, and write, com-pletely alone.

In May 1814 Schopenhauer quarrelled with his mother yet again – terminally this time. Johanna, tired of having him in her house even as a paying guest, had insisted he look for lodgings elsewhere so she could lead her own life, which, her son jealously suspected, now included a lover. They argued also over money, and Schopenhauer moved to Dresden. There, after cutting most ties with his family, he became a near hermit, albeit a theatre- and concert-going one. By now, still in his mid-twenties, the pattern of his life was becoming established: that of a nearly friendless eccentric intellectual, some-times admired, more often feared for his coruscating but mordant wit, and never loved.

Meanwhile, reinforced in his views by reading the *Oupnekhat*, Schopenhauer worked furiously on his masterpiece, *The World as Will and Representation* (*Die Welt als Wille und Vorstellung – Vorstellung*, normally translated as representation, also means performance of a play or opera in German, an ambiguity lost in translation). He saw in

the Indian concept of *maya*, the veil of illusion, the equivalent of his Representation, while his concept of Will paralleled Brahma, 'that from which all living creatures are created, that by which once born, they live, that towards which they die and towards which they hasten'. What especially appealed about Buddhism and Hinduism was the lack of a creator god. But his approach remained essentially Kantian in its wholly Western philosophical approach and language.

He had no false modesty about the value of his book. 'My work . . . is a new philosophical system . . . a chain of thought linked to the highest degree, such as has not previously entered any man's head,' he told his publisher Eberhard Brockhaus, who oddly also published Johanna's works. In December 1818 his masterpiece was finally published. Convinced, like Wittgenstein later, that he had solved all the great philosophical questions, he had already left for Italy and a well-deserved grand tour. Italy relaxed rather than stimulated him, but his mood, like that of so many northerners, lightened under southern skies. When he returned in 1819 he was expecting praise and acclaim or at least serious criticism. What he got was – nothing. On asking how many copies had sold, he was told none. This total lack of appreciation, which lasted most of his adult life, first amazed then embittered him.

Mainly to propagate his views, he began teaching in Berlin, chosen precisely because it was where Hegel, still his *bête noire*, had emerged as the wunderkind of German philosophy, proclaiming that God or history was being manifested in the rise of Prussia. Schopenhauer's determination to debunk such (to him) absurd views proved a humiliating flop, chiefly because he insisted on giving his lectures at exactly the same times as Hegel. (The controversial nature of his 'Indian atheism' may have also alarmed students in the notoriously repressive city. Even Hegel, who so enthused over Prussia's rise that it was joked he lectured in military uniform, faced problems over his rejection of Christianity.) Unsurprisingly, Schopenhauer's classes were usually almost unattended. Morose pride made him

refuse to alter his hours and ruined his chances of finding posts in Heidelberg or Würzburg when he applied in 1827. The Bavarian envoy in Berlin wrote in withering reply to their requests for a reference, '[Schopenhauer] enjoys no reputation here either as a writer or as a teacher.'

In Berlin in 1821 Schopenhauer fell in love with an actress and singer, Caroline Richter, then aged nineteen. They became lovers, but she often had several lovers simultaneously. When she had a child in 1822, he grew jealous on realizing he was not the father. Chest pains, possibly tubercular in origin, forced Caroline to quit her role in the National Theatre and nearly drove Schopenhauer away, too – he had already fled from a woman he believed to be tubercular in Italy. But Caroline seems to have mattered more to him than any other woman, and for a time he even toyed with the idea of marrying her, although she was in no way his intellectual or social equal. His behaviour towards Caroline at the end was far from gentlemanly, however. When he fled Berlin in panic at the cholera epidemic of 1831 – the epidemic that killed Hegel – he wanted her to accompany him, but insisted she leave her child behind. When she naturally refused, he moved to Frankfurt alone and never saw her again, although he did remember her in his will.

Schopenhauer had already fathered an illegitimate daughter in Dresden in 1818. To have this infant taken care of before his first Italian journey, he approached his sister Adele, whom he had hardly noticed earlier, asking her to help. Shocked at his request – she was still a virginal nineteen year old – she declined to do more than forward money to the baby's mother. The child's death soon after relieved him of further worries. Although Schopenhauer seemed to lack all paternal impulse, he was at least as highly sexed as any average man. But, as he recognized and loathed, he had an unusually cold-blooded, unappealing sexuality. As a young man, he later admitted, 'I was very fond of women – if only they would have had me.' The famous portrait of him in his twenties by Ludwig Ruhl shows a full, high white forehead

above red sensual lips. The effect is striking, even handsome, but the actual man failed to impress many women. In Weimar in 1813 he had conceived a wild but futile passion for Karoline Jagerman, the Duke of Weimar's beautiful mistress, who predictably ignored him. Such a snub, so common as hardly to be worth mentioning by most people, festered in Schopenhauer's gloomy solitude.

Admirably clear-headed, however, Schopenhauer was the first philosopher since Plato to accept sex's vital importance in life, but he saw it as the most cogent expression of the pernicious individual will rather than as a springboard to discovering ideal beauty:

> [Sexual desire] is so very much the chief thing that no other plea-
> sures make up for the deprivation of its satisfaction; for its sake,
> moreover, animal and man undertake every peril and conflict . . . It
> may be said that man is the sexual impulse made concrete, for his
> origin is an act of copulation, and his desire of desires is an act of
> copulation, and this impulse alone perpetuates . . . his phenomenal
> appearance.

He further anticipated Freud's discovery of the social omnipresence of sex by adding, 'It is the great Unspeakable, the public secret which must never be distinctly mentioned anywhere but is . . . always present in the minds of all . . . even the slightest allusion to it is instantly under-stood.' Yet his attitude to sex was essentially negative. 'Laughingly look upon the temptations of your body as you would at the playing of a practical joke planned against you but divulged to you.'

About that other perennial human concern, money, he showed neither magnanimity nor disinterest. In 1819 the Danzig bank in which his mother and sister had put almost all their money but Schopenhauer only a third of his failed. Schopenhauer, who got the news in Italy, perforce resumed dealings with his mother. The Schopenhauers were offered 30 per cent of what they were owed. After initially offering to 'divide what was left to him' with Johanna

and Adele, Schopenhauer demanded 70 per cent at once, even though he risked wrecking the whole settlement and leaving his mother and sister literally penniless. It took him a two-year legal battle to get the whole sum due him, while his mother and sister only recovered about a quarter of their original money. His obstinacy finally ruined his relationship with Adele, trapped once too often in the feud between her brother and mother.

He revealed even greater pettiness in a long dispute with the seamstress Caroline Marguet, which began in Berlin in August 1821. Schopenhauer complained that she and some friends were making too much noise outside his rooms – he may have been waiting for his lover Caroline Richter, so particularly wanted privacy. (And, like many musical people, he was always acutely sensitive to noise.) In the ensuing argument Marguet, who was then forty-seven years old to Schopenhauer's thirty-three, claimed to have been thrown down the stairs by him and hurt so badly that she could not continue her trade. This Schopenhauer denied. The legal battle lasted for five years, at one stage all his possessions in Berlin being placed under distraint by the court. Schopenhauer was finally found at fault, being obliged to pay her sixty thalers a year for the rest of her life – a tiny sum for him, not for her. When he heard of her death in 1852, he merely wrote, '*Obit anus, abit onus*' ('The old woman dies, the debt departs').

But, belatedly, Schopenhauer's fame now began to grow, helped in part by the general disillusionment following the failure of the 1848 revolution in Germany, which made the philosopher of angst and despair seem a more perceptively sympathetic guide than Hegel. In 1853 a laudatory review of *Parerga and Paralipomena* – his last, briefest book, aimed at a wider audience – in England in *The Westminster Review* (edited by George Eliot) hailed Schopenhauer as a genius. This enthusiastic article boosted his still negligible reputation back in Germany when reprinted in *Vossiche Zeitung*. In 1854 Wagner read Schopenhauer, rapidly coming to see him as a guide, even guru. In Schopenhauer's will-denying beliefs the composer found a revelation

of his own inchoate, hitherto unconscious, ideas and aims. Wagner sent the philosopher a copy of the libretto of *Der Ring des Nibelungen*. (The gift, typically, was not acknowledged; Schopenhauer adored Mozart, Beethoven and Rossini, not German romantic opera. Without Wagner's electrifying presence or music, the libretto must have made heavy reading anyway.) Yet Wagner's erotic masterpiece *Tristan und Isolde*, where insatiable erotic yearnings lead hero and heroine inexorably to their *Liebestod* ('love of death'), effectively gives musical expression to much at the heart of Schopenhauer's philosophy. Wagner composed it soon after discovering Schopenhauer, so beginning the fertile but perilous intertwining of German music and philosophy, and he himself did much to spread the philosopher's name.

The universities of Bonn and Jena now began to give courses on Schopenhauer's work; it was reviewed in France and Italy; on his birthday he was showered with gifts from strangers. Schopenhauer, who had always said he would be discovered one day, greatly enjoyed his new fame and was even seen to smile at people, but he did not enjoy it long. His death in 1860 from heart disease did not affect his reputation, however, which continued to grow, influencing later philosophers and writers. Nietzsche started his friendship with Wagner – the greatest in the former's solitary life – in mutual admiration for Schopenhauer. Nietzsche's trenchant, lapidary style owes much to his precursor, as he admitted, although his mature philosophy totally inverts the earlier man's pessimism. For Wittgenstein Schopenhauer was almost equally important. Some of the thoughts expressed in the opening passages of Wittgenstein's first great work, the *Tractatus*, echo Schopenhauer's ideas to the point of sounding like cryptic rephrasings of them.

To modern readers, Schopenhauer's pithy works can appeal when more systematic – or turgid – Western philosophers cannot. His recognition of the vital role sex plays in our lives, the parallels with Buddhism

that make his work a bridge between Eastern and Western thought and, most significantly, his stress on art and aesthetic appreciation as offering liberation from individual misery all retain their appeal. Late nineteenth-century French decadents, such as Jules Laforgue and Jean-Marie Villiers de l'Isle Adam, were delighted by his writings, which seemed to provide philosophical justification for their beliefs in art for art's sake and their recoil from the vulgar world. Marcel Proust was also much influenced by Schopenhauer's emphasis on the importance of aesthetic contemplation both in his novels – where this is repeatedly obvious – and in his life. Dragging himself painfully from his sickbed to view a Vermeer exhibition, the great novelist's almost transcendent experience before those small, brilliant canvases seems to vindicate Schopenhauer's belief that, at least for the right person, art can alleviate, if not remove, human suffering. With the museums never busier, this higher aestheticism can still appear very seductive.

But the question remains: does the essentially negative story of Schopenhauer's existence suggest radical faults in his philosophy as well as his life? In theory it should not, but preaching selfless detachment chiefly through aesthetic contemplation is of little use if it cannot prevent deep misanthropy and bitterness. For far from radiantly embodying his thought, like a Western Bodhisattva, Schopenhauer behaved with dismal consistency throughout his life as a self-centred, gloomy and petty individual.

3
FRIEDRICH NIETZSCHE (1844–1900):
THE SICKLY ÜBERMENSCH

'The most spiritual human beings . . . experience by far the greatest
tragedies: precisely for this reason they honour life, because it turns
against them its most formidable weapons.'
– Friedrich Nietzsche, *Twilight of the Idols*

Reading Nietzsche's work can be intoxicating – so intoxicating that
it ought perhaps to carry a health warning: 'Do not attempt to drive,
operate machinery or to *think* when under its influence.' Anarchists,
Fascists, Freudians, existentialists, postmodernists, neo-pagans,
transgressive hairdressers and footballers, feminists and misogynists –
even philosophers – have bathed in the foaming rhetoric of *Thus
Spake Zarathustra* (*Also sprach Zarathustra*), his most popular book,
and staggered off spouting hyperboles that would have appalled
him. 'Above all, do not confound me with what I am not!' he wrote
in perceptive alarm. But to distinguish the pith of Nietzsche's ideas
from his rhetoric can be hard:

> Behold, I am a prophet of the lightning . . . this lightning is called the
> *Übermensch* [superman] . . . All gods are dead: now we want the *Über-
> mensch* to live . . . Let this be our last will one day at the great
> noontide! . . . Life is a fountain of delight; but where the rabble also
> drinks, all wells are poison.

> All joy wants the eternity of all things, wants honey, wants dregs,
> wants intoxicated midnights, wants graves, wants the consolation of
> graveside tears, wants gilded sunsets . . .

> We build our nest in the tree Future; eagles shall bring food to us in
> their beaks!

Truly food in which no unclean men could join us! They would think
they were eating fire and burn their mouths!

No other philosopher writes remotely like this – Nietzsche, self-
anointed prophet of Dionysus, god of drama, intoxication and ecstasy.
Others, recoiling from this bombast, may prefer his calmer aphoristic
books:

Idleness is the beginning of all psychology.

Is man God's only mistake? Or God only man's mistake?

To stay cheerful when involved in a gloomy business is no inconsiderable
art.

Buddhism makes no promises but keeps them, Christianity makes a
thousand promises but *keeps none*.

No other philosopher writes like this, either. Nietzsche is among
the most readable, most *enjoyable*, of philosophers. W.B. Yeats, George
Bernard Shaw, Rainer Maria Rilke, D.H. Lawrence, August
Strindberg, Albert Camus, John Banville, Richard Strauss and Gustav
Mahler are among the eminent non-philosophers influenced by his
writings. And his impact on later philosophers, even – or especially –
when they rejected him has been huge.

At his most lucid – and he became pithier as he wrote – Nietzsche's
thought displays a mountain-like sharpness and clarity, suiting a man
who spent long years in or south of the Alps. They were also years of
increasing solitude. On his birthday in October 1888, the last before
his mind disintegrated, he received only one card. But in solitude and
exile Nietzsche gained the intellectual audacity less to proclaim the
death of God – he was hardly the first atheist – than to realize fully
what this implied for human morality, something many still have

not begun to realize. His call for a 'revaluation of all values' – and he meant *all*, not a neat rearranging of relationships between the sexes, races or classes – and the need for the *Übermensch* who would restore meaning to life in a god-free universe, remain fiercely relevant today.

Wagner – first Nietzsche's idol and friend, then his enemy, always his obsession – claimed to be writing the music of the future (*Zukunftmusik*). Nietzsche tried to write a philosophy for the future: *Prelude to a Philosophy of the Future* was the subtitle of *Beyond Good and Evil* (*Jenseits von Gut und Böse: Vorspiel einer Philosophie der Zukunft*). Shunning systematic philosophy, he wrote mostly in aphorisms, lacerating what he saw as embryonic trends, cultural, moral and intellectual, especially the popular *ressentiment* (resentment, sense of injury, victimhood), that twentieth-century dictators and subtler demagogues have since exploited. Nietzsche scarcely worried about politics, however. A supreme individualist, he despised all mass movements, subtitling *Zarathustra* 'A Book for Everyone and No One'.

Another peculiarity in the cerebral world of philosophy: Nietzsche *embodied* his thinking to an unparalleled degree. 'Of all writings I love only that which is written with blood. Write with blood and you will discover that blood is spirit,' he said. He actually wrote in a state of feverish exertion and excitement while he threw out every human value dependant on a transcendent world. As this meant not only Kantian–Schopenhauerian idealism but the whole Christian–Platonist tradition, the backbone of Western culture for 2,000 years, his rejection left a terrible void. Nietzsche was attempting to fill it with *The Revaluation of all Values* (*Umwertung alle Werte*), left unfinished at his collapse.

The effort exhausted the philosopher, as his letters reveal. For readers, however, Nietzsche can be stimulating, illuminating, even alarming. As he climbs ever higher into the mountains of the mind, scorning all safer paths, we must scramble after him, trying to ignore the vertiginous drops on either side. Looking up we see our guide,

moustache flecked with ice, vanish into a snowstorm, reappear on a distant ridge for a moment and then vanish again, this time permanently. When we look around we realize we are alone on the crevice's edge. 'Philosophy, as I have so far understood and lived it, is to live voluntarily in ice and high mountains . . . How much truth can a spirit bear, how much truth can a spirit *dare?*'

Nietzsche did not always live above the snowline, 'beholding the whole of humanity at a tremendous distance below'. He was also a philosopher of the senses, rejoicing in the sun and the Mediterranean. After he rejected Wagnerian romanticism, he turned to eulogizing Bizet's masterpiece *Carmen*, that most popular yet unsentimental of operas. He heard it twenty times, 'and each time it seemed to me I became more of a philosopher, a better philosopher . . . so patient do I become, so happy, so settled, so Indian'. His poetry – which he at least valued highly – hymns the south, anticipating the Mediterranean's twentieth-century appeal. Nietzsche wanted to become a *Ja-sagender*, saying 'Yes' to life with all its pains and pleasures and without the consolations of false philosophy or religion.

But those expecting the *Übermensch*'s prophet to live up to the famous images of him – photographs show huge moustache, majestic forehead, deep-set eyes – are going to be disappointed. Far from his bronzed muscular form greeting sunrise from an Alp top – the image evoked by Richard Strauss's tone poem *Also sprach Zarathustra* – Professor Nietzsche was a frail, half-blind neurasthenic, crippled by regular headaches that forced him to his bed. This was partly because he suffered from eye problems and sinusitis, recurring from an early age, partly psychological and probably later due to syphilis, the AIDS of the nineteenth century. 'Isn't there a neurosis of the healthy?' he cried once, despairing at his own ill health. Recurrent invocations to Dionysus, god of wine, disguise the fact that he was almost teetotal. His preferred tipple was cocoa, the low-fat version.

As for sex . . .

Zarathustra contains philosophy's perhaps most sexist lines, 'Are

you visiting women? Do not forget *the whip!*' This attempted humour was typical of Germany at the time, if seldom of Nietzsche. Elsewhere, he could be remarkably perceptive. 'There is something quite astonishing and extraordinary in the education of higher-class women; indeed, there is perhaps nothing more paradoxical. All the world is agreed to keep them as ignorant as possible *in eroticis* and to inspire their soul with a profound shame of such things.' What makes this comment – commonplace today, shocking then – remarkable is that Nietzsche, unlike, say, Wagner, had almost no sexual experience from which to draw his conclusions but had to rely on his phenomenal intuition. In truth, he was nearly celibate, although he made at least one disastrous trip to the bordello. His one significant affair – with Lou Salomé in 1882 – got no further than a kiss, and she kept the whip hand, quite literally. The notorious photograph shows Lou brandishing a whip over Nietzsche and Paul Rée, the other man in their short-lived *ménage à trois*. It was Lou who ditched Nietzsche.

The photograph suggests something else: near manic intensity on the suitor's part, although Nietzsche was never a photogenic philosopher. At times he claimed, half-jokingly, to be possessed by the spirit of Zarathustra, the ancient Persian prophet whose name he stole and whose views he inverted. He increasingly felt gripped by a *daemon* – Greek for a spirit, either good or evil. 'If one had the slightest trace of superstition left in one, one could hardly escape the idea that one is merely incarnation, merely mouthpiece, merely medium of overwhelming forces.' This was written shortly before he collapsed, early in 1889, from the third stage of syphilis. By then he was signing his letters Dionysus, or the Crucified One.

The Crucified One . . . But there are no crucifixions in the Greek pantheon. Beneath the paganism of the adult philosopher, the imprinted Christianity of a pastor's son survived, a classic case of *non-sexual* repression. Throughout his adult life Nietzsche was at war with an ancestry and upbringing designed to produce a learned pastor or pious professor. Although he later claimed descent from the Polish

nobility – because nationalist Germans despised the Poles and he hated German nationalists – he really came from a very *German* family. Friedrich Nietzsche was born on 15 October 1844 in Lützen in Prussian Saxony. His father Karl Ludwig Nietzsche, like those of so many German philosophers, was a Lutheran pastor, as were *both* his grandfathers. Later Nietzsche would fulminate, 'The Protestant pastor is the grandfather of German philosophy, Protestantism itself is its *peccatum originale* [original sin].' The women of this clerical dynasty, although barred from climbing into the pulpit themselves, were also intensely religious. Little Fritz proved markedly devout even in this household of suffocating piety. His favourite childhood game was playing at pastors, hence his family nickname 'Little Pastor'. In this he was assisted by his sister Elizabeth, who for a long time hero-worshipped her brother.

The death of his father from encephalomacia (brain softening) in 1849 at the age of thirty-five forced the Nietzsche family – Franziska his mother, still only twenty-four, Elizabeth, aged four, and Fritz himself – to move to Naumburg. In this small town overshadowed by its huge cathedral they lived in genteel poverty and piety. In retrospect Nietzsche savaged the 'Naumburg virtues . . . pretence of innocence, pretence of profundity, pretence of honesty and fidelity . . . What a poisonous atmosphere I had to breathe when I was a boy!' At the time, however, he was an exemplary pupil, in 1858 winning a scholarship to Pforta, Germany's top boarding-school, renowned for its classical studies and Christian ethos. Here, again, he excelled at the core Greek and Latin curricula, despite headaches that frequently kept him in bed. He compounded his physical weakness, however, by austerities such as taking cold baths in all weathers or, to prove a point about Mucius Scaevola, a Roman writer, holding burning matches in the palm of his hand. His classmates, impressed, called him *Quälgeist* (tortured spirit).

At Pforta he began writing poems and a play in the manner, he hoped, of Goethe. He also proved brilliant at improvising on the piano.

But, as a musician's career was thought improper for a clergyman's son, he enrolled at Bonn University in October 1864 to study classical philology (Greek and Latin) and theology. Obeying the conventions of the *Studentenkorp*, he also got drunk, suffered terrible hangovers and even fought a duel with another student, duelling scars being semi-obligatory badges of honour. During this rite the myopic Nietzsche staggered around blindly waving his sabre, received a scar on the bridge of his briefly spectacle-free nose and went to bed to recover.

Another rite of passage had far more serious consequences, although exactly what happened remains obscure. According to his friend Paul Deussen, Nietzsche, visiting Cologne in February 1865, was directed to a brothel when asking the way. Entering, he found himself 'suddenly surrounded by half-a-dozen apparitions in tinsel and gauze, looking at me expectantly. For a moment I was speechless. Then I made instinctively for the piano as being the only thing with a soul present. I struck a few chords . . . and I escaped,' he later said. Few believe, however, that he *did* escape. In Thomas Mann's *Dr Faustus* the hero Adrian Leverkühn, a composite Nietzsche/Schoenberg figure, has the same experience, returning to catch syphilis from a girl who has bewitched him. Whether or not Nietzsche returned to that particular brothel, he almost certainly contracted syphilis around this time. Such a long latent period between infection and final collapse is not exceptional; such student outings were disastrously common. Schubert, Donizetti, Paganani, Manet, Baudelaire, Maupassant, all caught the then fatal disease. Nietzsche later said that he had sought medical treatment for syphilis at this time. This meant, most importantly, that he could never honourably marry for fear of infecting his wife.

Illness did not check Nietzsche's academic career, however. Transferring to Leipzig University in August 1865 to follow his favourite professor Friedrich Ritschl, he dropped theology to concentrate on philology – a momentous decision for a pastor's son. Already he had upset his family by refusing to take communion at Naumburg

that Easter, an open breach only being averted by a tactful aunt who pointed out that all great theologians had 'doubts'. But doubt was not the word for his rejection of Christianity. Ancient literature had revealed an alluring world very different from the Christian ideal, but so far he knew no modern philosophy. Then the chance purchase in Leipzig that October of Schopenhauer's *The World as Will and Representation* revealed a new cosmogony. 'I took it in my hand as something totally unfamiliar and turned the pages. I do not know which daemon was whispering to me: "Take this book home." . . . Back at the house I threw myself into the corner of the sofa . . . and began to let that dynamic, dismal genius work on my mind.' Later, in *Schopenhauer as Educator* (*Schopenhauer als Erzieher*), he said that he knew 'after reading the first page that I will read every page, and will listen to every word he had to say. My confidence in him was instantaneous . . . I understood him as if he had written especially for me.'

Schopenhauer *made* Nietzsche a philosopher, helping a precociously successful academic become a solitary prophet through the example of his own intellectual independence and courage. 'Your educators can be no more than your liberators,' Nietzsche acknowledged. He now became a fervent 'Schopenhauerian', restricting himself to only four hours' sleep a night to mortify the body (not something Schopenhauer had ever attempted). While producing brilliant essays and getting articles published in philology journals, he felt increasingly drawn towards *philosophy*. His studies were interrupted by military service in the Prussian army – he was not quite myopic enough to gain exemption – from October 1866 to 1867. Although he disliked military life, he proved a skilled horseman, but an accident when he tore his chest jumping into the saddle meant months in bed with a septic wound. Then came his discharge, with his health weakened further.

Back in Leipzig, on 28 October 1868, he had a musical epiphany. Hearing the overture to Wagner's *Die Meistersinger* and the *Tristan* prelude, he was overwhelmed – 'carried away', as he wrote to Erwin

Rohde, then his closest friend. 'I cannot maintain a critically cool view of this music. It thrills every fibre, every nerve in my being.' Eleven days later he actually met the composer, then visiting Leipzig incognito. 'He is an astoundingly vivacious and high-spirited man, speaks very rapidly, is extremely witty and is very animated when in the company of friends. During the evening we had a long conversation about Schopenhauer, and you can imagine my unbounded joy at hearing him say . . . how much he owed to Schopenhauer,' he wrote in another letter. Schopenhauer and Wagner now became his twin idols, but such idolatry had its dangers.

Wagner was one of the greatest monsters, as well as masters, of classical music – monstrously charming, among other things. An exact contemporary of Nietzsche's father, Wagner reputedly even resembled the pastor. Nietzsche, long fatherless and unconsciously wanting a hero, was overwhelmed. 'Wagner embodies all the qualities one could possibly desire. The world has not the faintest idea of his greatness,' he told Rohde the following summer. By then Nietzsche was living in Switzerland, where he had just become Professor of Classical Philology at Basle University. Not only was he astonishingly young – still only twenty-four – he had not even got his doctorate. The recommendation of Professor Ritschl, who declared, 'He will simply be able to do anything he wants to do', had catapulted him to fame. The world of German academe – then the best in the world – seemingly lay at his feet. Nietzsche, however, was more pleased by the fact Basle lay only fifty miles from where Wagner was living at Tribschen on Lake Lucerne with Cosima, soon to be his second wife. He could and did visit his hero regularly, staying with the Wagners *twenty-seven* times over the next three years, including all three Christmases.

Wagner had decorated his house with the satin and silk furnishings, statues and other items he felt essential for his creativity. (These included eight servants and an aviary of golden pheasants.) Freed from debt by the generosity of Ludwig II of Bavaria, he now dressed theatrically in black velvet coat and breeches, reflecting his own

ideas about the proper garment for the *Meister*. Nietzsche, however, noticed only his genius. 'With him I feel in the presence of the divine', he wrote in August 1869. For all his later attacks on Wagner, he recognized this was the greatest relationship of his life: 'No cloud ever darkened our sky . . . My first contact with Wagner was also the first time in my life I ever drew a deep breath . . . I call Wagner the greatest benefactor of my life,' he declared in rose-tinted reminiscence near his own end.

The Birth of Tragedy from the Spirit of Music (*Die Geburt der Tragödie aus dem Geist der Musik*), his first book, appeared in 1872. Wagner lapped up Nietzsche's comparison of his own operas with Ancient Greek tragedies. Nietzsche, who then saw Wagner recreating their equivalents in nineteenth-century Germany, was later embarrassed by this work, calling it 'an impossible book . . . badly written, ponderous . . . image mad and image confused . . . sentimental in places'. But it was the first to demonstrate the central importance in Greek culture of Dionysus, the 'dark god' of drama and ecstasy, polar opposite to Apollo, god of rational thought and individuation.

> Dionysian emotions awake and as they grow in intensity everything subjective vanishes into complete self-forgetfulness . . . Under the charm of the Dionysian not only is the union between man and man reaffirmed, but nature, which has become alienated, hostile or subjugated, celebrates once more her reconciliation with her lost son, man . . . Each one feels himself not only united, reconciled and fused with his neighbour, but as one with him, as if the veil of *maya* had been torn aside . . . he now walks about enchanted, in ecstasy.

Nietzsche had found his distinctive voice, using brilliantly powerful imagery. As he said, 'It should have sung, this new soul, not spoken.' The book's villains are Socrates and Euripides, the last great dramatist, who, Nietzsche claimed, killed Greek tragedy by his sceptical rationality, turning mythic rite into mere theatre.

Wagner, who knew about myth, may have contributed ideas, both directly and through his library, to the young professor's exciting book. The work did little, however, to advance Nietzsche's academic career. In 1871 he had failed to secure the vacant chair in philosophy at Basle and had to continue teaching a subject, classical philology, in which he felt dwindling interest and which attracted few students. These, however, remembered him as a teacher who brought ancient languages and culture brilliantly alive. At Tribschen the musician and philosopher talked long and excitedly in their lakeside walks. Despite the gap in age and achievement between them – Wagner now enjoying ever-growing acclaim, Nietzsche almost unknown – both were geniuses and knew it. Elisabeth Nietzsche, visiting Tribschen, later recalled, 'Wagner, Frau Cosima and my brother began to speak of the tragedy of human life, of the Greeks, of the Germans and of their mutual plans and wishes. Never in my whole life . . . have I heard such marvellous harmony in three people so fundamentally different.' Wagner at this stage requited Nietzsche's feelings, saying that he was, with one (unnamed) exception, the only person 'who positively enriched my life'.

But no one could live long in Wagner's egocentric orbit unscathed. Nietzsche, at first so obliging that he ran petty errands for Wagner – to the point of buying his special silk underwear for him – harboured musical ambitions and once played some of his own compositions. Wagner dismissed them, as everyone else has since, as *kirklich* (churchlike) dirges, the drab music of a pastor's son. Nietzsche, wounded, claimed that Cosima found his improvisations at the piano better than her husband's, but Wagner was a surprisingly poor pianist.

Cosima now also became a crucial figure in Nietzsche's life. Photographs showing her as the dutiful Victorian *hausfrau* sitting meekly beside the Master are misleading. The illegitimate daughter of Franz Liszt and ex-wife of Hans von Bulow, the conductor whom she had left for this genius twenty-five years her elder, Cosima was a gaunt, almost ugly figure. Highly intelligent, very musical, strong-willed, she

73

was also strongly anti-Semitic and nationalistic. Nietzsche, generally pro-Jewish and seldom nationalistic, for a while swallowed his reservations, fascinated by this woman more sophisticated and educated than any he had met before. He was at least half in love with her. Wisely he kept his quasi-Oedipal feelings for her quiet until, on the brink of madness, he sent her a note saying, 'Ariadne, I love you, Dionysus.' Cosima did not reply.

Nietzsche volunteered for the Franco-Prussian War that broke out in July 1870. He had no need to, as he had given up Prussian nationality, but this was the very last time he felt and acted as a German. Serving as an ambulance orderly, he contracted dysentery and diphtheria. When he recovered, his mood had changed irrevocably. German triumph in this war led to the creation of a new, bombastic Prussian-led German Empire, from which he soon felt estranged. As early as November 1870 he urged Rohde to leave 'that fatal, anti-cultural Prussia, where slaves and priests sprout like mushrooms. Soon they will darken the whole of Germany for us with their vapours', and in 1873, on the opening page of *Untimely Meditations* (*Unzeitgemäße Betrachtungen*), he warned, 'Of all the evil consequences which have followed the recent war with France perhaps the worst is a widespread if not universal error . . . that German culture, too, was victorious in the struggle.' Fifteen years later he repeated himself more pithily, 'The moment Germany rises as a great power, France gains a new importance as a *cultural power*.' But for most Germans, the new Reich fulfilled long-frustrated national yearnings for unity.

The Wagners' move in April 1872 to Bayreuth in Bavaria, where a special opera house and sumptuous villa were being built for the Master, deprived Nietzsche of the home where he had felt happiest. But, freed also from the Wagners' mesmerizing presence, he began to have doubts about a music which promised – threatened – such seductive self-annihilation. A classicist by training, increasingly an admirer of French culture – chiefly for its lucidity – Nietzsche was

starting on his long, painful recoil from Wagnerolatry. He refused most invitations to Bayreuth and only finished *Richard Wagner in Bayreuth*, the fourth *Untimely Meditation*, belatedly in 1876. He was aware of a growing hypocrisy in its praise of the Master, as his notes show. (Wagner, sublimely unaware, wrote back, 'Friend, how did you get to know me so well?' Probably he never read it.)

In August 1876 Nietzsche went to Bayreuth to attend the first complete performance of *The Ring*. This proved more fiasco than triumph. (The dragon for *Siegfried*, ordered especially from England, arrived late and without its neck that had been sent to Beirut in the Lebanon; in *Das Rheingold* Wotan lost the ring; a curtain rose early on stage hands still at work . . .) But what upset the philosopher was finding, instead of the devout Wagnerites he had naïvely expected, a city teeming with the rich and powerful – 'the whole idle riff-raff of Europe', he protested. Kings and bankers were now essential to the debt-laden project, however, as Wagner realized. Worse for Nietzsche, the festival oozed German cultural chauvinism. With splitting headache and churning stomach he fled the city. It was not Wagner's music that drove him away but the realization that the composer had joined forces with the philistine new Germany. 'What did I never forgive Wagner for? . . . That he became *reich deutsch* [imperial German]'. This act of near parricide, which caused him much anguish, was vital to his intellectual and emotional independence.

Nietzsche had left Bayreuth with a new friend, Paul Rée, a novelist, psychologist – and a Jew. The last would, he knew, enrage Wagner, who had proclaimed in *Religion and Art* (*Religion und Kunst*), 'The Jewish race is the born enemy of pure humanity.' The two geniuses met just once more, that November in Sorrento. Nietzsche, granted a year's sick leave from teaching, was seeing Italy for the first overwhelming time at the age of thirty-two. ('I shuddered, sorry for myself at having been so old at the beginning of my life,' he said, dating his rebirth from the day he first watched the sun set over the Bay of Naples.) Wagner, working on *Parsifal*, rhapsodized about Christian

ritual, which he envisaged his last opera replicating on stage. Nietzsche claimed to be shocked by Wagner's bogus religiosity – the 'spirit of the Counter-Reformation'. But here he was being disingenuous, for Cosima had read him the libretto of *Parsifal* in Tribschen back in 1869. Nietzsche was now mainly reading French writers – Montaigne, La Rochefoucauld and Stendhal – whose psychological shrewdness thrilled him. Nothing could be more alien to Wagner than such francophilia. They parted in uncomprehending mutual disdain.

In *The Cheerful Science* (*Die Fröhlich Wissenschaft*) of 1882 Nietzsche gave a lyrical epitaph on their friendship:

> *Star friendship* . . . we are two ships, each of which has its goal and course; our paths may cross and we may celebrate a feast together, as we did . . . our life is too short and our vision too small for us to be more than friends in the sense of this sublime possibility. Let us then believe in our *star* friendship even if . . . compelled to be earth enemies.

From Wagner, no such magnanimity. He spread rumours that his ex-disciple's illnesses were caused by excessive masturbation – an activity many in the nineteenth century believed led to blindness and madness. Dr Otto Eiser, whom Nietzsche had consulted, supported Wagner's slander, saying that Nietzsche's subsequent works revealed signs of insanity, a breach of confidentiality that enraged the half-blind Nietzsche.

Intellectually, Nietzsche was heading in new, totally uncharted directions. In *Human, All Too Human* (*Menschliches, Allzumenschliches*), which appeared in May 1878 with the subtitle *A Book for Free Spirits* (*Ein Buch für Freien Geister*), he jettisoned Schopenhauer's transcendental idealism, itself a modified version of Kant's. From now on Nietzsche would proclaim the reality only of the phenomenal world, rejecting the main currents of Western thought which accorded greater importance to the noumenal. *Human, All Too Human* has an implicit attack on Wagner – 'the noblest type of beauty is that which

does *not* sweep us off our feet' – but its chief concerns are 'the small inconspicuous truths' of human life, demonstrating his new psychological acuity. 'As soon as we notice that anyone has to compel himself to pay attention when . . . talking to us, we have valid proof that he no longer loves us,' echoes La Rochefoucauld, as Jacob Burckhardt, the Swiss historian admired by Nietzsche, admitted. But 'the unresolved dissonances in personality and opinion between parents go on echoing in the child's character, forming the history of his inner sufferings' anticipates Freud. This volte-face alarmed many old friends. Rohde, bewildered, asked, 'Is it possible to divest oneself so completely of one's soul and substitute another?' Cosima, typically, saw the 'sleek' Rée bewitching Nietzsche as 'the relationship between Judaea and Germania in miniature'. For Nietzsche had attacked the 'growing obscenity of leading the Jews to slaughter as the scapegoats of every conceivable public and private misfortune'.

In June 1879 Nietzsche resigned his university post – belatedly rather than prematurely, for he had been dangerously ill that spring, having to cancel 118 lectures. His headaches now lasted weeks at a time, as did his vomiting attacks and periods of near blindness. 'Continual pain; for many hours of the day a feeling akin to sea-sickness, a semi-paralysis which makes it difficult to speak,' he noted in January 1880. These attacks may sometimes have been migraines; they were probably not syphilitic in origin, for they had started years before possible infection. Nietzsche guessed his physical ailments might be linked to mental turmoil, but, as he now existed only to write, he could hardly relapse into intellectual quiescence. For such a sceptic, however, he put an odd trust in quack cures. These included strange diets – only milk and fruit, or cocoa and dry bread – hydrotherapy or cold baths, all equally useless.

He tried to laugh at, even exploit, his sickness. 'The daily battle against headache and the laughable diversity of my ailments demand so much attention that I am in danger of becoming petty – but this balances those . . . high-flying tendencies that so dominate me that

without them I would become a fool.' This was brave rather than accurate. Forced back on his own company, he risked growing – eventually became – solipsistic. Meanwhile he led the nomadic life of the 'wanderer and his shadow', searching for somewhere his health might improve.

He acquired one faithful disciple, Peter Gast, a young composer who looked after him during his stay in Venice in spring 1880, taking notes that went into his next book, *Daybreak* (*Morgenröte*). Venice, for a while, soothed Nietzsche. 'With the high rooms and silence I sleep well, and the sea air reaches me before it has been spoilt by going through Venice,' he wrote to his sister. *Daybreak* strongly attacks Christian sexual morality. 'The passions become evil when regarded from an evil, vicious viewpoint. Christianity has succeeded in making Eros and Aphrodite – great ennobling ideals – into goblins and phantoms.' Few today outside the Bible Belt would disagree, but Nietzsche went on to attack the foundations of *all* morality:

> I deny morality as I deny alchemy, that is I do not deny that there have been alchemists who have believed in these premises and acted in accordance with them . . . It goes without saying that I do not deny that many actions called immoral ought to be avoided or resisted, or that many called moral ought to be done . . . but I think the one should be encouraged and the other discouraged for other reasons than hitherto. *We have to learn to think differently . . . to feel differently.*

Nietzsche was not celebrating the imminent collapse of morality but warning of its terrifying consequences.

In 1882 Nietzsche discovered Sils Maria, 6,000 feet up in the Swiss Alps, 'the loveliest corner on earth . . . I have never found anywhere so quiet.' It became his summer base; winters he spent in Italy or on the French Riviera, less cold but still chilly enough when a wandering philosopher could afford no heating. And in November 1881 he had had another epiphany, hearing *Carmen* for the first time.

Its Mediterranean passion seemed the perfect antidote to Wagner. Inspired, he continued writing in the same exalted vein. His next book, *The Cheerful Science*, carries his most famous announcement, the death of God:

> Have you not heard of the madman who lit a lantern in the bright morning, ran to the market-place and cried incessantly: 'I am looking for God! I am looking for God!' This produces mockery from bystanders. 'Have you lost him then?' said one. 'Did he lose his way like a child?' asked another. But their laughter dies as the madman pierces them with his glances. 'Where has God gone?' he cried. 'I shall tell you. *We have killed him* – you and I. We are all his murderers. But how have we done this? . . .Who gave us the sponge to wipe away the entire horizon? What did we do when we unchained this earth from its sun? Where is it orbiting? Where are we orbiting? Away from all suns? . . . Aren't we drifting through empty nothing? . . . Has it not grown colder? Is not endless night closing in on us? Don't we need lanterns in the morning? . . . Has the smell of God's putrefaction not reached our nostrils?' Then the madman smashes his lantern, announcing he has come too early: 'The tremendous event is still on its way – it has not yet reached the ears of men . . . *and yet they have done it themselves.*'

Even Schopenhauer had never been this bleak. Nietzsche had anticipated the twentieth century's endless angst. But to balance it came a determined, dynamic optimism. 'I want to learn more and more to see the necessary as the beautiful, so I shall become one of those who makes things beautiful. *Amor fati* [love of fate]: let that be my love from now on. I want to wage no war against the ugly. I do not want to accuse . . . All in all, I want some day only to be *ein Ja-sagender!*' His determination was soon to be sorely tested.

In Rome in April 1882 Nietzsche met and fell in love with Lou Salomé. Highly intelligent and attractive, seventeen years his junior,

Lou came from a Russian–German upper-class family – so satisfying both his latent snobbery and growing Germanophobia. Like him, she had lost her religious faith early. Lou was impressed by the poetic, intellectually overwhelming but half-blind and impoverished philosopher. She later said that his first words to her were: 'What stars have sent us orbiting towards each other?' However, she was neurotically virginal, perhaps because of an incestuous attachment to her father. The idea then arose that Rée, Nietzsche and Lou would live and study together that winter – but chastely. Nietzsche did not know that Paul Rée, whom he considered his best friend, had already proposed to her in vain.

Nietzsche, really in love for the first – and last – time, talked to her about his germinating ideas for *Zarathustra* and, on a mountain top, proposed to her, prepared to accept a celibate marriage. Celibacy had obvious attractions to a man with syphilis. Although Lou rejected his offer, the 'Trinity' as she termed it, met again in Lucerne in May. They made a pilgrimage to Wagner's former villa at Tribschen where Nietzsche, according to Lou, broke down and wept. They also posed for a photograph in a studio. This notorious picture is deeply disappointing. Far from suggesting a coven of high-brow flagellants, it shows only a small, mock-rustic cart 'drawn' by Rée and Nietzsche, in which Lou languidly waves a whip. Behind is an Alpine backcloth. The whip, like the cart, is obviously a studio prop, and if the idea was Nietzsche's – as Lou said – it was clearly a joke. Lou later showed the picture around as such.

But Nietzsche, who thought he had at last found a fellow 'aeronaut of the spirit', now became euphoric. He spent August with Lou in the Forest of Tautenburg, advising on her own writings, which included poems very like his, expounding his ideas. 'I wonder whether such philosophical openness as there is between us has ever existed before,' he wrote. Two serpents wrecked this paradise: Rée maliciously suggested to Lou that Nietzsche was only interested in using her sexually, and Elisabeth, Nietzsche's sister, seeing Lou as the

archetypal seductress, quarrelled violently with both Lou and Nietzsche. At first trusting Rée and Lou totally, Nietzsche grew anxious that autumn. In November in Leipzig he realized that the other two had gone off together without telling him. The *ménage à trois* was over.

Lou Salomé went on to publish novels and poems, praised at the time. In 1889 she married an academic, Fred Andreas; interestingly, their marriage remained unconsummated up to his death in 1930. She had other 'trinities', famously with the Nietzschean poet Rainer Maria Rilke, by whom she conceived but aborted a child. Later she became a disciple of Freud, specializing in anal sexuality. Rée vanished from sight. And Nietzsche, seething with useless hatreds – of Elisabeth, of Rée, of Lou – was left lonelier and sadder than ever. 'This last mouthful of life was the toughest I ever had to chew . . . If only I could sleep! But the strongest sleeping draughts [he was taking fifty grams of chloral hydrate a day] help no more than the six- or eight-hour walks I take. If I cannot find the magic formula to turn all this filth into gold, I am lost,' he wrote on Christmas Day 1882 to Franz Overbeck.

Virescit volnere virtus (Strength is restored by wounding) was Nietzsche's motto. Out of his despair came his longest, grandest work, his opera-in-prose, *Thus Spake Zarathustra*. Written in spurts of manic inspiration, often echoing or parodying the Bible, its first section was finished in 1883. It starts with a sonorous down-going into the world:

When Zarathustra was thirty years old, he left his home . . . and went into the mountains. Here he had the enjoyment of his spirit and solitude and did not weary of it for ten years. But at last his heart turned and one morning he rose with the dawn, stepped before the sun and spoke to it: Great star! What would your happiness be if you had not those for whom you shine? . . . Behold! I am weary of my wisdom, like a bee that has gathered too much honey; I need hands outstretched to take it. I should like to give it away, to distribute it, until the wise among men have become happy in their folly and the poor

happy in their wealth . . . Bless the cup that wants to overflow, that the waters may flow golden from him and bear the reflection of your joy over all the world!

So huge, so overflowing a book can support many readings. Two huge concepts dominate it, most famously that of the *Übermensch* (literally, superhuman, but the word does not really translate), a word that escaped its creator to gain an often dubious life of its own. By *Übermensch* Nietzsche meant not a species biologically different from current humanity, nor a genetically enhanced type, but a psychologically, morally, aesthetically greater being, of whom the 'great men' of the past – Julius Caesar, Beethoven, Goethe – were mere inklings. 'What is the ape to humanity? A laughing stock, or a painful embarrassment. And just so shall humanity be to the *Übermensch* . . . Once you were apes, and even now humanity is more apelike than any ape . . . Behold, I teach you the *Übermensch*. The *Übermensch* is the meaning of the earth.' With God dead the *Übermensch* must fill the moral and psychological void. What he would do in his exalted state Nietzsche left vague.

Complementing this is the doctrine of Eternal Recurrence. Everything – literally everything – would come around again and again in huge cycles. 'Have you ever said Yes to a single joy? . . . then you said Yes, too, to all woe. All things are entangled, ensnared, enamoured . . . All joy wants eternity!' This is a philosophy for strong stomachs. Nietzsche hammers home another vital message: '*Remain true to the earth*, and do not believe those who speak to you of otherworldly hopes . . . They are despisers of life, atrophying and self-poisoned men, of whom the earth is weary.' Equally crucial is his view of life itself as staggeringly, superbly, abundant, a view latent in *Zarathustra*, made explicit later. For all his acceptance of existential suffering, he saw the universe's natural state as 'one of superfluity and prodigality, even to the point of absurdity'. 'As for the famous struggle for existence . . . it occurs, but as the exception; the general aspect of life

is not hunger and distress but rather wealth, luxury, even absurd prodigality.' This was his main disagreement with the Darwinians, already claiming quasi-papal omniscience for the great biologist.

Nietzsche had just finished the first part of *Zarathustra* when he heard of Wagner's death on 14 February 1883. He fell ill again, then felt huge relief. 'It was hard, having for six years to be against the man one most revered', but it left him even more alone. *Zarathustra* is in part a hymn to solitude. His sister Elisabeth, long so attentive to her brother that some suspect incestuous infatuation, had become engaged to a rabid anti-Semite Bernard Förster. Förster founded the German People's Party, an ineffectual precursor of the Nazis, before emigrating to Paraguay to found an 'Aryan' colony. Elisabeth married him in May 1885 – with her brother's curse, but, aged nearly forty, she was desperate. The couple sailed to Paraguay in 1886, but the colony of New Germania was ill-fated; Förster committed suicide in 1889, after his embezzling had been revealed, and Elisabeth returned to Europe. Long before then Nietzsche had lost patience with 'a vengeful anti-Semitic goose'.

His earlier books had sold increasingly poorly. Nietzsche, although amazed that the world ignored 'the most exalted book that exists', had to pay for the publication of the last section of *Zarathustra* in 1885. Money was an increasing problem for the pensioned-off professor, although an elderly aristocratic admirer, Meta von Salis, helped at times. But, as if writing *Zarathustra* had sated his need for prophetic extravagance, he now wrote faster, more lucidly and better than ever. *Beyond Good and Evil: Prelude to a Philosophy of the Future*, published in 1886, was, in fact, concerned with truth. 'Do you suppose we *want* truth?' he demanded. 'Why not rather untruth? and uncertainty, even ignorance? Most people have, rather, an instinctive desire for the superficial.' (This is perhaps Nietzsche's least contentious statement.) He now praised self-confident, indeed rapacious aristocrats, saying, 'Life itself essentially consists of dispossessing, injuring, overpowering the foreign and the more feeble.' He was

thinking of Renaissance princes such as Cesare Borgia, who inspired him as they had Machiavelli. Burckhardt had argued that Renaissance 'despotism . . . fostered extreme individuality not only in the tyrant but also in the . . . secretary, minister, poet and companion'.

The Genealogy of Morals (*Zur Genealogie der Moral*), his next work, introduced his concepts of differing master and slave moralities. Judaeo-Christianity is essentially slave morality, he declared, the result of resentment against the noble warrior class, 'the *ressentiment* of those who, incapable of taking action, compensate by means of an imaginary revenge', that is punishment in hell. Socialism and anarchism he dismissed as forms of secularized, debased Christianity. He particularly detested Rousseau and the French Revolutionaries with their toxic ideals of equality. But politics hardly interested him compared with culture and psychology. He accepted asceticism as often essential for the self-mastery that gives the *Übermensch* the 'will to power' – another phrase to be disastrously misused after his death. But asceticism was just a phase before we can 'remove the concept of sin from the world . . . It is a disease, the bad conscience, that is indisputable, but disease as pregnancy is a disease.' The realm of the *Übermensch* would lie beyond such ordeals; it lay for ever beyond Nietzsche.

Early in 1887 he discovered Dostoevsky, hailing him as 'the only psychologist . . . from whom I learned something'. Nietzsche hardly needed to read the Russian's major novels; he knew as if by instinct the mentalities of the murderer Raskolknikov or the holy idiot Prince Myshkin. He later compared the 'strange sick world to which the Gospels introduce us' to 'a Russian novel in which the scum of society, nervous diseases and "childlike idiocy" seem to meet each other . . . It is regrettable that no Dostoevsky lived near this most interesting decadent [Jesus].' Nietzsche never denied that a Christian life of self-abnegation was possible, but he doubted if anyone really desired it. 'In truth there was only one Christian and he died on the cross . . . as he had lived, as he had taught – *not* to redeem

men but show how one must live . . . He does not resist, he does not defend his right, he does nothing to ward off the worst; on the contrary, he provokes it . . . Not to resist, not to be angry . . . to resist not even the evil person – to love him.' He saw non-resistance as the essence of Jesus' life and teachings, perverted by Paul and all subsequent Christians.

The year 1888 suddenly seemed to offer Nietzsche hope. In Denmark, the critic Georg Brandes praised his 'aristocratic radicalism', which delighted him, and began lecturing on Nietzsche at Copenhagen University. Soon after, in Sweden, the playwright August Strindberg began a correspondence, saying he was ending all his letters with 'Read Nietzsche!' And Nietzsche's health seemed to be improving, which he attributed to his discovery that spring of Turin. He loved its regal boulevards, cafés, bookshops and opera house, calling it a 'classical place . . . everything much more dignified than I had expected. The most beautiful cafés I have seen.' The whole city exuded 'aristocratic calm . . . there are no squalid suburbs'. Nietzsche, now claiming descent from the Niezky, Polish aristocrats, was enchanted, rejuvenated, inspired. 'Wonder upon wonders, I have had a remarkably cheerful spring so far. The first for ten, fifteen years,' he wrote to his mother in May. This productive euphoria survived even a filthy summer up in Sils Maria, and when he returned to Turin in the autumn it intensified into a golden sense of well-being.

He was now writing even faster, his handwriting so illegible that the printer could not read it. The Case of Wagner (Der Fall Wagner), perhaps the least fair and most entertaining book ever written on a musician, is almost an inverted eulogy, so intense remained his obsession with the dead Master. It opens with paeans of praise for Bizet's Carmen – 'This music seems perfect to me. It approaches lightly, supply, politely' – then lambasts Wagner as a decadent 'five steps away from the hospital', who offers 'the three great stimulants of the effete – the brutal, the artificial, the innocent (idiotic)'. And yet, as Nietzsche admitted, 'other musicians don't count compared to Wagner'; Brahms was a mere 'master of imitation'. If Wagner was decadent, he suited a

decadent age. (Unable to let sleeping gods lie, he returned to the attack yet again that year with the brief *Nietzsche Contra Wagner*.) German music in general he now condemned as 'constipated and constipating' – like German beer and religion.

Twilight of the Idols, subtitled *How to Philosophize with a Hammer* (*Götzendämmerung, oder Wie Man mit em Hammer philosphiert*), parodies in its title *Twilight of the Gods*, the immolatory finale of *The Ring*. In tone it is Wagner's utter opposite: pithy, witty, light-footed, xenophile. 'Nothing succeeds in which high spirits play no part,' declared its preface. Nietzsche attacked many varying modern ills as if aiming to upset everyone: philosophers, revolutionaries, dietitians, women, especially literary women, the people, especially the German people. But he focused first on Socrates' ugliness, somewhat overlooked by earlier thinkers. 'Ugliness . . . is among Greeks almost a refutation. Was Socrates Greek at all?' Anyway, 'Socrates was rabble . . . With Socrates Greek taste undergoes a change in favour of dialectics . . . It is above all the defeat of a nobler taste; with dialectics the rabble gets on top.' Yet Nietzsche still could not quite make up his mind about Socrates – or Wagner or even Christ.

About one hero, however, he was now unequivocal: Goethe

> . . . not a German event but a European one . . . What he aspired to was totality; he fought against the separation of reason, sensuality, will . . . a man to whom nothing is forbidden except weakness. Such a spirit who has become free stands amidst the cosmos with a joyful and trusting fatalism, in the faith that . . . in the totality everything is redeemed and affirmed – *he no longer denies* . . . Such a faith is the highest of all possible faiths. I have baptized it with the name Dionysus.

Nietzsche had found his *Übermensch*.

The Antichrist followed, repeating earlier polemics, not always religious. 'Progress is merely a modern idea . . . a false idea. The European of today is far less valuable than the European of the

Renaissance.' But Nietzsche's main target remained Christianity. 'If one shifts the centre of gravity out of life into the "Beyond" – into nothingness – life is deprived of its centre of gravity. The great lie of personal immortality destroys all rationality, all instinctive naturalness – all that is salutary.' He gave half-ironic praise to Buddhism 'a hundred times more realistic than Christianity . . . it stands, in my terms, beyond good and evil'. Even Islam and 'the wonderful cultural world of Moorish Spain' is applauded in passing – 'it said Yes to life'. The book ends with an anathema, 'I call Christianity the *one* great curse, the *one* great intrinsic depravity, the *one* great instinct for revenge for which no expedient is sufficiently poisonous, secret, petty.'

Nietzsche saw these books only as overtures to his planned *Revaluation of All Values*, itself a substitute for his even longer *The Will to Power*, whose inchoate notes were later published by Elisabeth in maliciously misleading form. But he wrote only one more work, the most original of autobiographies, begun on his birthday in October 1888: *Ecce Homo* ('Behold the Man', in reference to Christ's trial). Subtitled *How One Becomes What One Is* (*Wie Man wird, was Man ist*), it has sections, the titles of which – 'Why I Am So Wise', 'Why I Write Such Brilliant Books' – make some run for cover muttering 'General Paralysis of the Insane'. But Nietzsche was not yet mad – not quite yet, although the syphilis bacteria were spiralling into his brain as the disease moved into its third, catastrophic stage. Although principally a biography of his thought, *Ecce Homo* starts with a eulogy of his life:

On this perfect day, when everything has become ripe and not only the grapes are growing brown, a ray of sunlight has fallen on to my life. I looked behind me, I look before me, never have I seen so many and such good things together. Not in vain have I buried my forty-fourth year today; I was entitled to bury it . . . *How should I not be grateful to my whole life?*

For someone whose actual life had been a litany of suffering,

rejection, poverty and loneliness, this is heroically free of self-pity. Less laudable is the self-adulation peppering his lightning-quick résumés of his previous works. Self-praise was nothing new – writing so long without readers, he had grown solipsistic – but a side-effect of syphilis is to destroy the critical faculties.

Ecce Homo was written after Nietzsche had returned to Turin in September 1888, when he was delighted afresh by the 'superb and strangely beneficent' city. That autumn was unusually dry and clear, enabling him to think (wrongly) that Turin had the same invigorating climate as Athens or Rome. 'The clearest October light everywhere, the superb tree-lined road . . . alongside the Po, scarcely yet touched by autumn. I am now the most grateful man in the world, autumnally minded in every good sense of the word: it is my great *harvest time*,' he wrote to Overbeck. But delusions of grandeur were emerging fast. 'Here in Turin I exercise a perfect fascination. Everybody glances at me as if I were a prince – there is a special distinction in the way doors are held open for me, meals set out.' He asked his mother to send him smarter clothes, suitable for a prince living incognito. In fact, his landlord recalled later his lodger's extreme loneliness and how he spent hours on end playing the piano in his room. What he played was Wagnerian music.

Delusions of grandeur, delusions of health, delusions even of youth . . . Looking at himself in the mirror, he thought he looked younger and healthier than ever. He was now writing his *Dionysiac Dithyrambs* (*Dionysos-Dithyramben*), fragmentary but often beautiful poems that anticipate twentieth-century free verse. Increasingly, he began to believe he *was* Dionysus returned to earth, the god who would transform all values – and crush the German Reich. He wrote to Strindberg just after Christmas, 'I have ordered a convocation of princes in Rome. I want to have the young Kaiser [Wilhelm II] shot.' On 3 January 1889, trying to embrace a horse being whipped in the street, he collapsed. When he came to, he was clearly mad. He wrote to Meta von Salis, 'The world is transfigured, for God is on earth. Do

you not see how all the heavens are rejoicing? I have just seized possession of my kingdom and am throwing the pope into prison.' He signed this letter Dionysus. Overbeck, receiving a letter in Basle which ended 'I am having all anti-Semites shot', went at once to Turin. He found his old friend dancing naked in his room, which, he announced, was a temple to Dionysus. Overbeck persuaded Nietzsche to return to Basle. There he was admitted to a mental clinic until his mother took him back to Naumberg to look after him.

Nietzsche lived another eleven years in infantile dependence, his ferocious intellect completely gone. In a gross irony, fame and fortune, which had eluded him when sane, came at last. The beneficiary was his sister Elisabeth, who, on her return from Paraguay in 1893, cared for him after their mother's death and increasingly exploited him. She bought a house in Naumberg, which she turned into a museum, the chief exhibit being the mad philosopher. Robed in white like an Aryan high priest, his moustache vaster than ever, he stared uncomprehendingly at visitors, who duly admired his vatic silence. As royalties poured in, Elisabeth began to live luxuriously, acquiring servants and a carriage. Nietzsche died of a stroke on 25 August 1900 and was given a Lutheran funeral – just what he would have loathed. Elisabeth, perhaps deliberately, misunderstood her brother's ideas. In publishing *The Will to Power*, assembled from his *Nachlass* (posthumous notes), she turned him into an anti-Semitic German nationalist and prophet of imperialist Germany. This travesty culminated in a visit by Hitler to the Nietzsche Museum in 1934, when Elisabeth shook the dictator's hand. But unlike Hitler's regular visits to Wagnerian shrines – places of pilgrimage to an artist whose music and views the Führer genuinely adored – this proved a one-off visit. Hitler was no admirer of Nietzsche.

More than a century after his death, the questions Nietzsche was the first to ask – cultural, psychological, ethical – remain extraordinarily pertinent and the way he asked them extraordinarily seductive. His

view of life as an aesthetic rather than a moral challenge, or at least as one that can only be understood aesthetically, has proved almost dangerously inspirational, if more to writers and artists than philosophers. Yeats's tragic joy, Rilke's angels, Lawrence's ideas of the Greater Life are obviously indebted to him. Nietzsche can also be seen as warning of the banalities, *ressentiment* and self-pity of our culturally demotic age. Indisputably he was a pioneer in destroying Christian guilt – sexual and otherwise – as Freud acknowledged reluctantly. But if Nietzsche's intellectual intuition led him far beyond the cautious probings of the Viennese doctor, his own life led him nowhere.

'Character is destiny,' proclaimed Heraclitus, an enigmatic pre-Socratic philosopher Nietzsche much admired. For Nietzsche, both character and constitution predestined him to a far from superhuman life. He never came near to incarnating the *Übermensch*, remaining always a shabby, myopic ex-professor with abysmal health. But even if his health and wealth had allowed it, his puritan upbringing could have prevented guilt-free enjoyment of Dionysiac orgies. Beneath the heroic posturing of the *Übermensch* he remained for ever in part the pastor's son. In his attacks on early Christians for their 'inordinate fasting, continual sexual abstinence, withdrawal into the wilderness or climbing a mountain or on to a pillar . . . thinking resolutely of nothing except what provokes ecstasy and mental derangement', he was almost portraying himself, for once unwittingly. If he *had* taken a whip when visiting a woman, it would have been for her to goad him back to work, not to explore the wilder shores of sex together. The ascetic streak in Nietzsche verged on the masochistic. But, unlike Michel Foucault, who in philosophy has been his most alarmingly literal disciple, his was a psychological not sexual masochism, almost Christian in nature. A strange epitaph for the prophet of Dionysus and the *Übermensch*.

NIETZSCHE AND NAZISM

Nothing has damaged Nietzsche more than his alleged links with Nazism. Nazis such as Alfred Bäumler, professor of philosophy at Berlin, tried to enlist Nietzsche among Nazism's forerunners. Quoted out of context, various Nietzschean phrases – 'blond beast', 'will to power', etc. – sound Nazi enough. Yet thinkers as disparate as Hegel, Schopenhauer and even Kant, that pillar of the Enlightenment, suffered similar fates. One glance at what Nietzsche actually wrote about the Second Reich indicates what the writer, who admired French culture and so loathed his compatriots that he claimed to be Polish, would have thought of the Third. Above all, Nietzsche would have despised the Nazis' attitude to Europe's newly emancipated Jews. Nietzsche admired Spinoza, the first Jewish genius to escape the ghetto; he regarded (Jewish) Heinrich Heine, with his 'divine malice without which I cannot conceive the perfect', as the greatest nineteenth-century German poet, modestly placing himself second; he knew his adored Bizet had Jewish ancestors; and he applauded Offenbach, the Jewish operetta composer, as 'that most sophisticated and exuberant satyr who keeps to the great tradition as a musician'. In *Human, All Too Human* (1878) he openly attacked German anti-Semitism. Almost his last words as he fell into madness in 1889 were, 'I am having all anti-Semites shot.' On an intensely personal note, for nearly a decade his closest friend was the Jewish Paul Rée, the man who destroyed his one chance of romantic happiness with Lou Salomé. If Nietzsche had harboured a trace of anti-Semitism, it would have come boiling out then. Nothing of the sort happened.

If exculpated from charges of being anti-Semitic and a Nazi godfather, Nietzsche's admiration for 'great men', such as Julius Caesar, Napoleon I and Cesare Borgia, the most ruthless Renaissance tyrant, remains more controversial. It suggests that he might have had – as did writers such as Luigi Pirandello, Ezra Pound and W.B. Yeats later – potential sympathy for Fascism, that marginally less odious form of anti-democracy. Benito Mussolini, oddly literate for a dictator, read Nietzsche, making *Vivi Pericolosamente* (Live Dangerously) his motto. However, dictators ancient or modern have never really needed philosophers, and politics was an admitted lacuna in Nietzsche's thinking – he once called himself the 'last antipolitical German'. Nietzsche was certainly an elitist in every sense. His admiration for 'vigorous aristocracies' and dismissal of Judaeo-Christian (and Stoic and Buddhist) compassion for the weak, add a repellently brutal edge to some of his writing. But if Nietzsche's admirers include Nazi sympathizers such as Heidegger, left-wing Nietzscheans such as Herbert Marcuse, Karl Jaspers or Jean-Paul Sartre outnumber them.

4

BERTRAND RUSSELL (1872–1970):
THE MATHEMATICS OF HUMAN BEHAVIOUR

'I found great delight in maths . . . and hoped that in time there would be
a mathematics of human behaviour as precise as that of maths.'
– Bertrand Russell, *Portraits from Memory*

By the mid twentieth century Bertrand Russell had become for
many people around the world *the* philosopher, just as Einstein was
the scientist. With his white hair and noble craggy features Russell
certainly looked the part as he puffed away on his pipe. He also
sounded it, discoursing sagely on social or political topics. He gave
the first Reith Lecture on BBC radio in 1949, while his *History of
Western Philosophy* became the first philosophy bestseller. This made
Russell almost a household name and – for a philosopher – well
remunerated, but it was only one of his huge number of books, starting
with *German Social Democracy* in 1896, ending seventy-one years later
with *War Crimes in Vietnam*. Russell was never a narrowly academic
philosopher, and the award of the Nobel Prize in 1950 – for literature,
there is no prize for philosophy – must have seemed apposite.

Equally apposite was the document that he signed with Einstein
and five other Nobel Prize winners, which first warned of the cata-
strophic effects of nuclear war, and his subsequent campaigns against
nuclear weapons with the Campaign for Nuclear Disarmament
(CND) and Committee of 100. In 1961, at the age of almost ninety,
he endured prison for his 'sit-down' protests. Such heroism made him
seem a prophet of peace, a beacon of sanity and reason. He was, he
claimed, guided by 'three passions, simple but overwhelmingly strong
. . . the longing for love, the search for knowledge and unbearable
pity for the suffering of mankind'. Exactly what the public expects of
a philosopher.

But Russell had also fulfilled the academic world's expectations, chiefly through his *Principia Mathematica*, co-written with Alfred North Whitehead. This, his *magnum opus*, established his fame with his peers around the world. Applying mathematical logic to language, the *Principia* helped lay the foundations of analytical philosophy that became the dominant form of philosophy in the English-speaking world for much of the twentieth century. Ludwig Wittgenstein was won over to philosophy by Russell's writings. But Russell, when he had finished the *Principia* in 1913, felt intellectually exhausted, although only forty. By then, too, Wittgenstein's criticism of his thinking had undermined his intellectual self-confidence. In the First World War Russell's anti-war activities led to the loss of his Fellowship at Trinity College, Cambridge, and to imprisonment. There followed a second marriage, children and endless financial pressures.

As a result, Russell did almost no 'real' philosophy again for the rest of his life, although he lived to ninety-seven, dying in 1970. On a lecture tour of North America, Russell found himself asked by the head of a smart girls' college why he had given up formal philosophy. 'Because I found I preferred fucking,' he reputedly replied. But to pay his bills he wrote prolifically, an estimated average of 2,000 words a day throughout his life. Inevitably some of his writings were superficial, but in others he advocated then radical ideas on sex, marriage, divorce, education, child care, world government and disarmament. Such views – not unique to Russell but propounded by him with often persuasive brilliance – have since permeated the Western mind to become part of the liberal semi-consciousness, so widely accepted as to be almost unremarked. Russell's popular writings are important precisely because he anticipated or propagated so many later attitudes and trends. The priests and other conservatives who attacked him for 'immorality' were in a way right. Russell *was* propounding a social and 'moral' (that is, sexual) revolution that has, since his death, come about. We who live with a soaring divorce rate are partly the heirs of Dirty Bertie (one of his less flattering nicknames), who in his

life got through four wives and countless mistresses without apology.

His popular writings, often highly amusing, led to his being called 'the Voltaire of the twentieth century'. The comparison holds, for although Voltaire was never a profound thinker, both men were aristocratic liberals who at times espoused unpopular, even risky, causes. But while Voltaire ended his life fêted by all Europe, a benign smile on his octogenarian features, Russell ended his yet longer life amid devastating family feuds and recriminations. Behind and around him lay 'a long trail of emotional wreckage', in the words of his principal biographer Ray Monk, while he himself often seemed 'haunted by the ghosts of maniacs', his own phrase. Russell's will of 1966, for example, did not even mention John, his first son on whom he had once pinned all his hopes but whom he had later tried to have locked away as insane. Instead, his estate was to go to Ralph Schoenman, his controversial young press secretary. But Russell finally quarrelled even with Schoenman.

Rational, enlightened ideas did not prevent Russell, who greatly wanted children, from being as disastrous a father and grandfather as he often was a husband or lover. How far his personal failures invalidate his ideas, and how far they merely reflect Russell's own troubled character, are far from academic questions. Dealing with other individuals, as opposed to pontificating about humanity, Russell could behave with a cold callousness, suggesting 'two fundamental traits . . . a deep-seated fear of madness and a quite colossal vanity' (Monk's words again). Both came in part from his ancestors, some of the grandest in the land, but vanity was reinforced by academic triumphs. Elected a Fellow of Trinity College at the age of only twenty-three, he was made a Fellow of the Royal Society at thirty-eight for his work in logic and mathematics. From these intellectual and social summits Russell looked down with noble condescension on humanity. But only rarely, as when he declared that 'Darwin was worth more than 30 million ordinary people', did the mask of liberal humanism drop away and the icy arrogance of a Whig grandee emerge.

Bertrand Russell was born on 18 May 1872. His grandfather, the first Earl Russell, known as Lord John Russell, had twice been Prime Minister under Queen Victoria and earlier had helped guide the Great Reform Bill of 1832 (a less radical bill than its name suggests) through Parliament. But the dynasty's rise to power and immense wealth had begun in the sixteenth century with the first Earl of Bedford, one of Henry VIII's monastery-grabbing courtiers. The Russells long had radical sympathies, Lord William Russell being executed in 1683 for his part in the Rye Street Plot to assassinate Charles II. Russell's own father Viscount Amberley espoused such radical views – he was both an agnostic and a feminist – that he wrecked his political career, his advocacy of birth control particularly alienating the electorate. Amberley's friend, the liberal philosopher J.S. Mill, became Bertrand's godfather, stressing this radical connection. Russell's mother Kate Stanley was also highly aristocratic – her forebears could be traced back to 1066 – and high-mindedly radical.

But this golden inheritance was soon overshadowed by death. His mother and sister Rachel died of diphtheria in 1874. His father, sunk in melancholy, followed them to the grave less than two years later, with a pointedly non-Christian burial. Non-Christian, too, were the two guardians Amberley had appointed. But these proved totally unacceptable to Russell's grandparents, especially when it was revealed that Lady Amberley had, out of kindness or pity, let one of them, the tubercular biologist Douglas Spalding, sleep with her, although, as Russell later said, 'I know of no evidence that she derived any pleasure from doing so.' Instead, the three-year-old Bertrand and his brother Frank, seven years older, went to live with their grandparents at Pembroke Lodge, Richmond Park, a long, low building with spectacular views over the Thames Valley.

Lord Russell, affable but very old – he had visited Napoleon in exile on Elba – died in 1878, leaving Bertrand in the sole care of his grand-mother. Lady Russell was no diehard reactionary – she supported Home Rule for Ireland and accepted Darwinism – but she came from

a Scottish Presbyterian family, and life at Pembroke Lodge was Spartan. While Frank went off to school at Winchester, Bertie remained at home to be 'preserved pure, religious and affectionate . . . fitted to take his grandfather's place as Prime Minister and continue the sacred work of Reform', in the words of George Santayana, a philosopher who later became a friend. It was not a soft life. Every morning started with a cold bath, followed by piano practice in an unheated room; fruit, sugar, chocolates and even comfortable chairs were forbidden, but prayers were mandatory and even more frequent than in most Victorian households. For Lady Russell was suffocatingly, guilt-inducingly religious. On his twelfth birthday Russell received from her a Bible inscribed with her favourite texts: 'Thou shalt not follow a multitude to do evil . . . Be not afraid neither be thou dismayed; for the Lord thy God is with thee whithersoever thou goest.' The unintended result was to toughen Russell physically and mentally but half cripple him emotionally.

As a boy Russell met few children of his own age – his Stanley cousins, a noisy, rumbustious crew liked by his brother Frank, alarmed rather than charmed him. Instead, his unmarried neurotic Aunt Agatha and Uncle Rollo, who wrote psalms, provided suitably edifying company at Richmond. Many subjects were never mentioned in that sepulchrally quiet household: money, sex and, especially, the fate of Uncle Willy, committed to an asylum for murdering two men. Fears that such madness might prove hereditary haunted Russell all his life. But there were governesses and tutors – he became very attached to some of the former – to whom he could talk more freely, and Russell soon revealed intellectual promise. When he was eleven, Frank initiated him into the mysteries of mathematics. Russell was fascinated if disappointed that Frank gave no proof for Euclid's axioms, insisting they must be taken for granted. However, Russell had discovered a new world. 'This was one of the great events of my life, as dazzling as first love. I had not imagined there was anything so delicious in the world,' he later wrote. For a few months he had an

agnostic tutor, but he was sent away to avoid undermining Russell's faith – in vain, for the brilliant child increasingly took nothing for granted. When he expressed such doubts to his grandmother, however, she taunted him with the jingle 'What is mind? No matter. What is matter? Never mind!' 'At the fifteenth or sixteenth repetition of this remark it ceased to be amusing,' Russell recalled. He henceforth kept doubts about ethics and immortality to himself, writing his diary in Greek letters to baffle prying eyes

Life at Pembroke Lodge had consolations. In his grandfather's library Russell could find free-thinkers: Machiavelli, Swift, Gibbon, Byron, his godfather J.S. Mill and, above all, Shelley, whose poetry he always loved. Further, there were distinguished visitors. Russell once found himself entertaining Prime Minister Gladstone on his own, when the ladies had withdrawn after dinner. (The Grand Old Man spoke only to ask, 'This is very good port but why have they given it to me in a claret glass?') Such august but aged visitors scarcely compensated for the lack of livelier company, however. Russell later wrote, 'From adolescence onwards I was driven by a desperate misery of loneliness, for which I knew that love would be the only cure.' But the lifelong rebel always also spoke of the British government as 'we' not 'they', friends noticed.

In 1883 Uncle Rollo married and took a house near Hindhead in the Surrey hills. While visiting him, Russell at the age of seventeen met the Pearsall Smiths, rich American Quakers who had settled near by at Friday Hill. They were a colourful family. Robert, the father, had abandoned preaching because his love of certain women in his congregation proved more carnal than spiritual; his wife Hannah was 'a mixture of dormant sadism and religious fervour', who in 1895 suggested castrating Oscar Wilde after his trial; the son, Logan, became a literary dilettante, while Mary, the elder daughter, was about to leave her first husband for the art historian Bernard Berenson. But Russell fell in love with Alys, the shy younger daughter, blue-eyed, willowy, sweet-natured, five years older than him, a high-minded

graduate of Bryn Mawr Women's College in the USA. Although she did not at once requite his love, when she did her devotion never faded; in her eighties she was still vainly awaiting his return. But at the time Russell kept quiet about his feelings.

In 1890 this 'solitary, shy, priggish youth' (his words) went up to Trinity College, Cambridge, with a mathematics scholarship. (Russell chose mathematics because it possessed 'not only truth but supreme beauty – a beauty cold and austere, like that of sculpture', as he wrote in 1907.) Cambridge provided 'a new world of infinite delight'. Here were other people interested in the 'whole world of mental adventure', with whom he could talk the night through. Among his new acquaintances were the Trevelyan brothers – one of whom, the historian George, later, as Master of Trinity, helped Russell return to the college – and G.E. Moore, a philosopher of dazzling moral and intellectual integrity. Russell soon won Moore's respect but never his affection, for Moore became the first to sense Russell's abnormal lack of human feeling. Russell was elected to the Apostles, the exclusive debating club, still at this time rather austere – 'whale', that is, sardine, sandwiches were their main fare – and lacking the homoerotic atmosphere it acquired when Lytton Strachey and John Maynard Keynes later joined. Cambridge generally fitted him 'like a glove', and he discarded the last remnants of his childhood Christianity in its cheerfully atheistic air. What he could not for long discard was a passion to 'lay bare the most general features of reality'. Youthful enthusiasm for Pythagoras, Plato's precursor in mystical mathematics, disappeared very slowly in 'a gradual retreat from Pythagoras'. Russell's longing for intellectual certainty underlay his later quest for a logical basis to mathematics.

After getting a first in 1893, Russell, dissatisfied with a subject then taught as 'artful dodges and ingenious devices', switched to philosophy, that 'No Man's Land . . . intermediate between religion and philosophy', getting another first the following year. British philosophy at the time was dominated by Hegelian Idealism, which considered the whole universe, both mind and matter, to be one and indivisible, like a jelly:

99

shake one part of it and all the rest would quiver. Overcoming his scepticism, Russell 'for a while more or less believed it'.

By 1894 Russell, who had inherited £20,000 (a huge sum at the time), could afford to declare independence. The previous summer he had finally revealed his feelings for Alys. After much earnest wooing, in punts and on walks, always debating – Russell shared Alys's radical views on many things, especially the equality of women, but not her distaste for sexual contact – Alys finally agreed to marry him. They first kissed one snowy day in January 1894. Alys was only the second woman that Russell, aged twenty-one, had kissed; the first had been a housemaid at Pembroke Lodge. Soon after, at his insistence and against her wishes, she let him kiss her breasts.

If Alys's parents had some doubts about the engagement, Lady Russell was aghast that this 'baby-snatcher, a lower-class adventuress' should steal her beloved Bertie. She hatched plans to thwart theirs. A doctor was summoned to tell Russell something of the history of madness in the family; Russell, shaken, simply replied that Alys and he would always use contraception. Lady Russell, trying another approach, demanded he emulate his ancestors by entering public life. This had more effect. Russell, always torn between politics and academe, agreed to become the attaché of the British ambassador to Paris for three months. The family hoped that his ardour for the unsuitable American would be dulled by absence. In vain. Russell, disgusted by fin-de-siècle Paris, longed only to be with Alys. He was also unthrilled by diplomatic work, arguing with the French Foreign Office as to whether or not lobster should be classified as a fish. His many letters to Alys mingle premarital ardour with condescension: 'Don't be afraid I'm going to try to make thee into an abstract thinker, which thee [Russell had adopted the Quaker pronoun] isn't by nature . . . thee might wish to have some hours every day for bookwork of a historical or economical kind,' he wrote on 15 October.

Alys cried at times on receiving such letters, but on 13 December 1894 they were duly married – Russell swallowing his atheism for the

Quaker ceremony that most of his relatives avoided – and honey-mooned in Holland and Germany. Russell could now have sex with a clear conscience – this being among his strongest reasons for marriage, as for many men at the time – although he found Alys's flannel night-gowns to be passion-killers. Russell, emotionally and financially secure, had no need actually to do any work, even after his election as a Fellow of Trinity in October 1895. But sloth was never one of his vices. Another visit to Germany led to his first book, *German Social Democracy*, which appeared in 1896. He later said, 'I took no great interest in it as I had determined to devote myself to mathematical philosophy.' But it is astonishingly perceptive about Marxism (Social Democrats were half-Marxist at the time). He considered Marx's economic theories flawed but pointed out that Marxism's true appeal stemmed from its combination of the intellectual prestige of a (pseudo-) science with the emotional pull of a great myth or religion – this decades before Lenin or Stalin glared from a poster. The book had an appendix called 'The Woman Question in Germany' by Alys, making it their one collaborative work.

Political prescience took second place over the next fourteen years to intense work on mathematics and logic, years that saw Russell produce his masterpieces, *The Principles of Mathematics* and *Principia Mathematica*. Russell was trying to develop a new, wholly logical basis for mathematics. By 1898 he had rejected Hegelian idealism – feeling 'a great liberation, as if I had escaped from a hot-house on to a windswept headland' – and moved towards accepting Moore's empirical view that the world is 'like a heap of shot'. He wrote *The Principles* at speed, finishing the first draught of 200,000 words in 1900, but in doing so became aware of the intellectual problems towering before him, especially 'Russell's Paradox'. (This, put simply and non-mathematically, is typified by the conundrum of Epimenides, the Cretan who stated that all Cretans were liars.)

For his next, even greater, work on mathematical logic, Russell collaborated with Alfred North Whitehead, his former tutor, now a

friend, thinking it would take them a year or two. It took almost a decade. At times Russell would spend a whole day staring at a blank sheet of paper, unable to write. The mathematical trilogy that finally emerged over the years 1910–13 – so heavy that its manuscripts had to be trundled to Cambridge University Press in a cart and filled with such terrifyingly high maths that Russell later joked only six people in the world had read and understood them – made its authors no money. But it confirmed their intellectual reputations, being considered the greatest contribution to logic since Aristotle 2,200 years before. Although Russell decried any connection between his 'real' philosophy and popular writings, his authority as a social and political critic rested finally on these monumental works, even if few people ever read them. He did not win the Nobel Prize for pieces such as 'Who May Use Lipstick?' and 'Should Socialists Smoke Good Cigars?', both written for the Hearst press in the 1930s. He now felt qualified to pronounce on almost all human problems.

Among his first popular pieces was A Free Man's Worship, written while staying with the Berensons – now his in-laws, as Mary had by this time married Bernard Berenson – in Italy in 1902 and 'intended to provide intellectually acceptable solace for the non-religious'. Its majestic, lyrical tone echoed Berenson's Pateresque prose – 'To abandon the struggle for private happiness, to expel all eagerness of temporary desire, to burn with passion for eternal things . . . this is the free man's worship' – but also indicated the torment in Russell's own life. While his intellectual career bloomed, his emotional life had withered. Whitehead and his wife Evelyn, a beautiful, lively woman, younger than her husband, lived in Grantchester, which Russell often visited when in Cambridge. There Russell had a mystical experience. Returning after hearing a reading of Euripides' tragedy Hippolytus in 1901, he found Evelyn apparently suffering a heart attack:

> She seemed cut off from everyone by walls of agony and the sense of
> solitude of each human soul overwhelmed me . . . Suddenly the

ground seemed to give way beneath me, and I found myself in quite another region . . . I found myself filled with semi-mystical feelings about beauty . . . and a desire almost as profound as that of the Buddha to find some philosophy which should make human life endurable.

Russell did not mention his feelings for Evelyn that, if unvoiced, were far from unpassionate. They had totally replaced any love for Alys. 'I went bicycling one afternoon and suddenly . . . I realized that I no longer loved Alys. I had had no idea until this moment that my love for her was even lessening. The problem presented by this discovery was very grave,' he recorded in his *Autobiography*, a work far less candid than it appears. His bicycling revelation has struck many people as unconvincing, but the marriage now became unendurable for both partners. Russell, struggling to control his increasing distaste for Alys's company, refused to sleep with her – he seems to have been impotent when he tried – avoiding her as much as possible. Still in his thirties, he suffered a decade of celibacy and emotional aridity in which only work kept him sane or from suicide.

Alys, too, was miserable. Longing for death, she was dismayed to find that a lump in her breast was *not* cancer. Russell was ruthlessly, cold-bloodedly honest with her, as he now believed a philosopher should be. 'The next day came Alys's return [from an enforced 'rest cure'], the direct question and the answer that love was dead; and then, in the bedroom, her loud, heart-rending sobs, while I worked at my desk next door . . . Oh the pity of it! . . . And how my heart hardened from minute to minute because I left her to sob!' he recorded stonily.

Russell had not lost interest in politics, which offered an escape from marital woes. Long a friend of the Socialists Beatrice and Sidney Webb, he became a Fabian fellow traveller, although his views remained more Liberal than Socialist. As a keen supporter of women's suffrage he stood for Parliament in 1907, failing to win the seat of Wimbledon after a campaign in which rats were let loose and

eggs thrown at Alys. Although some thought that Russell employed in politics was like 'a razor being used to chop wood', he campaigned vigorously again in the January 1910 General Election on behalf of Philip Morrell, a Liberal whose views he shared and who was married to the flamboyant aristocrat Lady Ottoline. Ottoline and Russell had known each other socially for some time, Ottoline noting in her diary in September 1909, 'I don't think I have ever met anyone more attractive, but very alarming, so quick and clear-sighted and supremely intellectual.' Russell noted her horsy face and beautiful hair as well as her 'excessive' use of powder and perfume but was intrigued.

Russell was *en route* to a conference in Paris in March 1911 when he had dinner at the Morrells' house in London. Philip was away. After the other guests had left, Russell stayed on talking for hours to find that 'suddenly the long restraint gave way like the bursting of a dam. I found myself overwhelmingly and passionately in love.' Ottoline for her part was 'utterly unprepared for the flood of passion which he now poured out on me . . . It was as if he had risen from the grave . . . My imagination was swept away, but not my heart.' Next day Russell on the train to Paris wrote to her lyrically in the first of 2,000 letters, detailing not only his love but also his relations with men such as Wittgenstein.

Ottoline was Russell's greatest, most formidable lover. Towering over the small philosopher, her stature accentuated by huge hats, scarves and romantic clothes, she lived amid guests from the artistic and literary worlds, including the Bloomsbury set. From 1915 she entertained lavishly at Garsington Manor in Oxfordshire, where Lytton Strachey would totter around in her high heels. Many guests repaid her generosity by biting the hand that had fed and flattered them – D.H. Lawrence ridiculed her in *Women in Love*, Aldous Huxley in *Those Barren Leaves*. Certainly Ottoline could be over-powering. But for Russell she was a liberation, as his letters, at first written almost hourly, reveal: 'O my heart, I ache for you. I feel as if

I could hardly live through the joy of your kiss tomorrow . . . Wherever I go and whatever I am doing, you are always with me like remembered music . . . Everywhere the radiance of your love lights the world for me.' Ottoline was never quite so bowled over. In Russell's daughter Kate's words, 'She laughed at him. She surrounded herself with beautiful objects and delicious perfumes which worked strongly on his senses once he had got over his disapproval of them . . . Ottoline was different from his other loves because he was in awe of her.'

Ottoline was currently having affairs with the painter Henry Lamb and the art critic Roger Fry – she adored the arts – while still sleeping with her tolerant husband. Russell's early expectations that she would leave everything – including her daughter – were disappointed. Ottoline, almost as strong-willed if not remotely as egocentric as the philosopher, kept her marriage intact. She was in so many ways his opposite that their love encountered problems. One was that while Russell quivered with desire for her Ottoline did not find him very attractive physically. Scarcely good-looking – skinny, not tall, big-nosed – Russell also had acute halitosis at the time. His mind, however, fascinated her – relevant, as their affair was often conducted more by letter than in person.

A major difference between them was religion. Ottoline, piously Christian as a child, remained mystically inclined, something that Russell with his 'logic machine of a mind', as she called it, found hard to accept. Even so, with Ottoline Russell behaved much like a normal lover, counting the minutes until her arrival or agonizing over their partings. Aldous Huxley's phrase 'High brow, low groin', probably coined with Russell in mind, was for once inapposite. Russell rediscovered, too, the joys of poetry and music. He even thought of abandoning philosophy to become a novelist. His attempt at fiction, *The Perplexities of John Forstice*, revealed his literary shortcomings, however, and he put it aside. Much more successful was his 'shilling shocker', *The Problems of Philosophy*, written for the Home University Library in 1912. It begins by asking, 'Is there any knowledge which is so certain

that no reasonable man can doubt it? This question, which at first sight may not seem difficult, is really one of the most difficult that can be asked.' The slim book managed to deal, among other philosophical topics, with the real impetus behind Russell's major works, his quest for certainty, popularizing without trivializing it.

At Cambridge in October 1911 Russell met an intense young Austrian who was to affect his work as much Ottoline had his life. Ludwig Wittgenstein, unhappily studying engineering at Manchester, had been overwhelmed by reading Russell's *Principles of Mathematics*. At the advice of the German philosopher Gottlob Frege, he had sought out Russell but in agonized indecision. Abandoning engineering for philosophy would anger his father, an overpowering businessman. At first Russell treated Wittgenstein with amused condescension – 'He is armour-plated against all assaults of reasoning. It is really rather a waste of time talking to him,' he wrote to Ottoline. But this soon turned to appreciation. 'He is literary, very musical . . . and I *think* really intelligent.' Wittgenstein, during the Christmas vacation in Vienna, wrote a paper that convinced Russell of his genius. Soon Russell wrote, 'In discussion with him I put out *all* my force and only just equal his . . . I love him and feel he will solve the problems that I am too old to solve [Russell was not yet forty]. He has the theoretical passion *very* strongly . . . He doesn't want to prove this or that, but to find out how things really are.' He was touched by Wittgenstein's appreciation of the aesthetic beauty of the *Principia*, an extremely rare reaction. By July 1912 Russell could tell Wittgenstein's sister Hermine, visiting Cambridge, that he expected 'the next big step in philosophy to be taken by your brother'.

Wittgenstein grew from being Russell's protégé to becoming almost his master – a fact Russell tacitly acknowledged by dropping work on his new book *Theory of Knowledge* in 1913, after Wittgenstein had criticized it. Later he wrote, 'I saw he was right . . . that I could not hope ever again to do fundamental work in philosophy.' This realization was confirmed when Russell read Wittgenstein's *Tractatus*

in 1920, a book which he helped get published by writing the introduction that Wittgenstein, typically preferring truth to tact, attacked for its lack of perception.

If such open-mindedness testifies to intellectual generosity, Russell's behaviour elsewhere grew rapidly worse, perhaps to compensate. Love with Ottoline had uncorked a long-repressed but rampant libido, but she now wanted their relationship to be mainly platonic. This had little appeal, and Russell began a series of affairs. Visiting the USA on a lecture tour in the spring of 1914, he made a generally favourable impression. But he struck the young T.S. Eliot, then studying philosophy at Harvard, less as a sage than as a satyr. Eliot immortalized Russell as:

> Priapus in the shrubbery
> Gaping at the lady in the swing.

While grandly dismissive of life in the USA – Harvard was a 'one-horse place' – Russell liked at least one of its inhabitants. Helen Dudley, a 28-year-old graduate of Bryn Mawr and Oxford and the daughter of his hosts in Chicago, fell in love with the priapic philosopher. They slept together, and Helen believed they were engaged, although Russell was still married to Alys. Encouraged by Russell to follow him back across the Atlantic – not a cheap or easy crossing in those days – Helen arrived in London as Russell was striving to reignite his affair with Ottoline. As Helen had little money, Russell suggested she stay with the Morrells. Helen at first knew nothing of Russell's affair with Ottoline, who found herself forced to look after her nervous rival. Russell only wanted 'to get away from this horrible personal tangle', he confessed. But he continued to sleep with Helen – despite telling Ottoline all was over between them – and Helen confided in Ottoline. Helen would turn up and bang at the door of Russell's flat in Bloomsbury while Ottoline and Russell were inside. Only once did he open the door – to give her a glass of water – but he never let her

in. Helen finally returned to America where she suffered a break-down that left her paralysed and then insane. 'I broke her heart,' Russell noted briefly in his *Autobiography*.

Private passions were partly eclipsed, however, by the eruption of popular hatred at the outbreak of the First World War in August. The sudden conversion of formerly peaceful people into enthusiasts for the mass slaughter of Germans – including dachshunds, now feared as canine Fifth Columnists – astonished Russell and lastingly changed his views on human nature. Admiring German culture, he could not at first believe that the war was supported by the majority of Britons. But the majority included old friends like Whitehead and most members of Trinity, who in 1916 stripped him of his fellowship.

By then Russell was working for the No-Conscription Fellowship (conscription was introduced in January 1916), editing its journal the *Tribunal*. Watching 'young men embarking in troop trains to be slaughtered on the Somme . . . I felt an aching compassion . . . and found myself united to the actual world in a strange marriage of pain,' he wrote, recording a sea change in attitude. Early in 1916 he gave eight lectures, published as *Principles of Social Reconstruction*, dealing not just with war but with the role of the state, instinct versus reason – emphasizing the former more than earlier – education, marriage and the family. They are among his most eloquent and perceptive writings. He now thought capitalism as well as nationalism a cause of war, advocated a socialist world government – but typically gave no clues as to how this could be realized – and suggested replacing both British and German navies with an international force, a view that enraged millions. A typical apoplectic review in the *Spectator*, denouncing the book as 'thoroughly mischievous', delighted him.

Revealing unexpected gifts as a campaigner, he became the government's foremost critic, positively courting imprisonment. In 1916 he admitted that he had written a leaflet defending a conscientious objector. He was sentenced to a fine or imprisonment – 'the very thing I wanted', he told Ottoline, declining to pay. The court

ordered the seizure of his goods instead, but friends bought all his books and returned them to him. He was, however, increasingly restricted in his movements – he could not visit the USA or certain parts of Britain. All this made him a hero for opponents of the war, but the cause of his actual imprisonment was almost frivolous.

Staying at Garsington for Christmas 1917, he half-jokingly suggested that American troops now reaching Europe might be used against British strikers, an absurdity he repeated in the *Tribunal*. This time he was tried for prejudicing 'relations with the United States of America' and sentenced to six months' prison. But, as a result of strings being pulled, he was imprisoned in the more comfortable First Division, where he had his own cell, cleaned by another prisoner, and could write on uncontentious topics. (While opposing what he saw as a fratricidal conflict, Russell was not a total pacifist, however. He accepted wars might occasionally be necessary – for example, the British and American civil wars – or at least defensible, such as those which led to the extermination of North American natives, thus enabling the spread of Western civilization. Western civilization he considered humanity's greatest achievement, not then an unfashionable view.)

By the time he came out of prison the war was nearing its end. Through the riotous celebrators on Armistice Day Russell walked, feeling even more isolated. His problem, at the age of forty-six, with neither work nor family, was what to do next – and whom to do it with. But his war years had not been exactly celibate. In 1915 Russell had met and apparently seduced Vivien Eliot, wife of the poet. Although newly married, the Eliots' relationship was already in trouble, Eliot himself being very short of money. Russell helped them financially – he could be remarkably generous – and then, not exactly in return, slept with Vivien, whom Eliot left insouciantly in his care. Russell even lived in the Eliots' London flat when Eliot was away, buying Vivien 'silk underclothes and all sorts of silly things', according to Ottoline. Vivien was highly attractive – Aldous Huxley

described her as 'provocation incarnate' – but emotionally, if not mentally, unstable. While Graham Greene's statement that, 'Mrs T.S. Eliot's insanity sprang from her seduction and desertion by Bertrand Russell' over-simplifies, Vivien's affair with Russell, abruptly terminated by him when he tired of her, cannot have helped her fragile mental health. Vivien spent her last eighteen years involuntarily confined to an asylum by her brother and husband.

Russell had a far more serious attachment – concurrently at first with Vivien, with Ottoline still not out of the emotional picture – with Lady Constance Malleson, who as an actress called herself Colette O'Neil. Another aristocratic beauty with a complaisant husband, Colette had great erotic allure, but she also often had other lovers. 'Colette's capacity for being in love with several people at once was astonishing,' he noted indignantly, but they kept in touch for decades, at times renewing their affair.

But for Russell, now approaching fifty, philoprogenitive urges were becoming overwhelming. He wanted someone to be the mother of his children. The woman he finally chose was a Cambridge academic, Dora Black: intelligent, determined, twenty-two years younger than him, a socialist, but not keen on marriage. However, Dora *did* want children, and as Russell insisted on marriage – to safeguard the Russell title among other things, although Dora spat at the prospect of becoming a countess – she agreed. It was to be an open marriage, then very unusual. 'We both thought that marriage should be compatible with minor affairs . . . we made a compact in writing to the effect . . . But I stipulated that if she should have a child that was not mine there should be a divorce,' he wrote. Alys, ever amenable, agreed to sue for divorce, and Dora and Russell were married on 27 September 1921.

By then Russell had visited both Russia and China. In China he spent a year lecturing, and fell in love with its ancient, urbane, aristocratic culture, even then under serious threat. His feelings about Bolshevik Russia were utterly different. Arriving in 1920 with

guarded optimism – he had welcomed both revolutions in 1917 – he left disgusted. Granted a one-hour interview with Lenin, he found 'nothing in his manner or bearing suggests the man who has power ... He laughs a great deal; at first his laugh seems merely friendly and jolly, but gradually one finds it grim.' Russell could not share the Soviet leader's mirth at reports of landlords being hanged from the nearest tree. Once out of Russia he told Ottoline, 'Bolshevism is a closed tyrannical bureaucracy with a spy system more elaborate and terrible than the Tsar's and an aristocracy as insolent and unfeeling.' Russell's rejection of Russian Communism – exceptional at the time among Western intellectuals and not shared by Dora who made her own Soviet pilgrimage – dominated his world view for forty years.

Russell's first child, John, born in November 1921, filled him with atavistic paternal joy – he revived the old aristocratic custom of driving around London in an open carriage to display his wife and new-born. Russell had been thinking hard about child-rearing in the Modern Age, however. Rejecting Rousseau's *Emile*, he was impressed by Montessori's ideas as well as Ivan Pavlov's. Far more influential, alas, was the American behaviourist J.B. Watson, whose ideas dominate his book *On Education* of 1926. This declares:

> that education of character must begin at birth and requires a reversal of much of the practice of mothers and ignorant nurses ... All mothers wish their children to sleep because it is both healthy and convenient ... They developed certain techniques: rocking the cradle and singing lullabies. It was left for males, who investigated the matter scientifically, to discover that this technique is ideally wrong ... it creates bad habits ... Infants are far more cunning than grown-up people suppose; if they find that crying produces agreeable results, they will cry ... Some of these precepts might seem harsh, but experience shows that they make for the child's health and happiness.

'Whose experience?' wondered Kate Russell years later. 'Not mine either as infant or as mother.' Russell's second child, Kate, born in 1923, often felt the neglected junior but in fact proved the tougher of the two.

Despite such attempts at character-building, the children's first years were often happy, summers being spent at Carn Voel, a seaside house in Cornwall that Kate later called the Garden of Eden. Here Russell spent every morning writing articles and books. (His inheritance had been given away to the Eliots and others.) Some books, such as *The ABC of Atoms*, popularized subjects on which he was deeply knowledgeable; others, such as *On Education*, reveal more arrogance than insight. He wrote swiftly, 'covering page after page with his immaculate handwriting', Kate recalled, never crossing anything out. Afternoons were spent on the beach, where he rejoiced in 'the ecstasy of watching two healthy happy children learning the joys of sea and rocks and sun and storm'. These were among the happiest moments of his life. But even here Russell could not give up his quest to create a 'generation raised in fearless freedom'. He set out to overcome John's childish fears of the sea by behaviourist techniques. 'Every day for about a fortnight we plunged him up to the neck in the sea, in spite of his struggles and fears. Every day they grew less . . . Fear had not ceased altogether, but had partly been repressed by pride,' Russell recorded proudly. 'He was such a kind man, my father, yet his method of education seems full of brutal assaults on the childish mind,' Kate later remarked.

As their children grew, the Russells decided to found their own primary school – strange work for a philosopher but a logical outcome of Russell's current Utopianism. Frank, his brother, leased them Telegraph House high on the Sussex Downs, and in 1927 they moved in, hoping to give their children an education in which emotional needs would not be sacrificed to intellectual development. That, however, was exactly what happened. Russell, ensconced in a tower room, enthralled his young audiences talking on history, mathematics,

science or religion. He could communicate intellectually amazingly well even to small children and, as he chose the often heterodox teachers, the standard of teaching at Telegraph School was generally excellent. But he was useless at administrative duties and at dealing with the nasty reality of children's behaviour.

Kate remembered 'being just one of the children, having no special position and feeling vaguely unhappy', but her brother suffered worse. Unchecked bullying and teasing drove John – small for his age and seen by others (unfairly) as favoured by his parents – into hysterics and then, more ominously, into silent withdrawal. As Russell later admitted, 'To let the children go free was to establish a reign of terror in which the strong kept the weak trembling and miserable.' He found himself forced into the odious role of headmaster, not the apostle of children's liberation he had expected. Many of the children were simply trouble, arriving at Telegraph School only after serial expulsions from other schools. Dora, who later continued the school for a decade on her own, was more determined and tougher all round. She insisted that children sleep with dormitory windows open and no more than two blankets on their beds, no matter what the weather. Unsurprisingly, the children were often ill, John almost dying in 1929.

Telegraph School needed other finances than its fee-paying pupils, driving Russell back to lecture tours as well as writing. With such a famous founder and naked children leaping around the grounds, however, it soon became notorious. Reputedly, an investigating journalist exclaimed 'Good God!' when the front door was opened by a naked infant, only to be told there was no God. Rumours of sex among the pupils were rife but unfounded. More pertinent were the growing strains on the Russells' marriage. Dora had begun carving out her own political career when Russell was on a lecture tour of the USA in 1924. He had stood at two elections for the Labour Party, to which he had transferred his rather provisional allegiance after 1914. Now she stood for election for the same unwinnable seat of Chelsea (taking more votes than he had) and took up campaigning,

mainly to promote contraception, then still almost illegal. In doing so she met and began sleeping with Roy Randall, a Labour activist, for free love was one of her central beliefs.

At first this was not catastrophic, despite Russell's raging jealousy. He had become impotent with Dora in about 1925 – a sign of his fading ardour, not physical decay – and so started an affair with a glamorous young Swiss teacher, behaviour copied by other members of staff. Bedroom doors in Telegraph House may have opened and closed all night, but the Russells tried, for their children's sake, to keep the marriage going. In *Marriage and Morals* (1929) Russell wrote, 'adultery should not to my mind be a ground of divorce', and attempted to live up to his precept that jealousy, not infidelity, was the marriage-destroyer. (The book, while not extolling promiscuity, typically attacks Christian sexual attitudes and asserts that extra-marital affairs relieve intra-marital discord. Of mutual affection, loyalty and enjoyment in marriage Russell said nothing – a point picked on by the novelist John Cowper Powys when the two men debated marriage in 1928, Powys hymning fidelity.)

Then Dora, lecturing in the USA herself in 1928, fell madly in love with Griffin Barry, a bisexual Communist-sympathizing adventurer, who followed her back to Europe and went off to the Riviera with her. This strained Russell's tolerance to breaking point, something Dora ignored. But Russell could not ignore Dora becoming pregnant with Barry's child. Born in July 1930, Harriet was given Russell's surname, which angered him – he spent years getting her name removed from Debrett's, a sign of his deep dynastic feeling. Another Barry baby followed, but by then Dora was besotted with Paul Gillard, a feckless ex-lover of Barry, who claimed to be a Communist agent but spent his time pub-crawling. Russell, prepared to try to tolerate Barry, loathed this 'drunken homosexual spy', and the marriage collapsed in bitter hatred.

Russell, meanwhile, had fallen in love with Patricia Spence, called Peter, an Oxford undergraduate who helped to look after the older

Russell children in 1930. Then aged twenty (so thirty-eight years younger than Russell), tall and glamorous, Peter at first delighted Kate who recalled her as 'one of the most beautiful women I have ever seen . . . full of fun and zest for life'. She and Russell married in 1936. Peter seemed mainly a trophy wife for the new earl – Russell had inherited the title in 1931 on Frank's death – for, while she at times helped him with his work, Russell's friends admired her elegance not her mind. Inevitably, the children, shuttled between households, suffered in an acrimonious divorce in which neither partner showed goodwill, let alone the rational benevolence they had preached. Russell developed a contemptuous hatred for his ex-spouse, outwitting Dora in legal affairs and trying to use the children against her whenever he could. John, loyal to his mother, withdrew further into himself; Kate, half-guiltily, preferred the elegance of Telegraph House, where Russell and Peter now lived, to Dora's domestic chaos. Peter even knew how to display their furniture – mostly designed by Wittgenstein, so of a certain austerity – to good effect. Both children entered Dartington School in Devon in 1934, which Kate loved. 'It preserved my sanity, educated my mind and . . . provided a stable environment,' she remembered.

The 1930s was a grim decade for Russell, as his books reveal. *Education and the Social Order* (1932) takes a semi-authoritarian view of education, almost advocating Plato's division of mankind into rulers and ruled and shows his utter disillusionment with the school he had founded. In *The Scientific Outlook* (1931) Russell gloomily predicted a world controlled by technocrats where all human freedom would vanish. His ideas on scientific fallibilism were later taken up by Karl Popper and those on technocratic tyranny by the likes of Herbert Marcuse and Jurgens Habermas, gurus to the 1960s' radicals. (Russell at the time accused Aldous Huxley of plagiarizing his ideas in *Brave New World*, but Huxley's dystopic novel satirized a generation of utopians. Its precursor, if any, was Yevgeny Zamyatin's *We* of 1920.) Burdened by alimony payments and tired of writing endless articles – his investments

had vanished in the Wall Street Crash of 1929 – Russell tried to return to academic philosophy, first at Cambridge, where Moore cold-shouldered him, then at Harvard and then Oxford, where from 1937 to 1938 he gave some lectures. Ironically, while his *Principia* had become very influential between the wars, Russell himself now sounded dated, for he had ignored recent developments. Finally offered a post at Chicago, he sailed for America with Peter and their baby son Conrad in September 1938 during the Munich Crisis. Right up to the Nazi–Soviet Pact of August 1939 Russell advocated appeasing Hitler, his pacifism being based both on horror of war and ignorance of Nazi Germany. In 1936 he had urged Gandhian non-resistance to the Nazis in *Which Way to Peace?*, the one book he later disowned.

His American stay ended unhappily. Horrified by the threat to Britain – Russell was in his own way patriotic – he managed to bring Kate and John over to California in 1939, where he was lecturing at University of California at Los Angeles. Russell liked UCLA but not its president, so he happily gave notice when offered a post at New York City University. This proved a rash career move. Before the appointment was ratified, a campaign sprang up to stop this 'desiccated, divorced and decadent advocate of social promiscuity' – as the Catholic magazine *American* put it – from corrupting the young by lecturing on logic and mathematics. A hyenas' chorus of religious bigots threw back at Russell his more impish statements, chiefly from *Marriage and Morals*, and he was 'judicially pronounced unworthy to be Professor of Philosophy'. Russell was jobless, indeed penniless, until providence intervened in the shape of Alfred Barnes, the eccentric millionaire founder of the Barnes Foundation. Barnes hired Russell to lecture on the history of philosophy and paid for the Russells to move to Pennsylvania.

If Russell had briefly appeared a modern Socrates heroically defending intellectual and sexual freedoms, he now revealed his own bigotry. Far from growing up 'happy and free', the elder children had become disturbed adolescents, John especially being troubled by his homosexuality. He tried to disclose this to his family obliquely via the

Ouija board, which spelt out one evening 'John it [is] homo'. Perhaps deliberately obtuse, Russell treated this as a joke. He shared the then common belief that homosexuality was just the result of bad parenting, ergo it was impossible for his son to be homosexual. Kate and John soon became happy to leave a home where the marriage was under strain. Peter, tiring of a life of poverty with a husband thirty-eight years older than herself, was having affairs with other men, to which Russell reacted with icy courtesy. When Barnes sacked Russell – the millionaire had taken offence at an article comparing them – Russell worked up his lecture notes into his *History of Western Philosophy*, published in 1946. Attacked by academics for its reliance on secondary sources and often wild generalizations – the chapters on Kant, Hegel and Nietzsche are outrageously biased and inadequate for such great figures, it eccentrically includes a chapter on Byron, least intellectual of poets – this book is immensely readable, sparkling with acute perceptions and prejudices, and has probably introduced more people to philosophy than any other.

Suddenly the sun of official favour shone again on the elderly philosopher. Trinity offered him a new fellowship, and in 1944 he sailed home – in every sense. He now became the Establishment's darling, broadcasting regularly on the BBC, lecturing for the British Council in Belgium, Switzerland, Norway – where he owed a narrow escape in an air crash to his smoking, which placed him at the back of the aircraft – and Australia. In 1949 he received the Order of Merit, an honour restricted to just twenty-four people. Russell, long alarmed at the Soviet threat to freedom, found the Establishment now agreed with him as the Iron Curtain bisected Europe. But Russell surpassed every hawk in the Pentagon by proposing that the USA should at once use its current monopoly of nuclear weapons to launch pre-emptive nuclear war. 'I should for my part prefer all the chaos and destruction of a war conducted by means of the atomic bomb to the universal domination of a government having the evil characteristics of the Nazis,' he declared in October 1945, two

months after Hiroshima. Later he accepted that such a war might kill 500 million people and set civilization back centuries, yet thought this a price well worth paying. But the Soviets' explosion of their first atomic bomb in 1949 changed his mind, and his thoughts veered off in radically other directions. Soon he was denying that he had ever advocated atomic war.

Russell had not impressed his intellectual peers with these public statements, nor with his Cambridge lectures, let alone his *History*. Wittgenstein, now Professor of Philosophy, had not been a friend since their last meeting in 1921 in Austria, although Russell had reluctantly agreed to co-examine him with Moore for his doctorate in 1929. Wittgenstein regarded all Russell's work since 1913 as execrable – Russell's great mathematical works should be read by every philosopher, he declared, his subsequent output by none. Russell neither accepted nor fully understood Wittgenstein's later philosophy. This mutual disdain was the background to the famous poker incident in 1946. Normally, the two men avoided each other. Russell also saw little of Moore, being isolated intellectually at Cambridge, although students still crowded his lectures.

Russell's private life had again become deeply troubled. Peter finally left him in 1948 in jealous fury – Colette had resurfaced in Russell's love life, but this was only one reason for her departure. Gamel Brenan, wife of the writer Gerald, was actually in Russell's sights at the time, although he had no luck there, nor with the wife of a young Cambridge lecturer on whom he simultaneously showered amorous letters. Russell maintained his reputation as the 'philosophical rake' to an impressively advanced age, still looking for the ideal woman. As a friend commented, he was seeking an 'impossible combination of Cleopatra and Aspasia . . . of Boadicea and Joan of Arc'. Peter took Conrad with her, and Russell did not see his younger son again for twenty years.

Meanwhile Russell's evergreen hatred of Dora prevented them cooperating to deal with the growing problems of his other son John.

John had precipitously married Susan Lindsay in 1946, probably in an effort to 'overcome' his homosexuality, and they soon had two daughters to add to Susan's first child. But he proved incapable of earning a living – he had literary ambitions – so Russell provided a home for their whole family at his house in Richmond in the early 1950s.

According to Susan, who hero-worshipped 'Diddy' as she called Russell, yet who in some ways understood him oddly well, the octogenarian philosopher now seduced his daughter-in-law. Evidence for this is ambiguous, but their closeness cannot have helped John, whom Susan anyway abandoned for the writer Christopher Wordsworth. By late 1954 John had become insane, and all Russell's ancient fear of hereditary madness resurfaced. He reacted by trying never to see John, and it was left to Dora, now almost penniless, to try to save him. Russell wanted John's permanent certification – confinement against his will in institutions – although here he had no success. John remained uncertified but unbalanced for the rest of his life, living mostly with his mother. Russell would, however, see his granddaughters, finding Lucy, the youngest and brightest, particularly appealing.

Domestic disasters did not stain the august public figure of Bertrand Russell. With the Nobel Prize to confirm his eminence, when he spoke on radio in 1954 about the growing threat from nuclear weapons, made worse by the explosion of the first hydrogen bomb, the world listened. He ended his broadcast, 'Man's Peril', with urgent eloquence, 'I appeal as a human being to human beings: remember your humanity and forget the rest. If you can do so, the way lies open to a new Paradise; if you cannot, nothing lies before you but universal death.' Fine words were followed by actions. He buttonholed the Indian Prime Minister Nehru, passing through London in 1955, who made sympathetic noises, and got Einstein and five other Nobel Prize laureates to sign the Russell–Einstein Manifesto, almost Einstein's last action. It called for peaceful solutions to international crises and meetings of scientists from both sides of the Iron Curtain.

119

These started in 1957 at Pugwash in Canada – hence the name Pugwash Conferences – with Russell as first president and have continued very usefully since, helping bring about the partial Test Ban Treaty of 1964. Russell then became the first president of the new CND in 1958 but found its cheerful Aldermaston marches – duffel coats, beards, guitars and pacific goodwill – inadequate to a crisis he depicted in increasingly apocalyptic terms. In 1960 he joined the Committee of 100, which was dedicated to direct illegal action, and resigned from his CND presidency, paradoxically just as it was beginning to sway British public opinion.

The Committee had been proposed by Ralph Schoenman, a young, oddly bearded American student – he had no moustache – who turned up at Russell's house in 1960. Schoenman impressed Russell less by his intellect than his immense energy and charm, becoming his press secretary – a post that turned him into Russell's spokesman on almost every political issue. Schoenman seemed to many Russell's evil genius – 'Russell's viper' as the family termed him – but he was really his surrogate son, taking on the role Russell had envisaged for John. The secret of Schoenman's hold over Russell probably lay in the way he flattered the ageing philosopher's vanity. This grew in his last years in inverse proportion to the seriousness which greeted his ever wilder pronouncements. On Russell's ninetieth birthday in 1962 Schoenman organized a concert at the Royal Festival Hall at which he hymned the 'beauties of Bertie, for nothing touches this, not the meanness or the smallness or the hostility of pathetic men'. Russell simpered at such eulogy.

Russell, earlier prepared to address both sides equally – as in his open letter to the Soviet and American leaders in the New Statesman in 1957 – now viewed America as the global aggressor. This was partly because he got warmer, more frequent responses to his peace proposals from the Communists than from the USA, but it also reflected his growing acceptance of Schoenman's New Left views, a fashionable blend of Maoism and Trotskyism. A hyperbolic note first emerged

when he described Harold Macmillan and John F. Kennedy as 'much wickeder than Hitler' at a rally in 1961. But Russell redeemed himself that September by being imprisoned for civil disobedience after a mass sit-down in Trafalgar Square. He actually spent his week's incarceration in the hospital wing, reading detective novels and a biography of Madame de Staël, but the affair made the almost ninety-year-old philosopher a hero to the world. Such success encouraged his intervention in the Cuban Missile crisis of October 1962, the closest the world has come so far to nuclear war. Russell issued telegrams to the US and Soviet leaders, to which Khrushchev alone responded, and published leaflets, probably penned by Schoenman, starting, 'YOU ARE ABOUT TO DIE . . . WHY? Because rich Americans dislike the Government that Cubans prefer.' Russell's efforts had no discernible effect on defusing the crisis, but old friends and Pugwash colleagues such as Joseph Rotblatt were shocked by this crude propaganda from one of the world's greatest minds.

Undismayed, Russell, conscious that his grandfather had been Prime Minister (twice) and encouraged by Schoenman, decided that humanity's continued survival depended on his actions. To help pay for these, he set up the Bertrand Russell Peace Foundation in 1963, appealing for money to run it. He also decided to publish his *Autobiography*, long gestating, and to sell his papers and letters – Macmaster University of Hamilton, Canada, bought them.

While Russell's main target was the Americans in Vietnam, almost any enemy of the USA received his praise. He supported Mao's regime in China, Castro's in Cuba and Che Guevara's guerrilla war in Latin America. To focus the world's attention on US atrocities in Vietnam Russell agreed to co-found an International War Crimes Tribunal. This met in Stockholm in 1967 to declare – to no one's surprise – the Americans guilty of genocidal war crimes on a Hitlerite scale. (Russell did not attend its meetings. Schoenman, who did, found himself outmanoeuvred by more lucid outsiders such as Jean-Paul Sartre.) All this was ridiculed at the time, yet some accusations

121

turned out to be oddly accurate. The strident tones in which they were made, however, alienated most Westerners including Russell's daughter Kate. The decline in Russell's public image – from sage to senescent crackpot – was highlighted by a *Private Eye* article of 15 August 1966:

BERTRAND RUSSELL SWIMS THE ATLANTIC: In an amazing feat . . . the 94-year-old philosopher and 'Happy Pilgrim of Peace' yesterday swam the Atlantic in two hours. The news was revealed in a special dispatch from the Ralph Schoenman Press Bureau.

Russell's private life, however, was happier. In 1952 he had married, for the fourth and final time. Edith Finch, an American whom he had known for years, provided the stability and support he much needed. They moved to Plas Penrhyn, a house near Portmeirion in North Wales, a region he loved for its mountains and sea. Here they provided a home life for his grandchildren. These, however, suffered the same disastrous division of loyalties – between an adored grandfather and John and Dora, their father and grandmother – that had blighted John and Kate's lives. (Russell only saw John once after 1958.) In November 1969 Edith, long tired of Schoenman's erratic behaviour – deported from numerous countries, he was now travelling on a false passport – persuaded her husband to read and sign a memorandum disowning all his secretary's behaviour since mid-1966. This was not true, as Russell had known of and approved Schoenman's acts then, but Russell subsequently excluded him from his will.

Russell's life ended peacefully on 2 February 1970, but the misery he had created lived on. Behind him he left two bitter ex-wives, a schizophrenic son John, who was never again fully sane, one granddaughter, Sarah, who was classified as schizophrenic, and another, Lucy, who for a time promised well and long adored her grandfather. But at Dartington Lucy developed emotional problems and failed all her examinations, partly because she was doing mathematics, although

her talents were literary, mainly because of the family's divisions. Falling in love with a young Moroccan shoplifter (of books – Foyles was his chief victim), she lost her grandfather's affection so completely that by 1966 he cut off all contact and support. Not yet eighteen years old, rebuffed by other members of her family, Lucy was effectively homeless. A life of confused wandering, with spells in mental hospitals, ended in her horrific suicide in 1975, when she burnt herself to death in a Cornish graveyard. Only Russell's younger son Conrad wholly escaped the Russell fate. Defying his still furious mother, he turned up at Plas Penrhyn in late 1968 and delighted Russell with an unexpected philosophical knowledge, at last providing him with a son he could talk to. The fifth earl's happily married life, however, was the opposite of his father's.

'When I talk to an ordinary person, I feel I am talking baby language and it makes me lonely,' Russell had lamented to Ottoline Morrell in July 1915. She had been unsympathetic, with some reason. At Garsington Russell was rubbing shoulders with the brightest minds of the day – Lytton Strachey, Aldous Huxley, T.S. Eliot and John Maynard Keynes were fellow guests – so he could hardly complain of lack of intellectual stimulation. That he *was* isolated is revealed by photographs from around this time showing him stiffly upright in the gardens of Garsington in a dark three-piece suit with stiff collar, while other guests lounge around in flannels or bathing costumes. And he did not change later. A photograph of Russell and his over-extended family on the beach at Hendaye in France in 1932 shows the others in bathing gear – and Russell still rigid in dark suit and tie, his one concession to summer being a straw hat. He remained oddly Victorian, noted for his perfect, archaic manners. Asked once why he always bowed from the waist on being introduced, he said he did not know where else to bow from. But even Victorians relaxed, and Russell was far from Victorian in his beliefs. Many sexual and social freedoms now taken for granted were pioneered in part by him. His isolation, his rigidity, came from something else.

Throughout his life Russell was haunted by unconscious fears, as he finally admitted. 'The same kind of fear caused me for many years to avoid all deep emotion and live, as nearly as I could, a life of intellect tempered by flippancy,' he wrote in his *Autobiography*. Kate regretted that her father had not read more Freud, which might have encouraged him to look for his unconscious motives, something he was perhaps too frightened or too arrogant to attempt. Probably the most acute analysis of Russell was delivered by D.H. Lawrence. In many ways polar opposites, the two men – who had, inevitably, met at Garsington – yet attracted each other and agreed in 1915 to collaborate on a book. But Lawrence, disgusted by what he had seen of Cambridge life – Keynes in a dressing-gown for some reason to him epitomized corruption – turned violently against Russell, writing a letter that devastated the already troubled philosopher:

> You are simply full of repressed desires, which have become savage and anti-social. And they come out in this sheep's clothing of anti-war propaganda. As a woman said to me, who had been to one of your meetings: 'It seemed strange to me, so strange, with his face looking so evil to be talking about peace and love. He can't have *meant* what he said.' . . . You are too full of devilish repressions to be anything but lustful and cruel.

As this very English disciple of Nietzsche had intuited, repeated professions of universal peace and love came oddly from a man raging with inner conflicts, that no mathematics of human behaviour could ever hope to control.

5

LUDWIG WITTGENSTEIN (1889–1951): ANGER AND ASCETICISM

'God has arrived: he came by the 5.15 train.' – J.M. Keynes, 1929

'Don't think, but look.'

This advice, given by Ludwig Wittgenstein in his *Philosophical Investigations*, was intended to apply to the use of words, but it might equally be applied to understanding his own life and impact. Thinking about Wittgenstein is almost like thinking about God: the temptation to prostrate ourselves before such a towering intellect can be overwhelming. Looking at the man himself can be more rewarding.

Indisputably, Ludwig Wittgenstein was a seminal figure in modern philosophy, probably the twentieth century's greatest and most radical thinker, but he was also one to be approached with extreme caution. Every great philosopher reputedly gives philosophy a new direction: Wittgenstein, astonishingly, managed to do so twice and towards the end of his comparatively short life was seemingly about to do so yet again. *Tractatus Logico-Philosophicus*, his slim, aphoristic book of philosophy published in 1922, was immensely influential on the Vienna Circle of philosophers and the movement that became known as Logical Positivism, although Wittgenstein had little patience with his philosophical followers. Assuming that his book had solved all the problems of philosophy, he went off to do other things, at various times being a schoolteacher, gardener and architect.

His genius in philosophy was recognized immediately he turned to it, however. In 1911, after an acquaintance of only a few weeks, Bertrand Russell – first his delighted tutor at Cambridge, then his awe-struck colleague and finally his bitter enemy – called him 'perhaps the

most perfect example I have ever known of genius as traditionally conceived, passionate, profound, intense and dominating'. Maynard Keynes, the great economist and no intellectual slouch himself, later put it more pithily. 'God has arrived: he came by the 5.15 train.' Wittgenstein's posthumous fame has continued to grow until it has become a synonym for charismatic, uncompromising genius even among people who know nothing of his ideas. Books continue to appear about him in ever-growing numbers – there was even Derek Jarman's extraordinary, purportedly biographical film. The impact of his second philosophy, in *Philosophical Investigations*, was felt only after his death while that of his third, lesser known, phase is still affecting the intellectual world.

Wittgenstein's charisma stemmed from his conviction that he was absolutely right – and any who disagreed with him absolutely wrong and intellectually or spiritually feeble. Much of his appeal lies, of course, in the limpid persuasiveness of his thought. The famous opening statement of his first and most famous work, the *Tractatus*, 'The world is all that is the case', set the agenda for a careful and systematic definition of the function of language, and when he had finished defining what could be said closed with 'Whereof we cannot speak, thereof we must remain silent', so preventing others from having their say or going beyond his discourse. In part, it was the product of a mathematician's mind that could analyse with impeccable logic. Yet it left open the possibility that language cannot start to deal with the real questions of life, and his final statement can be taken as a challenge to allow for the mystical. By contrast, Wittgenstein's admirers in the Vienna Circle and Anglo-Saxon Logical Positivists regarded what could not be said as not worth considering.

Yet a significant part of Wittgenstein's impact, both during his life and posthumously, derived from the man, not the work. In person Wittgenstein was as cryptically impressive as his books. Although small and lightly built he invariably dominated gatherings, his deep-set blue eyes staring out passionately beneath a huge forehead criss-crossed

with lines like a chessboard. Such gatherings frequently saw him give vent to a fiery impatience when dealing with the stupidity of others. At times this could explode into physical anger, even violence. 'When I am furious about something, I sometimes hit the ground or a tree with my stick or the like,' Wittgenstein admitted. Even when he did not lash out at human beings, he tended to persuade – to convert – listeners as much through force of character as his logic.

At Cambridge in the 1930s and 1940s, where he was first a lecturer and then Professor of Philosophy, he attracted a ring of devoted, indeed overwhelmed, disciples, who not only accepted his teachings but aped their master's mannerisms, such as wearing plimsolls and tweed jackets with white open-necked shirts, eating plain food and sleeping on narrow beds. They even copied his mannerism of striking his forehead and saying, 'Ja!' when struck by a thought. Such imitation was often unconscious; it was certainly easier than understanding his notoriously abstruse thinking. Wasfi Hijab, an undergraduate who had, rather rashly, chosen Wittgenstein as his supervisor (tutor), was so overwhelmed by his close encounters that he abandoned philosophy for nearly half a century. He later described Wittgenstein as being 'like an atomic bomb, a tornado'. Another Cambridge pupil of that period, John Vinalott, described his teacher as 'incandescent with intellectual passion'. Some felt and confessed open adoration. J.N. Findlay, who later did become an academic, recalled, 'At the age of 40 he looked like a youth of 20, with a godlike beauty . . . awesome in its unearthly purity he looked like Apollo who had bounded into life out of his own statue, or perhaps like the Norse god Baldur . . . he was the *philosophe soleil*.'

Others were not so overwhelmed. Also at Cambridge in the later 1940s Peter Gray-Lucas, a brilliant linguist who had worked at Bletchley Park on the Ultra deciphering programme, found Wittgenstein a 'charlatan' as a philosopher but admitted, 'He was an absolutely marvellous mimic. He missed his vocation; he should have been a stand-up comedian. In his funny Austrian accent he could do all sorts

of mimicry of accents, styles and ways of talking.' Rudolf Carnap, a key figure in the Vienna Circle of Logical Positivists in the 1920s, had grown disillusioned with Wittgenstein as a thinker considerably earlier in Vienna. 'His attitude towards people and to problems was much closer to that of a religious prophet or seer [than a philosopher],' he said, unwittingly lighting on Wittgenstein's covert religious streak.

Philosophers are rarely considered prophets or seers or even ascetics. Many enjoy dinner parties, good wine and conversation, even sex – provided they can rule their passions. But a few, impatient of human frailties, have declaimed as if from a pulpit, anathematizing all who do not fall in line. They can start to resemble monks such as the twelfth-century St Bernard of Clairvaux. Founder of the ascetic Cistercian monastic order and opponent of lavish decoration in churches and abbeys – he almost proclaimed that decoration was a crime – Bernard used to sleep on a bed of rock beneath an open window, wearing only the roughest clothes. A savage persecutor of intellectual opponents such as Peter Abelard, Bernard retained the arrogance that came from his highly aristocratic family background. So, in his own way, did Ludwig Wittgenstein.

The Wittgenstein family, three-quarters Jewish in origin but Catholic in faith, was renowned both for its immense wealth and for a cultural brilliance outstanding even by the standards of early twentieth-century Vienna – the Vienna of myriad geniuses and neurotics, of Freud, Mahler, Schoenberg, Hofmannsthal, Musil, Klimt and Kokoschka. Ludwig's father, Karl Wittgenstein, was a phenomenally successful businessman. He founded and built up the Prague Ironworks, establishing a near monopoly of steel production in the huge Austro-Hungarian Empire, so becoming its richest man, among the richest in the world. After creating his business empire with a ruthlessness learned from his years in America, Karl retired. He then, with almost uncanny far-sightedness, transferred the bulk of the family fortunes abroad, principally to the USA, shortly before his

death in 1913. During the First World War Karl's brother Ludwig bought land with the rest of the family money. These measures ensured that the Wittgenstein fortune, almost uniquely, escaped the hyperinflation that ravaged all central Europe after 1918, ruining most middle-class families and wrecking the old order far more effectively than the war itself. When Ludwig inherited his share of the fortune in 1913 he was considered one of the richest young men in Europe. In 1920 the Wittgenstein dynasty's wealth was estimated at $200 million, equal perhaps to forty times as much today.

The Wittgensteins' main home in Vienna was the immense, opulently furnished house in the Alleegasse, called by others – although not by the cautious family – Palais Wittgenstein, the rooms of which opened off each other in noble enfilade above a grandiose marble staircase. Wittgenstein later said the palace contained seven grand pianos, although most people could remember only four. Brahms was a frequent visitor, his Clarinet Quintet being premièred there in 1891, and he taught Hans, the eldest Wittgenstein son. Ludwig Wittgenstein could not compete with this, long being thought to be more a mathematician and engineer, but even he was reputedly able to whistle whole concertos to astonished listeners and later he became a competent amateur clarinettist. Other eminent musical visitors included Gustav Mahler, Richard Strauss, Pablo Casals and Bruno Walter, already an assistant conductor at the Vienna Opera. Great musicians came to the Wittgenstein home as if to a prince's palace where, as Brahms remarked, the family 'all seemed to act with one another as if they were at court'.

Karl Wittgenstein, who sometimes enjoyed playing the rebel against the official Habsburg court, also patronized the breakaway artistic movement of the Vienna Sezession led by Gustav Klimt. In 1908 Klimt painted a remarkable portrait of Margaret Stonborough, Ludwig's sister, after her marriage – a portrait that stunned rather than pleased Margaret, who soon hid it in her loft. The Wittgenstein family owned several other large houses in Vienna, besides thousands

of acres in the country and a country retreat on the Hochreith, about an hour's drive from Vienna. Highly cosmopolitan in outlook, the peers of other great industrial dynasties such as the Carnegies or Krupps – and far grander than many Austrian nobles, although they had no title – the Wittgensteins kept very much to themselves as a family. Beneath their impeccable manners lay a colossal arrogance.

All this dynastic wealth and brilliance came at a price. Karl Wittgenstein, the all-conquering magnate, was overwhelmingly powerful at home, too, at times a bully to his five sons. Of these Ludwig was the youngest, spoilt by his adoring family, who only very gradually realized that he was the most brilliant of a very bright brood. Perhaps inevitably Karl wanted his sons to follow him into engineering and business, but they had very different ideas. The eldest, Hans, was a musical prodigy, performing in public to great acclaim at the age of twelve – Ludwig later recalled his brother practising endlessly alone in the Palais Wittgenstein in the small hours of the morning, utterly determined to become a professional musician. Under pressure from his father, however, Hans had to enter the business world. Highly strung and unable to adapt to the demands of commerce, he committed suicide at the age of twenty-six in 1902 by jumping off a ship. The third son, Rudolf, also killed himself in 1904. Another son, Kurt, killed himself at the very end of the First World War reportedly because his troops had failed to follow him into battle.

Suicide was often to be in the forefront of Wittgenstein's mind, stemming in part from anguish over his sexuality. Like his two brilliant suicidal brothers – Kurt was the one relatively easy-going brother, untormented by exceptional intelligence – Wittgenstein was homosexual at a time when this was not an accepted option. He clearly found no happiness in promiscuity, for his diaries suggest repeated determination to eschew it – and repeated failures. Possibly his fastidious nature tended to recoil from any sexual contact even while irresistibly drawn to it, but he retained also a strong residue of traditional Christian

guilt. Baptized a Catholic like the rest of his family – to avoid the increasingly vicious anti-Semitism of the time – he never freed himself from Catholicism's negative attitudes to all extra-marital sex. But, significantly, he never openly repudiated or attacked the Catholic Church. (In 1919 Russell, meeting him in The Hague after five wartime years, found 'that he has become a complete mystic . . . he seriously contemplates becoming a monk', which began the estrangement between the two men. Wittgenstein also disliked the foreword Russell wrote soon after for the English version of the *Tractatus*, thinking, not without reason, that Russell had misunderstood him.)

The most important book for the young Wittgenstein, however, was not by a Catholic but by a young writer who became notorious in turn-of-the-century Vienna after he committed suicide in 1903: Otto Weininger. Weininger wrote just one book, *Sex and Character* (*Geschlecht und Charakter*). This now reads very bizarrely but at the time was regarded by many, including Oswald Spengler, author of *Decline of the West* (*Der Untergang des Abendlandes*), as holding deep spiritual, cultural and sexual insights. The book reeks of misogyny and anti-Semitism, both supposedly justified by Weininger's belief, tortuously derived from Plato's theories, that all human beings are fundamentally bisexual or androgynous. Only the male element should be encouraged, however, for it is totally superior to the female. A woman could never achieve anything positive, beyond being a mother and/or whore. Lesbians, being more masculine, are preferable to heterosexual women, but a Jewish homosexual man ranked as the most contemptible of males. Weininger himself was both Jewish and homosexual, which probably explains both his own suicide and part of his appeal to Wittgenstein. But young Ludwig was most impressed by Weininger's rejection of sexual love – especially that between men and women – as a distraction from loving the divine soul within, the 'God who in my bosom dwells'. The only worthwhile thing in life was to become a genius, to which suicide was the only honourable alternative. Wittgenstein later ranked Weininger, along with Russell,

Gottlob Frege and Schopenhauer, as one of the cardinal influences on his life. It can hardly have been a positive one on the tormented teenager.

Karl Wittgenstein, after failing to make engineers of his older sons, determined that Ludwig at least should become one to carry on the business. Ludwig was accordingly sent off to study engineering, first in Berlin and then, in 1908, at Manchester, a centre of engineering excellence. Wittgenstein clearly had inherited some of his father's engineering genes, for he proved a brilliant if temperamental engineering student, doing important work on aero-propulsion which anticipated the jet engine. But increasingly he found himself more interested in the philosophy of mathematics. In Manchester he discovered *Principles of Mathematics*, Bertrand Russell's book that sought to show that mathematics was essentially based on logic. As a result, and at the suggestion of the great German logician Frege, in the autumn of 1911 Wittgenstein decided to study philosophy at Cambridge under Russell.

His decision to switch to philosophy – useless for the family business – exacerbated existing conflicts with his father and so aggravated his own already obvious neuroses. 'Are you thinking of logic or your sins?' Russell asked one day, when Wittgenstein had been pacing around Russell's rooms for hours muttering to himself. 'Both,' said Wittgenstein, with typically devastating candour. Russell became worried that his most brilliant pupil, whom he rapidly saw as his successor and for a while half regarded as a son, might go mad. 'Wittgenstein is on the verge of a nervous breakdown, not far removed from suicide,' Russell wrote in December 1912, later adding that the Austrian lacked 'a sufficiently wide curiosity or a sufficient wish for a broad survey of the world. It won't spoil his work on logic but it will make him always a very narrow specialist.' In fact, Wittgenstein took himself off to a hut in Norway to spend the winter of 1913–14 alone, thinking with almost manic intensity but writing very little.

Russell's comments came in letters to Ottoline Morrell, his most liberating mistress. Ottoline had half humanized the arid philosopher, who had endured many years' unhappy celibacy before their affair, helping him appreciate far more of life, including the arts, music and, above all, human conviviality. If Russell in his letters to Ottoline revealed a warmth rare in his glacial emotional life, Ottoline was never completely in awe of him, admiration for his intellect being balanced by other reservations and, being the half-sister of a duke, her equal social rank. Wittgenstein could never find anyone of comparably similar status, intellectually or socially. Before 1914 he was deeply attracted to a young, middle-class, cheerful, very English undergraduate called David Pinsent, taking him off to Iceland with him in 1912 in the greatest luxury available. Pinsent, who probably never guessed his friend's true feelings for him and certainly never reciprocated them, died in 1918 in a plane crash. News of his death intensified Wittgenstein's suicidal tendencies. The *Tractatus* is dedicated to Pinsent.

The outbreak of war in 1914, however, gave Wittgenstein an outlet for his death wish. He at once volunteered for the army, although his physical condition (a double hernia) could easily have gained him exemption. In 1920 he told Martin Scherleitner, a fellow schoolteacher, that he had done so hoping that death in battle would save him from suicide. Wittgenstein fought extremely bravely throughout the First World War, at first on the Polish front and later on the Italian front, being recommended for decorations several times, and rather despised Russell's pacifism when he heard of it. But, like many caught up less voluntarily in that conflict, he lacked all desire for martial glory. Instead, he read and reread Tolstoy's *The Gospel in Brief*, becoming deeply imbued with its renunciation of the flesh. 'Man is powerless in the flesh but free because of the spirit,' Tolstoy had written. Wittgenstein eagerly accepted the Russian novelist's reluctant conclusions that all sex is incompatible with a spiritual life, which seemed to confirm Weininger's teachings. His notebooks from

the war years are filled with prayers or thoughts that sound deeply religious, indeed Christian. He was also studying Schopenhauer intently, a philosopher whose works he ingested so thoroughly at the time that the opening lines of his *Tractatus* almost echo those of *The World as Will and Representation*, Schopenhauer's gloomy masterpiece.

After a period in captivity in Italy, during which he completed the *Tractatus*, Wittgenstein returned home to Vienna in August 1919 more depressed than ever. There he amazed his family by twin decisions: one was to become a teacher, not at a university but at a primary school. In 1920 he in fact moved to Trattenbach, an especially ugly, impoverished mountain village, to escape the world. This flight into the mountains or wilderness – a leitmotiv of Wittgenstein's whole life – was perhaps partly to escape Vienna's sexual temptations. According to the American philosopher W.W. Bartley III, who interviewed people in Vienna in the 1960s, Wittgenstein, while attending teachers' training college at this time began indulging a penchant for the rough trade to be found in the Prater, Vienna's largest park. Wittgenstein found 'to his horror that he could scarcely keep away from it. Several nights each week he would break away from his rooms and make for the Prater for quick liaisons that left him seething with self-hatred.' Or so Bartley maintains, but his claims have been disputed.

Whatever the truth of these allegations – Ray Monk, Wittgenstein's great biographer, leaves the matter open while stressing that the philosopher *was* homosexual – Wittgenstein was certainly in turmoil. A letter to his friend Paul Engelmann in April 1920 reveals his self-disgust. 'Things have gone utterly miserably for me lately . . . only because of my own baseness and rottenness. I have continually thought about taking my life and now, too, this thought still haunts me. I have sunk to the bottom.' It was partly to deny himself all possibility of succumbing to temptation that Wittgenstein, before he fled the metropolitan fleshpots, demanded that all his huge share of the Wittgenstein fortune be given over to his surviving siblings – his second, even greater, decision.

Such a dramatic renunciation of worldly riches recalls – was surely meant to recall, even if only to himself – St Francis or the Buddha renouncing worldly wealth before starting on their spiritual quests. Wittgenstein, who earlier had been happy staying in grand hotels, now became a notorious ascetic. Later his rooms at Cambridge would have only a few canvas chairs (not the normal comfortably shabby college furnishings) and a small table. As his obituary in *The Times* later said, Wittgenstein 'showed the characteristics of a religious contemplative of the hermit type'. But the hermit retained the lordly self-assurance of someone from Europe's richest dynasty, while his sisters and his surviving brother Paul remained ready to help financially if needed. His nephew Thomas Bernhard was unimpressed by this renunciation, commenting later, 'The multimillionaire as a village schoolmaster is surely a piece of perversity.'

If perverse, it was a role Wittgenstein played it with typical single-mindedness. Forty years later Bartley discovered that many villagers in Trattenbach and the surrounding villages still remembered their eccentric teacher with mixed awe, bewilderment and affection. The post-war years were ones of great hardship for most people in Austria, which Wittgenstein did his best to ameliorate, even though such hardships meant little to him personally. At one stage he climbed up a mountain track through heavy snow to bring his pupils bananas, which at the time were a rare luxury. Luxury was something he carefully denied himself, however, living mostly off cocoa. At one stage he moved into the school's tiny kitchen where he made a bed for himself and where he would, according to Georg Berger, one his pupils, sit gazing for hours through its window at the stars. His engineering talents were usefully deployed when a steam engine in a local factory broke down and Wittgenstein mended it, astonishing the villagers.

Wittgenstein's teaching methods were heterodox. He started classes each day with two solid hours of mathematics, including algebra, a subject primary-school pupils were not expected to learn. For bright pupils the sun of Wittgenstein's approval warmed the school day.

135

Proof of this is that some children were happy to remain in class after school while Wittgenstein carried on teaching. Photographs show Wittgenstein beaming avuncularly over his little brood. For those not mathematically adept, however, it was a very different matter, for they could rouse his sudden, often violent, anger. One girl, failing to understand, remembered him pulling her hair so violently that it came out in clumps; another was hit so hard that she bled behind the ears. Austrian villagers did not then object to corporal punishment for unruly boys, but this did not apply to girls, who anyway were not expected to understand mathematics. And this power to use corporal punishment had its limits, which Wittgenstein in impatient wrath transgressed.

His schoolteacher days ended abruptly and ignominiously in April 1926. Wittgenstein had lashed out at a sickly child, Josef Haidbauer, so hard that the eleven-year-old boy collapsed and had to be taken to the doctor. Wittgenstein then panicked and fled the village. At the subsequent investigatory tribunal, he lied about the degree of violence he had used. (To see Wittgenstein getting a sexual thrill from hitting children would be utterly wrong, however, for he was no sadist.) No charges were brought against the irascible teacher. None could probably have compared with the remorse Wittgenstein himself felt at his double failure: to control his temper and, more important for a man usually so utterly honest, to tell the truth.

Now, with his teaching interlude over, a grown-up audience awaited Wittgenstein: the Logical Positivists of the Vienna Circle, who regarded the *Tractatus* as holy writ and longed for their charismatic leader's presence, long denied them. They were at first to be disappointed. Returning to Vienna deeply shaken, Wittgenstein went to work as a gardener at Hütteldorf monastery near Vienna and for a while even thought of joining the monks. The abbot, however, would not accept him, suspecting that his motives were not properly religious. Wittgenstein then became involved in helping to design a house for his sister Margaret, although the real architect was Paul

Engelmann, a pupil of the great Adolf Loos. Wittgenstein proved a hyperfastidious designer, insisting on moving radiators by mere millimetres if they struck him as ill-sited and raising the ceiling of one room by three millimetres at the very last minute. The overall effect, square and devoid of all ornamentation, fulfilled his ideal of a 'certain coolness' but strikes even many Bauhaus admirers as chillingly austere. Its style in some ways recalls that of the *Tractatus*.

Wittgenstein's *Tractatus*, written in terse, sibylline sentences, covers, in only seventy-five pages, mathematics, logic, logical truth, metaphysics, representation, solipsism and mysticism. Its numbered statements start simply but each is then qualified by another subnumbered statement and it by yet others:

1. The world is everything that is the case.
1.1 The world is the totality of facts, not of things.
1.11 The world is determined by the facts, and these being *all* the facts.
1.12 For the totality of the facts determines both what is the case and also what is not the case.'

It continues with the main numbered points, each expanded and buttressed with subpoints:

2. What is the case, the fact, is the existence of atomic facts.
3. The logical picture of the facts is the thought.

The whole book is set out in this way, with deceptive simplicity and logical precision. Curiously, however, it ends on a quite different note:

7. Whereof one cannot speak, thereof one must remain silent.

Such laconic omniscience, deploying the Logical Atomism pioneered by Russell and Frege to brilliant effect, proved vastly influential, first in Vienna, then across the Anglophone world, for it seemed to

give a complete, succinct solution to all philosophy's problems. 'I am therefore of the opinion that the problems have in all essentials been solved,' Wittgenstein announced without undue modesty at its end. What Logical Positivists almost everywhere ignored was that its last proposition left open – rather than ruled out – a mystical viewpoint in strange contradiction to all the earlier propositions.

When Wittgenstein finally joined the Vienna Circle discussions in the summer of 1927, he had little patience for most of them, partly out of snobbery – he found the group vulgar and badly dressed. Only the 'cultured' Moritz Schlick, murdered by a Nazi student in 1936, appealed to him. (Even Schlick was later accused by Wittgenstein of plagiarizing his views, an accusation he repeated against many who had been in contact with him.) More importantly, Wittgenstein's thinking, never wholly dormant in his teaching years, although he actually wrote nothing, was developing in ways that he could not easily communicate. Wittgenstein had already begun moving away from the language-as-picture theory that impressed the Vienna Circle towards an appreciation of the creative function of language and the variety of ways in which it could be used. From now on language was to be understood by observation rather than by analysis. Having assumed that he had solved all of philosophy's problems at his first attempt, he recognized that there was much more thinking to do. Wittgenstein, Rudolf Carnap recalled, 'tolerated no critical examination by others, once the insight had been gained by an act of inspiration . . . The impression he made on us was as if insight came to him as through divine inspiration.' Not finding the Viennese an inspiring audience, Wittgenstein took to reading out the poems of the Bengali mystic Rabindranath Tagore, sitting facing a wall. His would-be followers were nonplussed. But by 1929 Cambridge was drawing Wittgenstein back.

In Cambridge he easily impressed his examiners Moore and Russell, Moore calling his thesis (the *Tractatus*) a work of genius. Russell, who now disliked Wittgenstein, was more equivocal. With

Wittgenstein's doctorate came a lectureship at Trinity and soon a circle of devoted followers. He quickly made enemies, too, not through his ideas but because of the *ex cathedra* way he proclaimed them. Julian Bell, the son of Vanessa and Clive Bell and a lover of the famous art historian (and later notorious traitor) Anthony Blunt, was an undergraduate at the time. Bell, like the Austrian both homosexual and a Communist, was to die fighting for the Republic in the Spanish Civil War. In 1933, voicing feelings about Wittgenstein probably widespread, he wrote a poem in the magazine *Venture*:

> In every company he shouts us down
> And stops our sentences, stuttering his own;
> Unceasing argues, harsh, irate and loud
> Sure that he's right and of his rightness proud . . .
> Whose learning, logic, casuistry's so vast
> He overflows the metaphysic waste . . .
> I pity Ludwig while I disagree,
> The cause of his opinions all can see,
> In that ascetic life, intent to shun
> The common pleasures known to everyone.

In the last couplet Bell hits on Wittgenstein's Achilles' heel: his fanaticism, now manifesting itself in literally 'shouting down' opponents and a quasi-monastic asceticism that cut him off from normal relationships in or out of college. (Wittgenstein refused to dine at High Table, a normal part of academic life, partly because he would have had to wear a tie, partly because of his distaste for discussing *anything* intellectual with academic peers.) He had his lighter side – he enjoyed detective novels and even P. G. Wodehouse, but his chief love was American detective novels, with their tough-talking heroes, and American gangster comics, which his favourite pupil, the American philosopher Norman Malcolm, used to send him. He also loved going to the cinema after a day spent teaching, again preferring

violent American films to gentler British ones, sitting in the first row 'so that the screen would occupy his entire field of vision, and his mind would be turned away from the thoughts of the lecture and his feelings of revulsion', Malcolm recalled. He also enjoyed sending friends 'nonsense' postcards, some showing a surrealist relish for the absurdities of human behaviour.

In the 1930s Wittgenstein had the greatest affair of his life, with Francis Skinner, a brilliant mathematics student twenty-two years his junior. Shy, silent, unassuming and gentle – all passive qualities Wittgenstein loved in a disciple – Skinner became obsessively devoted to his master, happy to work with him in Cambridge. Skinner even used to sweep Wittgenstein's floors after pouring tea over them – then an approved method of floor cleaning – following his lover's precise instructions. Skinner was ready to join Wittgenstein as a manual labourer in the Soviet Union, which the Austrian visited in 1935 hoping to settle there permanently. (In fact, Skinner was too ill to travel.) Wittgenstein's political beliefs – that the Soviet Union was well on the road to Utopia – were common at the time. The Soviets seem to have classed him among the 'useful idiots', the withering Soviet phrase for self-deluders such as the Webbs or Bernard Shaw, who ignored the Great Terror when Stalin killed tens of millions of his own people. But Wittgenstein showed little real interest in Soviet Communism. What attracted him was the idea of a Russia of quasi-Christian self-abnegation where intellectuals laboured contentedly with their hands. Fania Pascal, a Communist Party member who taught Wittgenstein some Russian, later wrote, 'To my mind his feeling for Russia would have had at all times more to do with Tolstoy's moral teachings, with Dostoevky's spiritual insights, than with any political or social matters.' Nietzsche would have recognized the syndrome. Anyway, Wittgenstein's Russian visit led to nothing.

However, in 1937 Skinner was allowed to visit the philosopher in his inaccessible mountain hut in Norway, and there, Wittgenstein recorded, he 'lay with him two or three times. Always at first with the

feeling that there was nothing wrong with it, *then* with shame. Have also been unjust, edgy and insincere towards him, and also cruel.' This seems to have been all of their physical lovemaking. Wittgenstein then recoiled with coldness or perhaps disgust from someone who loved him so uncritically that he gave up his academic career for him.

In 1936 Skinner, persuaded by his idol that he was useless as a thinker – a view few other dons shared – abandoned university life to become an apprentice at the Cambridge Instrument Company, meaning to spend his life on the factory floor. When Skinner died in 1941 from polio Wittgenstein reproached himself not with ruining his former lover's career but for having had 'impure' feelings towards him. Wittgenstein persuaded other devoted, gifted students such as Maurice Drury to abandon academe for manual labour at which none of them proved adept. He urged one of his brightest pupils, Yorick Smythies, to work with his hands, although Smythies was notoriously inept manually and developed schizophrenia. Wittgenstein seems to have offloaded his own ambivalence about the intellectual life on to his star-struck followers, with often disastrous results for them.

Despite urging his students to quit university, Wittgenstein himself stayed on teaching at Cambridge up to the war in 1939. As his family, whom he visited every Christmas in Vienna until the 1938 Anschluss, was still colossally rich, Wittgenstein cannot have remained an academic just for the meagre salary. The company of (nearly) equal minds, and the possibility of finding malleable young disciples, were Cambridge's main attractions. It had been the one place he had begun to find these before 1914. During his second Cambridge period Wittgenstein evolved an approach to philosophy radically different from that of the *Tractatus* and, by implication, from most mainstream Western thinking, at least since Descartes. His approach to language, typified by the requirement that one should *look* rather than *think*, was to study language in the context of its use rather than try to measure it against some ideal standard or fit it into a preconceived notion of its function.

When finally published as *Philosophical Investigations* in 1953, the second phase of his work had an immense influence on philosophy in the post-war years. The meaning of language was not given in terms of some external referent but in terms of a wide range of different 'forms of life'. If, for the *Tractatus*, the world had been 'all that is the case', in the *Philosophical Investigations* language determines a world that is far richer and more varied than he had previously thought. Language is what it is, means what it does and is not to be evaluated with reference to the narrow picture function ascribed to it in his earlier work. The world, too, is as it is, and no general theory can explain the whole range of life's complexities. Philosophy, Wittgenstein now thought, is not an exact science of any sort and it cannot explain the world, it can only describe or illustrate it.

Wittgenstein now saw language as in many ways resembling a game and to illustrate his point used numerous metaphors, examples and analogies. Often his analogies were deliberately commonplace. 'Think of the tools in a tool box; there is a hammer, pliers, a saw, a screwdriver, a rule, a gluepot, glue, nails and screws. The functions of words are as diverse as the functions of these objects.' He even used childish illustrations such as the Duck-Rabbit, an optical illusion, to demonstrate how what we see is conditioned by what we expect to see. A key feature of this approach, and one which was to dominate Western philosophy for two decades after his death, was that Wittgenstein offered no general theory to explain the world but saw the function of philosophy as one of clarification, describing or illustrating our use of language. Philosophy observes, it does not explain – an unbearable conclusion for many philosophers. While fundamentally undermining Western philosophy, he created often startlingly beautiful and illuminating aphorisms – a combination that in its way recalls Nietzsche.

However, these cryptic later utterances – 'Not how the world is, is the mystery, but that it is'; 'If a lion could talk, we could not understand him' – did not impress former colleagues such as Russell. Of his

later work Russell said, 'Its positive doctrines seem to me trivial and its negative doctrines unfounded.' Professor C.B. Broad, Knightsbridge Professor of Moral Philosophy in the 1930s, also pointedly absented himself from all the Moral Science Club (MSC) discussion group meetings, which Wittgenstein dominated. Broad could not stand the way 'Wittgenstein punctually went through his hoops and the faithful as punctually "wondered with a foolish face of praise"'. But even Broad agreed that to 'refuse the chair [of philosophy] to Wittgenstein would be like refusing Einstein the chair of physics'. In 1939 Wittgenstein duly became Professor of Philosophy, a subject he generally discouraged his students from studying, at Cambridge, a university he increasingly disliked. The tensions thus created in him at times erupted with unpredictable results.

Perhaps the most revealing – certainly the most notorious – eruption occurred at an MSC meeting on 25 October 1946, when he clashed with Karl Popper. Another brilliant Jewish philosopher from Vienna, Popper had recently finished his *magnum opus*, *The Open Society and Its Enemies* (1945). This work, flaying the ideological underpinnings of totalitarianism, at first found only a few admirers – among them Bertrand Russell – for it attacked both Plato and Marx. Marxism–Leninism was still revered by many intellectuals, and Wittgenstein himself still admired Stalin's Soviet Union. The regular MSC weekly meetings took place in the rooms of Richard Braithwaite, a philosophy don, amid the chilly Palladian splendours of the Gibbs Building, King's College. Popper, up from London where he was a Reader at the LSE, had tea in Russell's rooms in Trinity College before they walked over together. Popper vastly admired the older man, calling him the greatest philosopher since Kant; Russell had long turned against Wittgenstein. Views as to what exactly happened differ sharply according to the observer. About thirty people crowded into H3 where a fire was burning in the grate, as usual in those days before central heating. Popper began criticizing ideas in the *Tractatus*. This has damned him with Wittgenstein's followers, for

Wittgenstein had long since moved on. But Popper, whether or not aware of Wittgenstein's newer ideas, still circulating only in type-written form such as the Blue and Brown Books – typescript copies of his lectures made by his students in the 1930s that were published posthumously – was attacking Wittgenstein's exclusion of other philosophical problems, so his attack applied to all Wittgenstein's thinking. Popper had reason to be concerned about philosophy's practical implications. Although Nazi Germany had been defeated, Stalinist Russia was extending its grim power across Central Europe.

As Popper talked about what he considered real philosophical problems, Wittgenstein, still silent, grew obviously irritated at such irrelevances or trivia. One student, Michael Wolff, recalls him picking up the poker from the fireplace and nervously waving it around. When Popper questioned Wittgenstein about the status of ethics, Wittgenstein reputedly challenged him for an example of a moral rule. 'Not to threaten visiting lecturers with a poker!' replied Popper, presumably attempting a joke. Russell, who had been silent in the background, now took his pipe from his mouth and told Wittgenstein to put the poker down. Wittgenstein turned to Russell and said, 'You misunderstand me, Russell. You always misunderstood me!' Russell retorted, 'You're mixing things up, Wittgenstein. You always mix things up!' At this point Wittgenstein stormed out of the room, slamming the door behind him. Or so one version goes. Wittgensteinians maintain that someone else, not Wittgenstein, asked for an example of moral rule, that Wittgenstein left the room *before* Popper made his joke and that he always departed so abruptly. The argument continues inconclusively.

Wittgenstein's clash with Popper was not, however, uncharacteristic, for he always demanded unconditional loyalty from supporters – and unconditional surrender from opponents, after which he could be pleasant enough. Alan Turing, the mathematical genius who invented the Turing machine, had quickly given up trying to argue with Wittgenstein in 1939 when visiting Cambridge, for Wittgenstein

shouted *him* down. Philosophers of a literary bent fared no better. Isaiah Berlin, the urbane Oxford philosopher, visited the MSC in the 1940s and began to give a talk on how one could have knowledge of other people's mental states. Wittgenstein turned up late, listened for a few moments without sitting down, visibly lost patience and took over saying, 'No no *no!* That is not the way to go about it! Let me. Don't let's talk philosophy. Let's talk business with each other, *ordinary* business.' After an hour's ordinary business Wittgenstein shook Berlin's hand, saying, 'Very interesting discussion, thank you', and left the room. Berlin crept back to Oxford.

Berlin got off lightly compared with some. When the Nobel Laureate economist Friedrich Hayek, a distant relative of Wittgenstein's, attended another MSC meeting around the same time and the discussion turned to 'matter', he recalled that, 'suddenly Wittgenstein leaped to his feet, poker in hand, indignant in the highest degree, and he proceeded to demonstrate with the implement how simple and obvious matter really was. Seeing this rampant man in the middle of the room swinging a poker was certainly rather alarming and one felt inclined to escape into a safe corner. Frankly, my impression at the time was that he had gone mad.' (G.E. Moore, the one Cambridge philosopher whom Wittgenstein always revered ethically, if not intellectually, did get a reluctant apology for such rudeness, after Wittgenstein had attacked him, 'talking continuously for two hours' in 1939, as Malcolm later recalled. But Moore was considered a near saint by many in Cambridge besides Wittgenstein, who even retained a comfortable armchair for him at his classes.)

More typical in his reactions was Gilbert Ryle, Waynflete Professor of Philosophy at Oxford. Ryle wrote that on his few visits to the MSC 'veneration for Wittgenstein was so incontinent that mentions, for example, my mentions, of any other philosopher were greeted with jeers. This contempt for thought other than Wittgenstein's seemed to me pedagogically disastrous for the students and unhealthy for Wittgenstein himself.' Ryle was broadly sympathetic to Wittgenstein's

thought, but he deplored the way Wittgenstein encouraged his students *not* to read other philosophers.

Wittgenstein once dismissed Plato's Socratic dialogues – renowned for their wit and style as much as their content – as 'a waste of time'. This was part of his general rejection or ignoring of most Western art and literature. Wittgenstein particularly hated Shakespeare for his refusal to 'regard himself as a prophet or as a teacher of mankind', unlike Tolstoy, who certainly saw himself as both. (Shakespeare was then almost as much admired in German- as in English-speaking countries.) This dismissal was not through lack of aesthetic sensitivity, for Wittgenstein remained a fastidious ascetic – his simple, rough clothes came from the best tailors in Cambridge, the minimalist décor of his rooms had to fit exacting specifications. It reflects rather the willed narrowness of vision Russell had noted in 1912.

Wittgenstein's teaching methods at Cambridge were as unconventional as they had been in Trattenbach. He not only did not talk from notes – he regarded notes as 'corpse-like' and hated his students taking any – he often did not talk at all but spent the hour of his seminars or lectures in self-torturing silence, his face screwed up waiting for the words to emerge The carefully chosen few who attended these seminars – they were never advertised in the normal way – listened enraptured, seldom daring to speak. Wittgenstein's method of 'anti-lecturing' bears some resemblance to Socrates' early informal approach, but Socrates himself was a man of immense, if ironic, conviviality. A closer parallel is with Plotinus (AD 204–70), the founder of Neoplatonism and one of the greatest philosophical mystics, who influenced thinkers from Augustine to Hegel. Plotinus was also an ascetic 'ashamed of his own body' who refused to write anything down. (His thoughts were recorded by his disciple Porphyry.) The atmosphere at his lectures similarly varied from sublime lyrical rapture to an almost pathologically stressed silence as he struggled to express the inexpressible. But Plotinus never threatened to hit anyone.

*

'Tell them I've had a wonderful life,' said Wittgenstein in April 1951 as he lay dying of cancer near Cambridge. Wonderful is not the obvious adjective for a life so tormented, friendless and restless, but Wittgenstein meant it. He had spent most of his last years, typically, wandering around Ireland looking for somewhere simple and remote where he could think and write undisturbed. (He ended up in a Dublin hotel.) Certainly, he *was* still thinking and writing – his last entries are dated just two days before his death – on what has become known as his third philosophy. This shows Wittgenstein moving towards a foundationalist viewpoint. Whereas earlier the various 'language games' or 'forms of life' determined their own validity, without reference to any absolute criterion of truth, he now started to explore how these might be 'supported' by foundations or grounds that are fundamentally certain. 'Isn't the question this: "What if you had to change your opinion on even those most important things?" And to that the answer seems to be: "You *don't* have to change it. That's just what their being fundamental is."' Wittgenstein's thought appeared to be starting to turn back to the recognition of the need to ground the various forms of discourse in some form of fundamental certainty, without which language and meaning are free-floating. He did not live to develop fully this third, foundationalist, strand to his thinking, and its implications are still being explored and questioned by scholars.

Wittgenstein, although he had disciples in plenty (at least compared with Nietzsche or Schopenhauer), also felt isolated intellectually and personally. Norman Malcolm, one of the few disciples whom he wholly respected – perhaps because Malcolm resisted his urgings to go to work on a 'farm or ranch somewhere' – and who probably knew him better than anyone else in his last years, argued in a book at the end of his own life that his teacher was profoundly religious, even Christian, at heart. Malcolm said that Wittgenstein only chose to become a schoolteacher rather than a priest in 1919 because of the four years' training in a seminary that priesthood required.

Wittgenstein had once told Russell that he could understand why medieval stonemasons had carved gargoyles and other statues on the roofs of cathedrals and churches where no one except God could ever see them. Later he said of his *Philosophical Investigations*, 'If I could, I would dedicate this book to God.' Later still he admitted, 'Life can educate one to a belief in God', even asking for a Catholic priest to visit him in his last illness. But because he could never accept Catholic teachings on subjects such as transubstantiation, there was no question of a 'return' to the Catholic Church. He certainly did not follow Catholic teachings on humility either. He died, as he had lived, an outsider, free from the constraints and comforts of any church not just intellectually but ethically.

About the overwhelming importance and significance of Wittgenstein's thinking in the twentieth century there can be little dispute. The *Tractatus* remains one of the century's seminal tracts, while his later philosophy effectively tries to redirect the mainstream of Western philosophy since Descartes, if not since Plato. Only Heidegger comes close to rivalling such audacity. But about the way he taught, and the whole personality cult which he allowed to grow up around him, there should surely be every debate. Wittgenstein repeatedly behaved in ways arguably unacceptable in a philosopher. If Wittgenstein had been the Western equivalent of a Zen master he might have retreated into a mystic's radiant wordlessness when faced with human obtuseness. 'Those who know don't speak' sounds not unlike the Wittgenstein of the *Tractatus*. But Wittgenstein not only lacked a mystic's calm benevolence, he *chose* to spend much of his adult life as an academic in a key centre of the Western intellectual tradition.

The term egomaniac fit him as well as mystic, as Julian Bell had intuited. When he could not at once convince listeners he was not prepared to stay and argue. For Wittgenstein's followers, overwhelmed by his numinous presence, his occasional explosions or frequent silences were of no real consequence. To them he appeared a magus

or sage, a reincarnation of Heraclitus, Merlin or Meister Eckhart – dubious antecedents philosophically. Even the literary critic F.R. Leavis, another dogmatic puritan, who for a while maintained a tentative friendship with the philosopher, admitted that 'Wittgenstein's discussions were carried on by Wittgenstein.' Such manic solipsism recalls another noted Austrian

Heresy as it will appear to Wittgensteinians, there is a strange, unremarked similarity between Wittgenstein's charismatic method of teaching – or conversion – and the *magnetische Kraft* (magnetic power) of his former schoolmate Adolf Hitler. For by bizarre coincidence Wittgenstein and Hitler, exact contemporaries, attended the Linz Realschule at the same time, although Wittgenstein was in a higher class than Hitler. (Having been privately tutored earlier, Wittgenstein had not learned the Latin required to enter a gymnasium or grammar school.) It is unlikely, however, that any fellow pupils guessed Wittgenstein was Jewish, for he was a Catholic and German in name and appearance, being blue-eyed and blond-haired. But Wittgenstein, mocked as the aloof posh kid from Vienna, perhaps fell foul of Hitler, who was already revealing a genius for bullying.

There are other similarities. Neither man could long maintain a halfway equal relationship, sexual or social, with another human being. Both gathered around them devoted, even fanatical, disciples, acolytes of their respective personality cults; both were given to explosions of wrath, lashing out physically; both were personally frugal; and both dogmatically rejected huge areas of Western thought and culture that seemed to them irrelevant and fit only for the feeble-minded. Of course, in other *far more important ways* they were total opposites. Wittgenstein and his thought reveal both blinding light and self-lacerating honesty when compared with Hitler's crushingly dark and bottomless self-deception. Hitler seethed with lifelong murderous hatred – not just of Jews – frequently exploding into anger, while Wittgenstein burned with a passionate impatience for the truth that only sometimes manifested itself in anger at human

stupidity. But the similarities remain. Perhaps something in the febrile air of *Mitteleuropa* at the time – that 'laboratory of the twentieth century' – could drive men half-mad. Or perhaps the verdict of Oskar Fuchs, a shoemaker from Trattenbach and pupil of the philosopher during his schoolteaching years, makes the fairest epitaph. 'Wittgenstein was an ascetic. Such men are thought to be mad, but one ought not to measure them just by ordinary standards.'

MARTIN HEIDEGGER (1889–1976): MAGICIAN, PREDATOR, PEASANT AND NAZI

'Let not propositions or "ideas" be the rules of your Being. The Führer himself and alone is the present and future German reality and its law.' –
Martin Heidegger, November 1933

Sometimes clothes can say it all. In a photograph taken around 1922 Martin Heidegger, still a youthful assistant professor, walks besides his now elderly mentor and former teacher, Edmund Husserl. Husserl is wearing a suit and broad-brimmed hat and carries a gold-topped walking stick, suggesting urbanity and civilization. In deliberate, aggressive contrast, Heidegger is wearing the peasant costume of his native Black Forest village: lederhosen and thick white knee-socks. He looks muscular, even brawny, very much the tough country boy, not fully at home in the urbane, liberal, often Jewish-influenced world of academe. His rustic dress might have been simply amusing if it had not spoken of a deeper sense of self, one that would dominate his entire thinking.

Behind the two men another figure is approaching – invisible in this photograph because she belongs to the men's near future – a slim girl with hair cropped in the fashion of metropolitan Berlin: Hannah Arendt, fated to become Heidegger's most famous pupil and lover. Like Husserl she is Jewish, not a problem in academic circles in Weimar Germany. Like Husserl she will play a crucial role in Heidegger's life and thought – and his reputation.

Paradoxically, Heidegger, who personally owed so much to German Jews (the most assimilated, the most cultured, the most *brilliant* in all Europe), was to become an ardent, indeed messianic prophet of Nazism. In the fateful April of 1933, when Germany was experiencing the *Gleichschaltung* (synchronizing of control) of the new Nazi

Reich and Hitler, who had gained full power only weeks before, was uprooting the Weimar Republic's institutions with terrifying speed, Martin Heidegger was elected Rector of Freiburg University and joined the Nazi Party. His inaugural address led one listener to wonder whether he should be 'studying the pre-Socratics or joining the storm-troopers'.

It is a further paradox that, despite all this, Heidegger was to become in the mid twentieth century a towering inspiration to a whole generation of left-inclined thinkers of the most sophisticated and urbane sort – the cosmopolitan café society of Paris who hardly shared his deep-held, almost mystical beliefs in blood and soil (Blut und Boden). Many French philosophers, led by Jean-Paul Sartre, Maurice Merleau-Ponty and Jacques Derrida, helped elevate Heidegger to rank with Wittgenstein as the most influential philosopher of the twentieth century, a position which has not since been seriously challenged.

It was not as if the existentialists' leader (a pertinent word) had experienced any profound change of heart. While fêted by those he despised, he made little effort to excuse his earlier behaviour and was never able to bring himself to reject the Nazi ideology in an unam-biguous way. His later protestations – that he had accepted the Freiburg post only under duress, had done his utmost to protect Jewish students and had rapidly become disillusioned with the Nazis – are now known to be false. How can this intellectual giant have allowed himself to endorse one of the most murderous and un-intellectual of political regimes?

It is possible to say that philosophers are only qualified to philos-ophize and that in the world of relationships and politics they remain naïve and easily misled. Such an interpretation of Heidegger's Nazi connection will see it as regrettable but as having little impact on the significance and value of his philosophy. More damaging is the approach, taken by Professor Richard Wolin and others, which looks at his philosophy for features of his interpretation of life and its goals that predisposed him, when the opportunity arose, to take the Nazi path.

But whatever conclusion is reached, there is no doubt that this brilliant, adulterous, country-loving Nazi-sympathizer, whose heart seems to have been for ever tucked away in his country retreat where he could find contentment among his forests and in his traditional dress, has contributed hugely to modern thought – whether through his writings on the dangers of technology, on our tendency to enframe and value things only in so far as they are useful to us (with enormous implications for our treatment of the environment and other species) or through his contribution to existentialism and the meaning of life. Apart from anything else, one only has to look at the influence of philosophers who studied under him: Hannah Arendt, for whom Heidegger was mentor as well as lover; Hans Jonas, who went on to contribute in a major way to environmental thinking, especially in Germany; Herbert Marcuse, author of *Eros and Civilization* and *One-Dimensional Man*, both seminal tracts for 1960s revolutionaries; and Karl Löwith, influential in the area of social and political thought. Among theologians, both Rudolph Bultmann and Paul Tillich – who taught alongside him in Marburg – were influenced by his work. His philosophy travelled across the world, the first serious published studies of his work coming from Japan. Although known especially for *Being and Time*, his list of publications and lectures is immense; he was, above all, a dedicated academic, who, in the midst of the chaos of war, was still capable of writing and lecturing on a whole range of subjects.

And herein lies one of the strange paradoxes of twentieth-century thought. In the decades after the Second World War existentialism was *the* philosophy of choice for many cultured and artistic people, as well as those who self-consciously rebelled against social conformity. It was a philosophy that translated well into literature and theatre: it could be worn like a garment, identified with the café society led by Sartre in Paris. It was, above all, a philosophy and style that promoted the individual, freeing him or her from social conformity. It was the antidote to the depression of living in a Europe so recently crippled

by the Nazis and the war. Although he did not accept the term itself, Heidegger – Nazi sympathizer, rural traditionalist from the deepest Black Forest – had established the principles upon which much twentieth-century existentialism was to be based. In fact, what the average amateur existentialist, enthusing freedom into the small hours in the heady days of the 1950s or 1960s, would have made of the founding fathers of such philosophy remains a mystery: Kierkegaard, an intense nineteenth-century religious thinker, for whom seriousness counted; Nietzsche, who, had he lived to see it, would hardly have regarded café life as heralding the arrival of the *Übermenschen*; Heidegger, traditional Catholic right-winger! Only after Sartre had come to its rescue could existentialism become fashionable along with sexual freedom and left-wing politics.

Heidegger was born in Messkirch, in the Baden region of Germany, on 26 September 1889, the son of Friedrich and Johanna Heidegger. His father was a cooper and also sexton at the Catholic church of St Martin. Heidegger was therefore rooted in a rural and religious community, with a strong sense that he belonged to peasant stock. He was the eldest child, followed by Marie in 1892 and Fritz in 1894.

This small Black Forest town was to be key to much of his life – it enshrined his sense of identity as a German, and to it he retreated when times were difficult, eventually being buried there. He frequently portrayed himself as a rural and provincial person, unhappy with the culture of large cities. In his view Germany needed strong central government in order to hold it together, and he was suspicious of any liberal democratic approaches that, along with international culture, could undermine German national identity. Another local place of importance for establishing Heidegger's sense of himself was the local Benedictine abbey at Beuven, where he was to retreat from time to time, both in the 1920s when he was establishing himself as an academic and later, during the 1940s, when he was banned from teaching.

Had it not been for his theology and then philosophy, he would probably never have left the community of Messkirch. Indeed, his brother Fritz remained there all his life, working as a bank employee. During the Second World War, when all around was vulnerable to destruction and Heidegger's own reputation was challenged on account of his Nazi associations, his manuscripts were safely tucked away in the vaults of this bank under the charge of his brother. Scratch the surface of the internationally known academic, and you find a small-town rural family, traditional, defensive, sure of its solidity and of the environment within which it finds itself.

At the age of fourteen, helped by funds raised by the local priest, Heidegger went to a Jesuit secondary school in Constance, and three years later, thanks to a scholarship from the Catholic Church, transferred to Bertholds Gymnasium in Freiburg, staying at the Catholic Seminary of St Georg. In 1909, at the age of nineteen, Heidegger received his baccalaureate and left school to start training as a Jesuit novice in Austria but had return home after only two weeks, probably on grounds of poor health. Committed to the Catholic Church, he then again started studying for the priesthood in Freiburg.

It was at this time that Heidegger may have recognized some affinity with a religious hero who had been born in Messkirch, an obscure seventeenth-century Augustinian monk called Abraham a Sancta Clara. As a local preacher Abraham promoted rural simplicity and opposed urban sophistication; he was also anti-Semitic. We do not know the extent to which Heidegger may have identified with Abraham's views, but he was sufficiently impressed to give a lecture on him in 1909 and a year later he was invited to speak on the occasion of the dedication of a monument to Abraham in Kreenheinstetten where his father had kept a tavern. His shadow was to fall over Heidegger's life.

In 1911 Heidegger abandoned his theological studies and turned to mathematics and philosophy. It was to be another decade before he abandoned Catholicism as a theological system, and it certainly

did not mark a complete break from the Catholic Church, for he attended mass when he returned home to Messkirch, but it was a first step away from his theological roots.

About this time Heidegger read Husserl's *Logical Investigations* (*Logische Untersuchungen*). Husserl was teaching at the University of Freiburg and was to be a great influence on the development of Heidegger's thought. Husserl's approach to philosophy is known as phenomenology – concerned with the actual phenomena of experience. Empiricists such as Hume had pointed out that our senses may deceive us about the external world, and Descartes had concluded that the only thing we can know for certain is ourselves as thinking beings, but Husserl considered that the one thing we can genuinely discuss without fear of contradiction is the world as we experience it – what he called our 'lived-in world' or *Lebenswelt*. Whenever we are conscious, we are conscious 'of' something and our mind brackets and divides up our experience in various ways, always examining the world for a particular purpose – what we might broadly call intentionality. Our experience is defined in terms of its significance for us. Phenomenology is the study of that process of experiencing the lived-in world. But what is this lived-in world like? What are we aware of when we are aware of our own existence? This question provided the starting point of Heidegger's philosophy and particularly of his principal work *Being and Time* (*Sein und Zeit*).

In July 1913 he passed his doctorate examination and chose to remain at the University of Freiburg as an assistant to Husserl. With the coming of war in 1914 he volunteered for the infantry but, after serving for only eight days, was released on health grounds. Two months later he was drafted into the same battalion but was again released after a few days. Eventually the army realized that he was never going to be fit for combat duty, and he was drafted for service as a military censor in the postal service in Freiburg. Given the opportunity, he was willing to fight – an attitude he was later to recommend to others.

Life was not all philosophy and censorship, however, for it was at

that time he met Elfride Petri, whom he was to marry in 1917. Since she was a Protestant, they had two weddings, the first conducted by Father Krebs, whom Heidegger had been assisting by lecturing in theology, the second – a week later – in a Protestant church. Then after a brief spell in which he was drafted yet again, survived basic training and served at a meteorological station, he was discharged from the army at the end of the war.

The years that followed saw the birth of his two sons, Jorg and Hermann, and Elfride had a ski hut built for him in Todtnauberg. There he could live a simple peasant existence in the mountains, escaping from the sophistication of the academic world. It was to be a feature of his life for many years. He invited students there, threw parties and settled quietly to do his most important writing. It was his rural retreat, his point for touching the earthiness of his roots.

In 1923 he moved to Marburg as associate professor. Marburg was a small, provincial town with a medieval atmosphere, charming but socially claustrophobic. It was not a place in which to get up to mischief unobserved. A fellow academic, Paul Tillich, later to become well known both as a womanizer and an interpreter of Heidegger's ideas into Christian existential theology, was rather horrified when he arrived there the following year. He found the atmosphere very restricting and immediately regretted leaving the social delights and sexual freedoms of Berlin. Marburg in 1924, he decided, was not a place conducive to his particular lifestyle.

Across the university, however, Heidegger was doing his best to make it so, for he had encountered a new student by the name of Hannah Arendt and they had become lovers. She was only eighteen, beautiful, highly intelligent, Jewish and clearly mesmerized (as were many of his students) by his style. He was a 35-year-old father of two, with a watchful and suspicious wife and a reputation for attracting students. Theirs was not a relationship between equals, and he has been described by Elizabeta Ettinger as a 'ruthless predator who bedded a naïve and vulnerable young student, dropped her when it

suited his purposes', and Richard Wolin says of the relationship that it was 'profoundly exploitative'. But their surviving letters to each other suggest something more profound: a passionate fusion of the erotic and the intellectual that Plato might have recognized. On 27 February 1925 he wrote in typical ecstasy to her, 'Dear Hannah, the demonic has seized me . . . The like has never happened to me before. In the rainstorm on the way home you were even more beautiful and wonderful, and I would like to have walked with you for nights on end.'

Had they ever dared to appear together in public they would have looked an incongruous pair. Heidegger had already settled into his standard form of dress: in the summer he generally wore his loden suit and knickerbockers, looking very much the Black Forest peasant – or perhaps just the overgrown Boy Scout; in the winter he was likely to plod around in skiing gear. He was always solid, stocky and looked every bit a manual worker. She, by contrast, was young, stylish and cosmopolitan, with her hair cut short.

An affair with any student was never going to be easy for Heidegger, not least because Marburg was a small place, and discovery would have led to his dismissal. They were also restricted by the fact that Elfride kept a close eye on him, and on his students, perhaps particularly Arendt because of her Jewishness. Elfride herself was known to be anti-Semitic.

Arendt lived in an attic room near the university. She and Heidegger met there in secret and the terms of the relationship seem to have been determined almost entirely by Heidegger. She became his muse during what was to be a most productive time for him – he was writing *Being and Time*, the book that was to establish his reputation. The intense secrecy must have been a strain, and the following year, prompted by Heidegger, Arendt moved to Heidelberg, a move helped by the fact that Heidegger's friend Karl Jaspers was in the faculty there. She claimed that she did so in order to take the pressure off Heidegger but maintained her independence by not immediately

giving Heidegger her address. He eventually found her, and they continued to meet from time to time, often in station hotel rooms, at a safe distance from Marburg. Arendt took other lovers and told Heidegger as much, but he saw their relationship as central and her other affairs as being of little consequence. However much she tried to distance herself and carve out her own life and relationships, it seems that – during those years – she was always available when Heidegger wanted to see her.

Meanwhile, on the academic front, it was a time of mixed blessings for Heidegger. In both 1925 and 1926 he applied for the Chair at Marburg but was rejected. He also applied for a Chair at Berlin but was turned down for lack of publications. That was soon to change, however, for in 1926 Heidegger presented Husserl with the manuscript of *Being and Time* at a party given in Todtnauberg, Heidegger's mountain retreat, to mark Husserl's sixty-seventh birthday. The following year it was published in the *Yearbook for Philosophy and Phenomenological Inquiry (Jahrbuch für Philosophie und phänomenolgische Forschung)* which was edited by Husserl. With its publication Heidegger was offered a full professorship at Marburg.

Being and Time is a major work by any standards. In it Heidegger built on the work of philosophers such as Kierkegaard, Schopenhauer and Nietzsche and prepared the way for Sartre, Derrida and many others. It is concerned primarily with the nature of being and more particularly with what it means to be a human being.

The task of the book, and the method used, was based on the work of his mentor Husserl, for it examines human life from a phenomenological perspective. Heidegger recognizes that human existence is embedded in time – indeed we are time incarnate, we live by past, present and future and it is these that define who we are. We are in a process of moving towards the future, our life shaped by our choices. We are equally defined by the circumstances into which we have been thrown by our birth.

To avoid ambiguity Heidegger coined the term *Dasein*. A literal

translation 'there-being' is of little help in understanding it. It refers to the being which we are ourselves – the human individual, determined by our birth and shaped by our choices; a being with a past and a future, with limitations and with hopes; a being that can show character. *Dasein* is confronted above all by the knowledge that life is limited, certain only of death, and also by the flux of life, with constantly changing circumstances that demand decision and choice. Above all, we have to face our future and, in the absence of God, define our own meaning. This is very much the challenge laid down by Nietzsche, to live in a world where God is no more, a world floating free of the lines that originally moored it to a sense of absolute meaning and purpose.

Heidegger's reputation was now well established, and by the following year (1928) he was appointed to succeed Husserl as Professor of Philosophy at Freiburg. He moved away from Marburg, ended the relationship with Hannah Arendt and stepped into his former mentor's shoes.

His inaugural lecture was entitled 'What Is Metaphysics?', and he was soon contributing to and editing a Festschrift in honour of Husserl, marking his seventieth birthday. It must have been with some satisfaction that he was later able to reject an offer of the Chair at Berlin, preferring small-town life. Within five years he had grown in stature as an academic, had attracted a significant and influential circle of students, and his book had established him not just as the heir to Husserl but as a major contributor to philosophy in his own right. He had already gained for himself a formidable reputation as a lecturer, attracting huge numbers of students and nicknamed 'the magician of Messkirch' for the way he could keep his audiences spellbound.

If only the story could end there, Heidegger's life – save perhaps for his behaviour towards Hannah Arendt – would have seemed to be a steady and purposeful rise from rural obscurity to academic fame. But it was not to be. He had, for some time, supported the rise of

National Socialism; now he was to find himself its academic spokesman.

In April 1933 the faculty elected Heidegger Rector of the University of Freiburg: it was to be his decisive moment. The following month he joined the National Socialist Party, and on 27 May he delivered his rectoral address, 'The Self-Affirmation of the German University'. He stood as the most academically prestigious convert to the Nazi cause, his speech shot through with the language of 'folk', 'mission', 'fate', 'decisiveness', 'will' and the 'forces of blood and soil'. His thought may have ranged from the pre-Socratics to his own *Being and Time*, but the language in which it was couched and the impact it had clearly linked it with National Awakening. He saw no place for academic independence, but thought that the work of a German university should reflect the sense of ethnicity and nation-hood and participate in what he saw as the spiritual mission of the German *Volk*. Everything was to give way before the heroic values displayed through *Kampf* (struggle). He immediately set about promoting *Gleichschaltung*, in which academic institutions were to be subordinated to the political control of Hitler's regime.

Clearly, for Heidegger, academic knowledge was no longer a dis-interested pursuit, providing its own justification; it had to be given a political purpose. He started to organize military training for the students and held 'camps' at his hut in Todtnauberg, at which the students were encouraged to wear Nazi uniform. Thus he demon-strates a link in his mind between National Socialism and his own sense of being rooted in German soil, his almost mystical love for the natural environment now linking in with what he perceived as a love of and pride in the German people.

Certainly when Karl Jaspers visited Heidegger in June of that year he found him intoxicated by the revolution being brought about by National Socialism. For a time Heidegger almost seemed to turn against philosophy itself, complaining that there were too many pro-fessors of philosophy in Germany and seeing philosophical debates as

a sign of indecisiveness. He wanted everything to be rooted in the primitive, the inner sense of urge and drive – rooted in blood and soil.

This was not an entirely new direction for Heidegger. Like many in inter-war Germany he had never really supported the Weimar Republic, regarding it as excessively metropolitan and democratic, tainted by its association with Germany's crushing defeat in 1918. The Republic had been doomed by the economic slump, for the German economy had been severely hit by the Great Depression that had started in late 1929 and which affected Germany more rapidly and deeply than any other European country, for it was dependent on short-term US loans that were rapidly called in. Coming so soon after the Great Inflation of 1922–3, this doomed the Weimar Republic. With six million unemployed in Germany by 1932, something radical was needed. Heidegger looked for a moment of decisive self-affirmation for the German *Volk*, turning away from mediocrity and compromise. The political option may have been a crude one, but he saw the arrival of National Socialism as a positive step forward and an opportunity for a new start. The same month that saw Heidegger's election to the rectorship also saw action taken against the Jews. Jewish businesses were to be boycotted, and from 7 April Jews were no longer allowed to work as public employees and therefore could not hold academic posts.

But was Heidegger's Nazi commitment merely an unfortunate political choice or did it reflect his philosophy? Central to his thinking, as presented in *Being and Time,* is historicity. He is not dealing with abstract and eternal truths but with the experience of a being that is essentially thrown into time. Human existence is related to its *Dasein,* its location at a particular time and place, thrown into a particular historical context. Mortality is a key to understanding Heidegger at this point. We are defined by the fact that we are limited, and that informs all our self-understanding and decisions.

We make choices based on our hoped-for future and on our past, and thus we shape our life. We encounter the world and relate to it

as though it were a tool in our hand with which to shape and construct *Dasein*.

What is more, we adopt masks in dealing with situations and people, convenient ways of not confronting our own unique reality. But for Heidegger the goal is to be authentic, to intensify *Dasein*, to act with decisiveness in shaping the future. There are no fundamental values built into the universe, and we are therefore free to construct our own valuation and to explore our own experienced world. This could lead to nihilism, but Heidegger thinks that *Dasein* is to be understood against a deep sense of nothingness. Everything is radically contingent; we can understand ourselves only within time and only in the light of our own death. Nothing is known in any eternal or essential sense – there is no ultimate or eternal level to be experienced; rather, everything is known in its finitude, as it appears to us.

For Heidegger it is crucial to take responsibility for personal decisions and thus to shape the future. The person who is authentic is able to give leadership, to give direction and dynamism in a particular historical setting. It does not take a great leap of imagination to recognize that the Führer and National Socialism were the very epitome of decisiveness, of self-affirmation for the German people of their historical destiny. Heidegger was looking, in his philosophy, for resolve and decisiveness as constituting the authentic hero. Given the challenges of the historical moment, authenticity demands the grasping of one's destiny.

Hardly surprising that he saw in the National Revolution under Hitler just such an affirmation of the historical destiny of the Germans. To claim that, in some way, Heidegger was right in his philosophy but mistaken in his political commitment – as though the philosophy had no essential part to play in his Nazi sympathies – is to overlook the fundamental nature of his philosophy.

For a moment he was caught up in Plato's dream of the philosopher-king: he may have seen himself as providing the whole philosophical underpinning of National Socialism. Its promise of

German national resurgence also fitted his deep-seated mistrust of international liberal culture. He may indeed have been naïve not to recognize that his young students in Hitler Youth uniforms, meeting in his Todtnauberg hideaway, might lead to brutishness, but his resolve and commitment to it was done with all the force and backing for which his philosophy had prepared him. The rise of Hitler gave him a moment of decisiveness in which to affirm his *Dasein*.

In the context of that moment in history Heidegger may perhaps be forgiven for his initial view of the potential of the National Awakening. Influenced by Nietzsche, he may have seen the life-affirming values of his philosophy as an answer for a Europe that had been torn apart by the First World War and seemed to be sinking into nihilism. He wanted to halt that decline and promote heroic values – sadly, cometh the hour cometh the wrong man: Hitler.

Richard Wolin, an academic who has examined the relationship between Heidegger's thought and his actions in 1933, presents a fundamental criticism of Heidegger's philosophy. He argues that Heidegger did not establish criteria by which to distinguish an authentic call of conscience from an inauthentic one. In other words Heidegger's is a philosophy that can promote decisiveness but with little objective guidance about what it is one should be decisive about! Self-affirmation and the development of *Dasein* do not themselves guarantee moral integrity, nor do they link to any moral system or values. If a heroic 'will to power' (to use Nietzsche's term) is the only criterion by which actions are to be judged, then the world rapidly descends into a chaos of titanic struggle and mutual destruction.

The results of reshaping the university to fit the demands of National Socialism were painful and profound. Until that time Heidegger had taught many Jewish students, including, earlier, Hannah Arendt, who at that time had married and was leaving Germany, later to establish herself in the USA. As rector Heidegger was now able to block Jewish students from receiving their degrees, and he also agreed that Husserl should be banned from using the

university library. This radical step against the man who had for years been his mentor must have been deeply hurtful to Husserl. In a letter dated 4 May 1933 he wrote, 'In recent years he has allowed his anti-Semitism to come increasingly to the fore, even in his dealings with his groups of devoted Jewish students. The events of the last few weeks have struck at the deepest roots of my existence.'

On a personal level Heidegger severed his friendship with Karl Jaspers, who had supported him and befriended Hannah Arendt (without knowing of their affair). Jaspers' wife was Jewish, and throughout the Nazi years they went in fear of arrest, later carrying suicide tablets with them, but Heidegger did nothing to help. For Heidegger, both academic community and friendships were to be set aside in favour of the new anti-Semitic stance of National Socialism.

By the end of that year, he was still enthusiastic about the Nazi cause. He ended his 'Appeal to German Students' with the words, 'Let not propositions or "ideas" be the rules of your Being. The Führer himself and alone is the present and future German reality and its law.' He claimed that 'this revolution is bringing about a total transformation of our German existence'. Here there is a clear link with his philosophy – for 'existence' here refers to *Dasein*. He saw what was happening as not merely the change in a political regime but as a fundamental shift in the national self-awareness. Clearly, for Heidegger, Hitler was in a deep sense the personification of Germany. He concluded his lectures with 'Heil Hitler!'

This was no superficial political error. Although it does not make him responsible for the horrors that were to follow, Heidegger was guilty of attempting to give philosophical legitimacy to an utterly repugnant Nazi ideology. This is not to claim that *Being and Time* was in any way responsible for the development of National Socialism, any more than Rousseau's *Social Contract* was responsible for the French Revolution, but, surely, philosophers behave well when they guard against the possible misuse of their ideas. Whereas with Rousseau we had a philosopher whose thinking was used to justify

the terror of the French Revolution and repression (in the name of the people) in later regimes, with Heidegger, by contrast, we have a philosopher who has deliberately offered his thought to the service of a revolution. He did not see his ideas as being misused but believed that their hour had come, with himself as the philosopher-king in a wonderful new world that the Nazi revolution would bring about in the German *Volk*.

Fortunately, others were able to take his work and apply it very differently. Rudolf Bultmann and Paul Tillich, who had worked alongside Heidegger in Marburg, were able to use his work in the critical interpretation of New Testament literature and in liberal and socialist interpretations of Christian theology. Sartre and others were inspired by his work in spite of his Nazi connections, recognizing it as far greater and of far more universal relevance than the cause to which, in those heady months of 1933, Heidegger himself chose to apply it.

However, it soon became clear that the Nazi Party was not ready to adopt Heidegger as its philosophical adviser, and by April 1934 disputes within the faculty and with local Nazi officials led him to resign as rector. It was not long before he was discussing National Socialism critically and was himself under the surveillance of the Gestapo. But by then the damage to his reputation had been done. It is said that one of his colleagues quipped, 'Back from Syracuse?' – a reference to Plato, who had gone to Sicily in the hope of trying to convert the young Dionysius to philosophy and justice: Plato failed and Dionysius remained a tyrant; Heidegger had no better luck with Hitler. Much of Heidegger's work in those years centred on his interpretation of Nietzsche, on whom he gave a series of lectures. Clearly, it was important for Heidegger to clarify his views on Nietzsche, not least because certain aspects of Nietzsche's philosophy were being used by some Nazis in an attempt, later abandoned, to enrol him, too, in the Nazi Valhalla.

By the end of the 1930s Heidegger had become disillusioned by the direction the Nazi movement had taken, although he did not

repudiate his former views, for in conversation with Karl Löwith in 1937, he still argued that National Socialism was the proper course for the German nation. To what extent he was attempting to distance himself from the Nazi Party is a moot point. Perhaps, having seen himself briefly as their philosophical champion, he was now concerned to justify his fundamental views of the German National Revolution and thereby maintain the validity of his original commitment, even while distancing himself from its blatant anti-intellectualism.

It was not until an interview with *Der Spiegel* in 1966 – an interview that was not to be broadcast until after his death – that he admitted that 1933 had represented his 'great blunder'. Mistakenly, he had seen the National Awakening under Hitler as an act of self-affirmation, perhaps as an expression of the Will to Power and of the coming of the *Übermensch* of which Nietzsche had spoken.

With the coming of war, he continued his work as an academic, except that in November 1944 he was drafted into the *Volkssturm* to dig anti-tank ditches along the Rhine. The following month Freiburg was bombed and he took refuge back in Messkirch while the faculty itself moved to the nearby Schloss Wildenstein. By the following February Messkirch, too, was bombed, and in April the French occupied the area. For Heidegger, the time had come to resign from the National Socialist Party.

Initially he was able to continue with his work, delivering a lecture on Friedrich Hölderlin in June. In that same month the French even tried to arrange a meeting between Heidegger and Sartre – it did not come off, but the two philosophers were at least brought in touch with one another and started to correspond. Unfortunately for Heidegger this cooperative attitude on the part of the authorities did not last long.

Towards the end of July he was the subject of Denazification Commission hearings. For these his former friend Karl Jaspers wrote a report on Heidegger's involvement in the National Socialist movement, suggesting that he was a political innocent caught up in the

movement and that he should be allowed to write and publish but not to teach and that he did not 'perceive the depths of his earlier mistake, which is why there is no real change in him but rather a game of distortions and erasures'. Happily for Heidegger the Commission agreed with Jaspers, who had acted with great generosity for, having ignored Jaspers and his wife during the years when they were vulnerable, Heidegger had made contact with him only that year when, faced with his own downfall, he had asked for help. By the end of the year even his own faculty at Freiburg, having considered his case, presented him with a set of twenty-three questions to which they required answers. But by then it had all become too much for Heidegger. He had a nervous breakdown, was hospitalized for depression and may even have attempted to take his own life.

Banned from lecturing at any university, he continued to write and was occasionally able to give talks. He applied for emeritus status, and this was initially approved by the university, but the decision was rejected by the authorities and the Denazification Commission. At the end of 1946 the University of Freiburg stripped him of his professorship.

In 1947 he published *Letter on Humanism* (*Brief über den Humanismus*), a title that alludes to Sartre's famous 'L'Existentialism est un humanisme' ('Existentialism Is a Humanism') of the previous year. In it Heidegger sought to distinguish his phenomenology from French existentialism. Heidegger did not want to be seen as an existentialist philosopher – but it is less clear whether that is because his own work is so very different from existentialism or simply because he did not want to be identified with what had become very much a French and left-wing approach. With this work he also acknowledged a 'turn' in his philosophy, moving beyond the themes he had presented in *Being and Time*. It is therefore common to hear references to the 'later' Heidegger (rather as one might to the earlier and later works of Wittgenstein). If this distinction is made, there is a difficulty, since the earlier work is embodied in a single work of immense importance,

whereas the subsequent work is spread through his lectures and papers of the post-war years.

But the past was not forgotten. Herbert Marcuse wrote to Heidegger in 1947 asking for a clear statement of his views on the Holocaust. His response was that a genocide charge against the Nazis could only be sustained if a similar charge were to be applied to the treatment by the Allies of the East Germans. Whatever one's views of the latter, this was hardly the response of a man who had fully turned away from his past political leanings.

One important concept he produced in his later work is that of enframing. As we examine the world, we understand things in terms of what use they are for us, how we can manipulate them and how they can help us achieve our goals. We do not see life objectively but enframe every experience in a way that makes it useful for us. Our world is a set of situations to be moulded to suit what we choose to do. And we also, in the way in which we project ourselves within the world, see ourselves as serviceable to others. I want to have a role, a purpose, and therefore I make myself (enframe myself) in a way that enables that to happen.

However, even this concept is not free from association with his political past. Although not permitted to give academic lectures, Heidegger was able to speak on various occasions, and one such talk, given in Bremen in 1949, was entitled 'The Enframing'. In it he used the analogy of industrial production to depict the death camps. In his study of Heidegger's later work, George Pattison quotes from it thus, 'Agriculture is now a motorized food industry – in essence the same as the manufacturing of corpses in gas chambers and extermination camps, the same as the starving of nations, the same as the manufacture of hydrogen bombs.'

There are many ways of interpreting these views. At one level there can be horror that the Holocaust is so casually identified with other motorized processes. But could not the same be said, genuinely, about the hydrogen bomb? Perhaps one should accept that Heidegger

is indeed probing the deepest structures of our existence, both as individuals and as a society. Of course, the Holocaust was made possible by modern technology – although history has plenty of examples of slaughter that did not depend on it, but does that diminish any of the horror we should feel? Does it make such actions banal or trivial, their scale simply depending on the tools that we have to hand for carrying them out? For those campaigning for animal rights the treatment of factory-farmed animals may indeed be seen as parallel to the Holocaust. A judgement needs to be made on whether such comments display the objectivity of Heidegger's perception of the fundamental structures of human society or whether they are deliberate attempts to escape the burden of having supported the Nazis by spreading the load of human misery more widely.

In 1948 Jaspers, by then in Switzerland, wrote to Heidegger wondering if they could rebuild their relationship. 'I greet you of the distant past, over an abyss of time, holding fast to something that once was,' he said. Heidegger responded with grateful letters, but they did not broach the subject of Nazism until 1950. Then Heidegger, in a famous letter, said that he had not stopped seeing Jaspers because his wife was Jewish but because he was 'ashamed'. Jaspers was at first delighted by this seeming repentance, seeing him as someone who had been foolishly misled. But Heidegger went on to attack those who were currently ruining Germany, comparing German suffering to that of the Jews. Only the advent of a mystical something or someone could, he declared, save Germany. This was too much for Jaspers, who now saw in Heidegger an anti-philosopher, irredeemably lost to Nazism.

Perhaps one should be charitable towards Heidegger: a lesser man might have at least remained silent. His comments, pointing to the dehumanizing and mechanical nature of the extermination, could be taken to illustrate the general impact of technology. But to make such links, in the absence of any other expression of the horror of what is being done in that context, is a lapse that might be excused in a less rigorous thinker. But, for a philosopher who had emphasized that

human self-understanding is related to an awareness of finitude and death, to take such a matter-of-fact and dehumanized view of the Holocaust shows a fundamental failure to relate to the reality he described.

Ethical theory does not lead to good behaviour in any sense that 'good' is commonly understood. It merely sets out a rational framework within which issues of what is 'good' may be considered. Similarly, existentialism sets out the framework for examining the significance of human life; it does not, in itself, prescribe how human beings should behave. In this sense, existentialism is neutral on questions about good or bad behaviour.

If there is bad behaviour on the part of Heidegger it is his deliberately using his philosophy to endorse a particular political movement, and a movement that many at the time could see as destructive of the whole philosophical and academic milieu within which Heidegger had been happy to develop his thought.

Overall, these post-war comments can only be excused for the very worst of reasons, namely that he was thinking at such a high level of abstraction or generality that the concrete realities, even of genocide, seemed but trivia. It is almost as if Plato's philosopher, returning to the cave and the fellow prisoners, sees the Holocaust depicted among the images on the back of the cave but considers it no more than an unfortunate and motorized aspect of a life that is altogether superficial.

Given that he points to the danger of enframing – taking the objects of experience only as there to be used or manipulated – he might have argued that the Holocaust was the result of an 'enframing' of the questions of Jewishness and German Nationalism. If he had, then at least the Holocaust could have been presented as an example of the dangerous tendency in human thought to manipulate and organize for its own benefit. But he appears not to have taken that step, and hence the Holocaust remains largely unexamined in his later thought.

There is another possibility, which raises serious questions about Heidegger's early work. In his study of Heidegger Pattison suggests that a fundamental problem was that Heidegger distinguished the deep ontological structures of life from the particular and the superficial but then forgot that distinction at the point at which, in his enthusiasm, he applied them directly to the National Socialism of his day. The nearest he came to recognizing it was in 1935 when, in a lecture entitled 'An Introduction to Metaphysics', he contrasted the actual philosophy of National Socialism as it was developing at that time with what he calls 'the inner truth and greatness of this movement (namely the encounter between global technology and the contemporary man)'. Perhaps he should have taken more care with the distinction made in his early work between the ontological (ideal) and the ontic (real), which might have prevented a confusion between the actual and the ideal form of National Socialism. If that is the case, then we may find here a lapse in intellectual perception, brought about by deeply held emotional convictions: a deliberate turning of a blind eye to the unacceptable. Whether for a philosopher in his position such a lapse in itself constitutes 'bad behaviour' is a matter of debate.

Two Festschriften were published to celebrate his sixtieth birthday in 1949, and that was also to be the final year of his official silence, for when the final report on him was published by the French authorities he learned that the ban on his teaching was to be lifted. The winter semester of 1950, therefore, saw him back in his teaching position at Freiburg, his first lecture series also being the last before his official retirement. The Senate then voted to give him the status of emeritus professor, being rather more generous towards him than he had been towards Husserl.

In 1950 Hannah Arendt returned to Germany from the USA and was reconciled with Heidegger. This time their fortunes were reversed. With an established international reputation she was able to help him secure publication of his work in the USA. She had

earlier been highly critical of his pro-Nazi position, although she saw it as partly an expression of German romanticism. Now she was to do her best to minimize the significance of the pro-Nazi elements and revised her earlier criticism. For her, their reconciliation was a completion of her earlier infatuation. Heidegger was vulnerable and in need; she had the contacts and influence to help him.

They were to maintain contact with one another throughout the remainder of their lives. However, it is clear that Heidegger never wanted to acknowledge her own success as a philosopher. It did not stop her indulgent interpretation of his behaviour, and her own writings on the Nazis and the Holocaust, including the sense of the banality of the evil, remains controversial. Ironically it was Arendt rather than Heidegger who was to address the key issues in political philosophy. Even given her support, he was not able to revisit his past in any systematic way. Arendt died suddenly in Manhattan on 4 December 1975; Heidegger did not long survive her.

Heidegger's later works cover a variety of themes of considerable social and political interest. He was very critical of the mechanization and industrialization of all aspects of life, and he was highly suspicious of mass society and its perceived superficiality. He was also particularly interested in art – in terms of the levels of reality that it was able to reveal but also in recognition of the limitations imposed by its specific nature. Although he continued to write and lecture through his retirement, and by the end of his life was involved in organizing the publication of his entire output, there is no single title from that later period to match the importance of *Being and Time*.

In 1959 Heidegger was made an honorary citizen of his home town of Messkirch. Speaking about the concept of 'home', he pointed out that watching television in one's own home one is not actually 'at home' but wherever the television programme is showing. He said, 'There is a danger that what was once called home (*Heimat*) will dissolve and disappear.' He feared that humanity was moving into a state of homelessness, where the world had become simply a resource.

173

If he was right, it would have be the ultimate threat of an 'enframing', utterly contrasted with his childhood in Messkirch, serving as an altar boy and helping his father in the graveyard.

In the interview he gave for *Der Spiegel* in 1966 he at least attempted to explain his links to the Nazi movement. In the article he said that he felt that democracy was inadequate as a political ideology to deal with the impact of technology on society. Clearly, he preferred National Socialism but criticized it for being too narrow in its thinking. This may have reflected the failure of the Nazi Party to live up to his hopes for National Socialism in the early 1930s. Had this interview been published twenty years earlier it might have helped his post-war reputation.

He died on 26 May 1976 and was buried, appropriately enough, in Messkirch; the wheel had turned full circle.

How then are we to evaluate his 'bad behaviour'? It would be unrealistic to portray Heidegger as somehow approving of all the actions that the Nazis were to commit subsequently. He could not, in the early 1930s, have foreseen the scale of the horror and brutality of Nazi rule. This point is made strongly by Pattison in his work on Heidegger. However, it is more troubling to find that after the war and the revelation of the Holocaust he did so little to distance himself from the ideology that had led to those events. The dilemma is that, according to his own philosophy, there are moments that shape one's *Dasein*. One such moment, for him, was 1933 and his longing for a new start and a self-affirmation for the German people. To have admitted it to have been an utter mistake must have taken courage, and it was only at the end of his life that he was able to do so.

His 'bad behaviour' with respect to the treatment of Arendt is no worse than that of many others. Adultery does not disqualify a person from presenting good philosophy. His actions in going along with discrimination against his Jewish students and colleagues, and, perhaps worst of all, his actions against Husserl, are more difficult to condone. Having dedicated *Being and Time* to Husserl, he subsequently had the

dedication removed – a sad act of covering up an intellectual and personal debt that had become an embarrassment – a petty act, perhaps, but a bitter one. He must have been aware that, in promoting National Socialism within the university, it was the Jewish community that would be paying the price.

Perhaps more disturbing is the recognition – which we find also in Nietzsche and for the same reason – that philosophy, particularly where it is related to personal self-understanding and self-affirmation, can have an immediate impact both morally and politically. If the criticisms of Wolin and others are accepted, a terrible burden hangs over the existential philosophy of Heidegger – the burden of having given people will and impulse without having also given direction. Without some criteria for the assessment of self-affirmation, anything is possible. Existential thought becomes a convenient cover for any form of bad behaviour, since it fails to establish an adequate criterion for evaluating behaviour. Existentialism is philosophy's loose canon.

Commenting on Heidegger, Ninian Smart said that 'he had his own sort of cultural nationalism' and also described him as 'a guru'. This probably encapsulates the difficulty in getting to grips with Heidegger and his Nazi connection. For some philosophers included in this book, their sense of self-worth was established in the early years by doting parents, guardians or grandparents – both Rousseau and Sartre admitted in their autobiographical works that they encountered the adult world certain that they only had to speak to be acknowledged as brilliant. They were natural sophisticates. The same could not be said of Heidegger. He grew up rooted in a rural community and was gradually helped into the academic sphere through the Catholic Church. He was essentially a country boy who never lost his sense of identity with that place and its naturally conservative culture.

But he was clearly also treated as a guru, in the sense that he spoke with a power and an ability to entrance and mystify which made him immensely popular with students and attracted such an

able following of philosophers. The temptation of every guru is to dispense with critical self-evaluation and to start to believe the adulation of followers to be deserved. Perhaps, in Heidegger's wider self, as an embodiment of German nationalism, he reached a point at which he could genuinely see himself as the philosophical voice of National Socialism and was therefore able to suspend his critical judgement of Hitler. And later, confronted with the horrors of the cause he once espoused, he would be oblique in his comments, unwilling to let go of his deeply held sense of the traditions within which he had grown up. He preferred to remain at such a level of abstraction that he could see the Holocaust as an example of the evils of technology rather than face its reality.

His hoped-for resurgence of the German people and their cultural identity had not materialized – indeed, it had been severely damaged by the very man and party to which he had aligned himself. Perhaps, as a result, he continued to believe that there was an issue to be addressed that could not be dismissed because of the actual behaviour of the Nazis, however horrific that had turned out to be. Whereas in *Being and Time* he had argued that every choice and every *Dasein* is rooted in a particular time and place, he had fallen into the trap of overlooking the brutish reality of the Nazi regime and projecting on to them the hopes of a nationalist revival his own roots demanded.

At the very time that Heidegger, a most challenging wizard in the lecture room, was throwing out ideas but forcing students to think things through for themselves, dazzling but never spoon-feeding, he was also hankering after the simple life of a peasant farmer, his retreat from life.

Where then was his true home, Freiburg or Todtnauberg? Was he a genuinely committed intellectual or was he a peasant who wanted a simple and life-affirming existence? It seems that it was the latter that might have done most to push him into a positive evaluation of National Socialism – perhaps even seeing the Jews as typifying the

cosmopolitan and intellectual. He found such sophistication exciting enough to attract him – whether in the person of Hannah Arendt (who was so clearly the very opposite of his very Germanic wife Elfride) or in the early temptation to apply for a post in Berlin. Once established, however, he was able to say that he preferred to stay in a provincial university. He also stayed near his hut at Todtnauberg and his birthplace. If his thought embodied a kind of German cultural nationalism that is hardly surprising, for it formed his *axis mundi*.

Lectures or lederhosen, Heidegger seemed to supply and fit both, and their combination in a way constituted his philosophy. To endorse an anti-Semitic political ideology after enjoying the benefits of a Jewish mistress and a Jewish mentor, however, smacks of the worst form of ingratitude: but he did so, and as the result of some deeply held and romantic notions about his own roots and those of German culture.

THE HELOISE COMPLEX

The erotic and the intellectual have intertwined throughout history. Heloise and Abelard are among the most famous lovers in history, but their doomed relationship is merely one in a line that stretches back to Socrates and Alcibiades and forward to Heidegger and Hannah Arendt, among others less illustrious. The intimate relationship between master and pupil, especially a young female pupil, is central to this pedagogy. Often involving elements of hero-worship with a strong erotic charge, it is termed the Heloise Complex.

Heloise, although still in her late teens, was renowned for her learning as well as her beauty even before she met Peter Abelard. He, however, born in 1079 was nearly quarter of a century older than her and the most brilliant mind of his age. Called the Master of Masters, Abelard was drawing students from all over Europe, for he had revived the study of dialectic for the first time since the fall of Rome, making his school in Paris a magnet for the intellectually avid. Tradition has it that he had more than 5,000 disciples, of whom fifty later became bishops, cardinals or abbots and three became popes, the cream of the intellectual and political aristocracy of Europe. But none mattered to him remotely as much as Heloise, the passionate and tiger-bright niece of Fulbert, his landlord, who hired him to teach her philosophy.

Besides philosophy and theology – their official subjects – together they studied Ovid, that most adept of Latin poets. Heloise later wrote: 'I blindly fulfilled all his commandments.' These seem to have included interesting variations for the historic Oatmeal. Abelard's memories allude clearly to corporal punishment with an obvious sexual element. Centuries later Lou Salome was to invert and burlesque this relationship in the famous photo showing her lazily brandishing a whip over her would-be masters over the unhappy Nietzsche. But for Abelard and Heloise there was a genuine d of rare blazing of desire and minds together. a convincing contrast to the German variant, Abelard's castration by thugs hired by Fulbert son his vengeance from them like.

The sidelong subsequent non-spontaneous shows Heloise the stronger and less self-pitying of the two, as she urged him back to the monastic and academic life. Today any professor of philosophy or literature rash enough to lay even a finger on one of they students faces not castration but other more common penalties, drastically limiting contact between teacher and pupil – arguably to the detriment of both.

THE HELOÏSE COMPLEX

The erotic and the intellectual have intertwined throughout history. Héloïse and Abelard are among the most famous lovers in history, but their doomed relationship is merely one in a line that stretches back to Socrates and Alcibiades and forward to Heidegger and Hannah Arendt, among others less illustrious. The intimate relationship between master and pupil, especially a young female pupil, is central to true pedagogy. Often involving elements of hero-worship with a strong erotic charge, it is termed the Héloïse Complex.

Héloïse, although still in her late teens, was renowned for her learning as well as her beauty even before she met Peter Abelard. He, however, born in 1079, was nearly quarter of a century older than her and the most brilliant mind of his age. Called the Master of Masters, Abelard was drawing students from all over Europe, for he had revived the study of dialectic for the first time since the fall of Rome, making his school in Paris a magnet for the intellectually avid. Tradition has it that he had more than 5,000 disciples, of whom fifty later became bishops, cardinals or abbots and three became popes, the cream of the intellectual and political aristocracy of Europe. But none mattered to him remotely as much as Héloïse, the 'passionate and tiger-bright' niece of Fulbert, his landlord, who hired him to teach her philosophy.

Besides philosophy and theology – their official subjects – together they studied Ovid, that most erotic of Latin poets. Héloïse later wrote, 'I blindly fulfilled all his commandments.' These seem to have included interesting variations, for the *Historia Calamitatum* (Abelard's memoirs) alludes clearly to corporal punishment with an obvious sexual element. Centuries later Lou Salomé was to invert and burlesque this relationship in the famous photo showing her lazily brandishing a whip over her would-be master/lover, the unhappy Nietzsche. But for Abelard and Héloïse there was a genuine if rare blazing of bodies and minds together – a conflagration too fierce to last. For then came catastrophe, Abelard's castration by thugs hired by Fulbert and his withdrawal from public life.

The ex-lovers' subsequent correspondence shows Héloïse the stronger and less self-pitying of the two, as she urged him back to the monastic and academic life. Today, any professor of philosophy or literature rash enough to lay even a finger on one of their students faces not castration but other more common penalties, drastically limiting contact between teacher and pupil – arguably to the detriment of both.

7

JEAN-PAUL SARTRE (1905–80):
INTELLECTUAL TYRANNY, CHARM AND BAD FAITH

'Since I have lost the chance of dying unknown, I sometimes flatter
myself that I live misunderstood.' – Jean-Paul Sartre, *Words*

It is Paris, 1974, and the great Jean-Paul Sartre, who has dominated
the philosophical life of that city for almost three decades, is blind
and ill, his body worn out by the excesses of his life. He does not stop
thinking and reflecting, however, and records two series of interviews
– one with his long-term partner Simone de Beauvoir and the other
with his secretary Benny Lévy. The former appears at the end of her
tribute to him, *Adieux: A Farewell to Sartre* (*La Cérémonie des adieux:
Entretiens avec Sartre*), published in 1981, and it reveals the extent to
which his neurosis, his fear of being swamped by women and the
ambivalence of his incestuous feelings towards his mother had
dominated his sexuality and his thought. His fear of being abandoned
to and by her had prevented him from ever being able to give himself
totally to a woman, and – more significantly and amazingly – he
admitted that this lay behind much of his philosophy. In many ways
his life and philosophy were shaped by the need to free himself from
the influence of his mother and from the super-ego that he pretended
not to have. From a precocious childhood of playing games to manipu-
late his family to the tyranny of being an acknowledged philosophical
giant, his life may be examined in the light of his own criterion: to see
if he acted with authenticity or in *mauvaise foi* (bad faith). The fact
that he was French, brilliant, prolific and opinionated, and that he
disliked both children and animals, may be enough for some to con-
demn him. Whether this might be called 'bad behaviour' is quite
another matter.

Sartre was amazingly prolific and multi-talented: playwright, novelist, political campaigner and founder of the influential journal *Les Temps modernes*, as well as being a philosopher of distinction. By the end of the 1940s he had developed, popularized and embodied existentialism, a philosophy that emphasized the creative freedom of the individual to shape and define his or her own life. Through the 1950s and 1960s he tackled the key political issue of that time: the relationship between Western thought and Marxism. Such was his influence and popular appeal that his death on 15 April 1980 dominated the French press: *Le Monde* devoted eight pages to an account of his life and work; *Le Figaro* described him as 'the last master of French thought'; and *Le Matin* announced that 'with him dies one of the truly free men of our age'. His international reputation put his photograph and the news of his death of the front pages of both the *New York Times* and the *Washington Post*, and tributes poured in from across the world. The French President Valéry Giscard d'Estaing went to the hospital and sat alone for an hour in vigil by his coffin. More than 50,000 people filled the streets of Paris as his funeral procession made its slow progress to the cemetery at Montparnasse. For all his failings Sartre had become the embodiment of French life and culture.

Jean-Paul Sartre was born on 21 June 1905. His father died when he was only a year old and his widowed mother, Anne-Marie Schweitzer, a cousin of Albert Schweitzer the famous missionary and theologian, moved back to live with her parents. For the next five years, Sartre found himself living with a strict, dominating but doting grandfather, a rather more distant grandmother and a mother who was treated by them as a child. It was not an auspicious start in life. His autobiography *Words* (*Les Mots*), published in 1964, flaunts the precociousness of his intellectual development in childhood but also illustrates the roots of his neurosis and ambivalent attitude towards women.

He admitted that during his childhood everything he did was for

show – he was play-acting, concerned to please others and be what they wanted him to be. He was mortified if what he did failed to meet with amazed pleasure and praise and felt horror at realizing that he might be normal, nothing special. He developed a rich fantasy life, and his first childhood writings were stories that focused almost exclusively upon himself as hero, as coming to the rescue and as modestly accepting praise. He had no hero father and was therefore busy creating fictional heroes in his own magnified likeness. As for his dealings with adults, he clearly learned how to manipulate them: 'I respected grown-ups provided that they idolized me.' He even started to believe what he was told by his limited band of family admirers: 'Playing at virtue, I never forced or constrained myself: I invented. I enjoyed the princely freedom of an actor who holds the audience in suspense and improves on his own performance. I was adored, therefore I was adorable.'

All except one, that is, for he found that his grandmother did not admire him enough and that she saw through his play-acting, which caused him great anxiety.

A key feature of his life was his relationship with his mother. He says that he could not respect his mother, since nobody else did. He and his mother were treated almost as sister and brother by her parents, and for a decade they slept in twin beds in a single room. She was like a little girl whose role in life was to wait upon him, and in turn he, the hero of his own fiction, would take care of her. Hardly surprising that he developed incestuous inclinations towards her. It was also predictably traumatic for him when she remarried. He found himself moved out of Paris to La Rochelle, where Joseph Mancy, his new stepfather, was an engineer in charge of the naval dockyards. He regarded his stepfather as an intruder, guilty of usurping his own place in his mother's affections and found in him a suitable hate figure. Emotionally he was utterly unable to accept that his mother might have married Mancy for love. In his childhood stories Sartre enjoyed telling of the gory retribution for tyrants – hardly the fantasy of

someone who claimed to have no super-ego. Perhaps he wished a similar end for his domestic tyrants – his stepfather and perhaps also for his grandfather. Significantly for his later views, his resentment of his stepfather grew to encompass the bourgeois lifestyle and everything associated with it that Mancy represented.

But Sartre was also afraid of abandoning himself to his mother. In the interviews with de Beauvoir he said that at the age of thirteen he had spent three weeks in hospital, and his mother slept in a bed made up next to him; he admitted pretending to be asleep in order to watch her undress. He hated both stepfather and La Rochelle, rebelled, stole from his mother and was eventually sent back to his grandfather in Paris.

Sartre seems to have had something of a blind spot when it came to the psychology of his own childhood and hence was less aware than he should have been of its impact. Writing an autobiography – even one as lucid and entertaining as *Words* – does not guarantee that one is immune from the effects of childhood. He believed that the death of his father had freed him from life under the rule of an authority figure. 'If he had lived, my father would have laid down on me and crushed me.' He conveniently used Freud to interpret the significance of this. 'Was it a good or a bad thing? I do not know, but I am happy to subscribe to the judgement of an eminent psychologist: I have no Super-Ego.'

This is a curious conclusion for him to have reached. Both his grandfather and later his stepfather fit into that super-ego-creating role. As a child Sartre read voraciously but wondered whether it was all done to please his grandfather, whom he described as having an almost God-like appearance: elegant, yet powerful and authoritarian. He was not sure whether his grandfather actually loved him or whether he simply enjoyed the experience of being generous towards a grandson who depended on him for everything. Significantly, however, Sartre claimed that this lack of a super-ego meant that he was not preoccupied with power. 'I am not a leader and do not aspire to

be one. Giving orders and obeying them are one and the same thing
. . . I have never in my life given an order without laughing or mak-
ing others laugh; the fact is that I am not eaten up by the canker of
power: I have not been taught obedience.'

However, that did not stop him from attacking all forms of authority
in the name of liberty of the individual, from tormenting those set
over him, from schooldays onwards, and also working obsessively in
order to dominate those around him by the strength of his intellect.
He was frequently accused of what amounted to intellectual bullying
– he needed to dominate with his mind. For all the self-deprecating
references in Words, it displays the arrogance of the intellectual giant,
whose life has also been dominated by the need to be admired and to
be loved.

He claims that his life at school contrasted with life at home, and
among friends he was able to drop his domestic 'play-acting'.
Frequently ill, short in stature and with an eye defect that affected his
vision caused by the poor treatment of a childhood illness, he must
have been all too well aware of his physical appearance. Notoriously
ugly, he strove to becoming intellectually interesting in order to attract
women.

After the unhappy exile in La Rochelle, he returned to Lycée
Henri IV, one of the best schools in Paris, later transferring to Lycée
Louis-le-Grand, and ended up as a student at the prestigious Ecole
Normale Supérieure, in the company of Simone Weil, Claude Lévi-
Strauss, Maurice Merleau-Ponty and Jean Hippolyte. He found him-
self with the right password at the gates of fame!

As a student Sartre divided his time between voracious reading
(Descartes, Bergson and Nietzsche were among those who had a pro-
found influence on his thinking), drinking and partying. Known for
his practical jokes, his sharp wit, his reviews, his fantasies, scandals
and mischief, his humour was at once charming and merciless.

To his dismay he failed his final examinations at the first attempt
(no doubt caused by his contempt for conventional thinking and the

mundane demands of examinations) but took first place the following year. Coming a close second to Sartre in his final examinations in 1929 was a brilliant young student of twenty-one who had skipped a year of study and whom a fellow student had nicknamed 'le Castor' (the Beaver), seeing in her that creature's industry and energy. Her name was Simone de Beauvoir. Sartre had found his match. She civilized him socially and in terms of his appearance. She also challenged him in terms of his thought. They established the basis of their life-long relationship. They would not marry (far too bourgeois!) but agreed that their relationship would take precedence over others and that they would spend times apart. They would not remain sexually faithful to one another, except in the sense that theirs would always be the most significant of their relationships. Theirs would be necessary; other relationships merely contingent. Each would remain free to take lovers, neither would be trapped and they would be transparently honest with each other. For a student who was already establishing something of a reputation for beer and women it must have seemed an ideal arrangement and an opportunity to shun superficial respectability. In her autobiography *The Prime of Life* de Beauvoir frankly admitted her agreement that he would not be expected to renounce the 'tempting variety' of women.

However, there were complications. De Beauvoir was bisexual, and enjoyed a wide range of lovers. She was not above sharing some of her friends with Sartre, and the most intense of these was the relationship with Olga Kosakiewicz.

Olga was an eighteen-year-old student of de Beauvoir, whom she introduced to Sartre. The intention, which de Beauvoir and Sartre had earlier discussed as a possibility, was that they would set up a *ménage à trois*. It did not work out, because for a period of two years Sartre was passionately in love with Olga and found it difficult to maintain the primacy of his relationship with de Beauvoir, who was later to use the affair as the basis for her novel *She Came to Stay*. Even after the *ménage* ended Olga remained within their circle of friends,

for she married Jacques-Laurent Bost, one of Sartre's students from Le Havre. However, this did not prevent him from adding her young sister Wanda to his harem.

Indeed, in the year before the outbreak of the Second World War Sartre seems to have managed a number of lovers simultaneously. Annie Cohen-Solal's biography delights in recording that Wanda, Lucile, Martine and 'Louise Vedrine' (a pseudonym for Bianca Lamblin) all came to share Sartre's nights in Montparnasse.

With Bianca Lamblin, who ended up feeling deceived and victimized by both Sartre and de Beauvoir, we have another example of a *ménage à trois*. She, too, was a young student of de Beauvoir who fell under Sartre's spell. In the spring of 1939, taking her to a hotel room for sex, she recalls – in her book A *Disgraceful Affair* (*Memoirs d'une fille dérangée*) – that he said to her (in 'an amused, smug manner'), 'The chambermaid will really be surprised, because I already took a girl's virginity yesterday.' She also commented that Sartre seemed to have a casual, almost brutal, approach to sex, confirming the neurosis that prevented him from fully giving himself to women. This contrasted with his letters, which were emotionally warm and romantic. Clearly, the part of him most suited to lovemaking was his pen! The affair ended abruptly, with a letter from Sartre saying that his feelings for her had 'dried up'.

In moving from one woman to another – both in Paris and during his vacations – Sartre gave de Beauvoir a detailed description of his sexual adventures. She later published these letters, which show the extent to which Sartre enjoyed telling her details, in a way that confirmed her position in his life but which also had the effect of making his relationships with the other women duplicitous.

But, for all his sexual adventures, the early 1930s were not happy years for Sartre since they were mainly passed (except for a few months spent in Berlin soaking in Husserl's philosophy) in what he saw as the cultural wilderness of Le Havre, stagnating in the role of a provincial teacher. He was in the doldrums, far from the delights of

Paris. His novel *Nausea* (*La Nausée*), eight years in the making, was twice rejected by publishers before it was accepted in 1938.

That was soon to change. Sartre moved back to Paris, war came, and in June 1940, after some months setting off balloons as a member of a meteorological unit based in Alsace, the real war caught up with him, the Germans advanced and he and his colleagues were captured. His time as a prisoner of war in Stalag 12D does not seem to have done his creativity any harm, however, for, while there, he claims to have finished *The Age of Reason* (*L'Age de Raison*, the first book in the 'Roads to Freedom' – 'Les Chemins de la liberté' – trilogy) and to have drafted *L'Etre et le néant* (*Being and Nothingness*), his major work of philosophy. It is ironic that a Frenchman, captured by the Germans, should spend his time captivated by a German thinker and Nazi – none other than Martin Heidegger. Sartre's development of existentialism in *Being and Nothingness* was in many ways a response to Heidegger's *Being and Time*, both of them, of course, building on the work of Husserl.

The Germans routinely released from the camps those whose medical conditions were such that they should probably not have been in active service in the first place. No daring escape on the 'road to freedom' for Sartre, then, but the rather more banal fact that a fellow prisoner provided him with a forged certificate claiming that the partial blindness in his right eye was causing him difficulties in orientation. It was enough to gain his release from the camp, and he was allowed to return to Paris, where he took up teaching once again. He also helped set up a Resistance group of intellectuals, including de Beauvoir and Merleau-Ponty, and wrote a pro-Resistance play, *Les Mouches* (*The Flies*), which was performed in Paris in 1943 under the noses of the Nazis. That year saw the publication of *Being and Nothingness* and the following year his play *In Camera* (*Huis Clos*), also translated as *No Exit*, was performed and he was finishing two novels in his 'Roads to Freedom' trilogy – *The Age of Reason* and *The Reprieve* (*Le Sursis*). His wartime output was absolutely astounding.

With the ending of war, he founded the literary journal *Les Temps modernes* and gave up teaching. It marked a decisive turning point in his life and fortunes.

His novels – including *Nausea* and 'The Roads to Freedom' trilogy – explore the experienced reality of which his existential philosophy speaks, with feelings of despair and alienation. Existentialism grew, for him, out of reflection on the individual's struggle to make sense of his or her life with all its limitations. He wanted to explore what it is to have an authentic involvement in the world, as opposed to one that merely follows the expectations of others in an inauthentic way. In this he was developing the ideas of Heidegger, who also looked at the issue of wearing masks and adopting public roles rather than acting authentically.

Faced with a life that is radically contingent (in the sense of being limited, always liable to change and vulnerable to the actions of others) and futile, there can be no ultimate justification of anything: no absolute right or wrong to be read from a rule book. Through fear we may be tempted to refuse to accept responsibility for our actions and choices – and to fall back on an explanation of them in terms of outside influences, to accept a role that others would give us. And that, for him, is *mauvaise foi* – bad faith. It parallels his fiction, in which people face situations of uncertainty and ambiguity and are therefore forced to confront themselves and their choices. The classic example is his story 'The Wall' ('Le Mur'), where a person faces life or death and the choice of whether or not to betray a comrade. He expounded the concept of bad faith, acting out of self-deception, and, perhaps especially, the separating out of unconscious desires as though not part of the self. In particular, bad faith is acting a part, not being true to oneself. He also criticized the temptation to promote what-we-might-become rather than what-we-are, which allowed fantasy to dominate over reality, and the danger of becoming what we think others want us to be rather than being ourselves.

Sartre opposes acting in bad faith by an ethic of seriousness. He

is concerned that people should act with integrity and not simply respond to what is expected of them. Clearly, he found fixed rules stifling but was prepared to go along with a seriousness of personal decision that seems to reflect the earlier existentialism of Kierkegaard, who had rejected speculative philosophy in favour of an approach based on the dilemmas and angst of individuals and their life-choices.

Being and Nothingness, published in 1943, is the key work for understanding French existentialism. In it he developed the ideas of Kierkegaard and Heidegger, setting out the dilemmas of human freedom and the desire for authenticity. Its success, and that of existentialism in general, was related to its appropriateness to those who, in a situation of war, were forced to live for the moment, for ever threatened by the unknown.

Central to his thinking is the contrast between two types of being: the active, self-aware, thinking, questioning for-itself and the impersonal, material in-itself of encountered objects. In the simplest of terms, these might be compared with Descartes' fundamental division of reality into mind and matter. We have responsibility for thinking and choosing – that is what makes our being for-itself. But that can be threatening, because the for-itself is also a nothingness: it does not have the solid, physical reality of the objective in-itself world. There is therefore always a temptation to escape from the threat of nothingness by accepting an impersonal, stereotypical image of the self, making it an object rather than a thinking subject. To understand oneself simply as trying to be 'a waiter' or even 'a philosopher' is to deny one's individual, thinking, choosing self. This is what Sartre calls acting in bad faith, the opposite of his existentialist ideal of acting authentically.

Although buried in serious ontological analysis, *Being and Nothingness* contains clear indications of Sartre's sexuality and the fact that he sees the love relationship as leading either to sadism or masochism, never a balance of equals. He speaks of the feminine as

that which 'gapes open' and the male desire to fill it. Clearly, the feminine represents the in-itself, while the masculine is the for-itself. Women are therefore unliberated; males must fight off the danger of being smothered by the in-itself in order to protect their freedom.

To overcome his fear of the temptations of incest, Sartre makes the in-itself as unattractive as possible. In the section on 'Doing and Having' he explores the implications of encountering something that is 'slimy' – the fact that it is soft, pliable and that it tends to stick to your hands. Whereas normally the for-itself is affirmative and active, as against the passive, fixed and defined in-itself, the slimy aspect of the in-itself tends to cling to and absorb the for-itself. His descriptions of the slimy, like the honey which slips off a spoon, includes a deflation of a blow-up doll or the spreading and flattening of her full breasts when a woman lies back. The slimy appears docile, but just as one goes to possess it one finds oneself possessed by it:

> It is a soft and yielding action, a moist and feminine sucking, it lives obscurely under my fingers, and I sense it like a dizziness; it draws me to it, as the bottom of a precipice might draw me. There is something like a tactile fascination in the slimy . . . In one sense it is like the supreme docility of the possessed, the fidelity of a dog who gives himself even when one does not want him any longer, and in another sense there is underneath this docility a surreptitious appropriation of the possessor by the possessed.

This might well be the nearest that abstract ontological analysis can get to the moment of orgasm!

But it is no joyful sexual release, rather the fear of a male who sees his life sucked from him by the female. He goes on to describe it as a 'sickly sweet feminine revenge', as being 'leechlike'. He also fears that man will be castrated in the amorous act. Hence the for-itself frees itself from the in-itself through rational thought, which represents a kind of clear and clean male activity. This seems to reinforce the

male-dominated view that rationality is for the male and that the female is always going to be emotionally sucking and slimy.

The sexual link is confirmed by his play *Huis Clos*, in which he presents three people who arrive together in a closed, windowless room. Significantly, there are two women, one of whom, Estelle, is particularly young and the other, Inez, is more of a challenge to the single male, Garcin. Before long he is saying to Inez, 'I won't let myself get bogged in your eyes. You're soft and slimy. Ugh! Like an octopus. Like a quagmire', phrases that mirror his description of the in-itself feminine in *Being and Nothingness*. Inez also describes the moment of death, when she knows that she will never accomplish all her dreams, recognizing that 'You are – your life, and nothing else', reflecting the key existentialist theme that existence precedes essence.

At the very end of the play, as the relationships between the three become intolerable, there comes the famous line 'There's no need for red-hot pokers. Hell is . . . other people!' Sartre should know, since the cast of that play reflects the triangular hells he and de Beauvoir created in their *ménages* with Olga and, later, with Bianca Lamblin. There is no clearer point at which Sartre's life and tortured dealings with women link with his literary work and with his philosophy.

Since he could not abandon himself to women, it became impossible to achieve a relationship of genuine reciprocity. He admitted to de Beauvoir in the interviews he gave towards the end of his life that the in-itself was nothing to him since he was in that moment the active principle. In other words he treats the woman as object, whereas he acknowledges that the norm should be reciprocity. Hence the impression is that in the last years of his life Sartre was able to see the limitations of *Being and Nothingness* and recognized the extent to which his philosophy had been shaped by his relationships with women.

Other limitations of *Being and Nothingness* were encountered by Heidegger, the philosopher who had inspired so much of that work,

in 1945. While admiring Sartre's literary talent and descriptions of human behaviour, he found it unreadable. In those days, some books proudly proclaimed their virginity, since the pages were folded together just as they had been printed and required to be slit apart before they could be read. No chance, then, to claim to have read the book without at least having given it the attentions of a paperknife. Heidegger cut only forty pages of *Being and Nothingness*. Later, in 1952, Sartre went to meet him in Freiburg but returned in a bad temper, exasperated, complaining that Heidegger looked like a retired colonel and that he had found himself speaking to a chamois hunter's hat! After that he seldom mentioned Heidegger. One can imagine what the old Nazi made of the French existentialist!

In October 1945 Sartre's lecture Existentialism Is a Humanism denoted his arrival as a popular force in French post-war culture. Pushing his way to the stage through a packed and chaotic meeting, he spoke with power, but without notes, to an enthusiastic and enthralled audience. It is difficult to appreciate the impact of material he had produced in the preceding years: *Nausea*, *The Wall*, *Being and Nothingness*, the first two volumes of his 'Roads to Freedom' trilogy and the founding of *Les Temps modernes*. Existentialism had arrived, and in this lecture he reinforced his most fundamental position – that existence precedes essence. In other words, that each person is able to construct who they are, to affirm the life they choose, nothing is fixed or given.

It caught the spirit of the moment, becoming instantly fashionable even for those who would never have a clear idea what existentialism was. It affirmed the freedom of choice, the possibility of shaping one's own future, of affirming one's own lifestyle, of rejecting tradition. Clearly, from a conservative viewpoint, Sartre was seen as a corrupter of youth, preaching a new and dangerous philosophy. In 1948 all of his works were put on the Index (of books prohibited to Catholics) by the Catholic Church. This was hardly surprising, since a key feature of Sartre's work is that there is no fixed human nature (whether

God-given or otherwise) but that people are challenged to shape their own lives. This not only undermines any form of absolute moral ethic but even the very sense of a purposeful and designed nature, human or otherwise. From a Catholic standpoint, what Sartre seemed to be offering was moral anarchy. Bernard-Henri Lévy's biography records many other accusations made against Sartre at this time, accusing him of an obsession with filth and sex. *Huis Clos* was banned in Britain.

If, for the individual, self-creation was to be achieved through action, for the philosopher it was important to be committed. Sartre's views develop through his many comments on political and social issues. It is curious to reflect that for someone for whom self-expression and determination are seen as crucial – the very heart of existentialism – Sartre was so automatically dismissive of all things bourgeois. Having had a privileged background, he seemed committed to destroy the very means by which he had achieved his position. By concentrating on the individual, he may (consciously or unconsciously) have ignored that social matrix that enables the individual to find a voice. It was exactly that narrowness which led Michel Foucault and other post-modernist and structuralist thinkers to criticize him. However, the individual only finds himself and his meaning in a social setting – just as in *The Wall* the prisoners only contemplate death because they are told they will be shot in the morning.

But with the achievement of fame and power Sartre could be utterly insensitive, promoting himself at the expense of others. Sometimes he could act in ways that he deemed to be right, even if they brought extreme pain to other people. His treatment of Jean Genet might illustrate this. In 1952 Sartre, having set out to write a preface to the works of Jean Genet (who, although a writer, was indeed the ultimate non-bourgeois, being a working-class, homosexual criminal in an age which did not admire either homosexuals or criminals), allowed his work to expand to 690 pages and to be

published as *Saint Genet*. In the book he praised Genet, setting him up as a hero; but at the same time he swamped him. Ostensibly about Genet, the book is really about Sartre – Genet is merely the opportunity for another marathon of self-exploration and promotion. Genet himself admitted in 1964 that he felt stripped naked by Sartre's book, and it led to a period of six years during which he felt almost unable to continue writing. Yet Sartre opened the book by an account of Genet's fear of the gaze of the world. Sartre knew very well the effect that such exposure might have on his subject – but went ahead and wrote it anyway! It may not necessarily have been cruel, since he also presumably hoped to achieve something for Genet, but it does reveal an arrogance that is free to prescribe medicine that he knows will be bitter for its recipient.

Worse was the arrogance and extreme cruelty with which he finally ended his friendship with Albert Camus. Camus had developed his own particular approach to existentialism, emphasizing – almost as a starting point – that life is 'absurd' and looking to the moral and political commitments that can arise in such a situation. The two writers had been on friendly terms for a number of years. Sartre had enjoyed Camus' company at parties, where they shared the same bawdy humour, and he admired his work. Sartre wrote *Huis Clos* for Camus and invited him to join the editorial board of *Les Temps modernes*. But tension between the writers may have been inevitable, given that their work and interests were so close, and Camus could be volatile when challenged.

The final dispute arose over the consideration of Camus' book *The Rebel* (*L'Homme révolté*) by the editorial committee at *Les Temps modernes* in 1952. When it was reviewed negatively, Camus objected. In response Sartre published an open letter in which he displayed nothing but contempt for Camus, using all that he knew of his weaknesses in order to hurt him. It was the work of an intellectual bully, damning someone who had dared to challenge his judgement. Full of bitterness and deliberately wounding, it showed how Sartre, with his

privileged background and education at the Ecole Normale Supérieure, could slap down a largely self-taught colonial from Algeria with literary flair and serious political commitments. But it was also a sign of bad faith. What had his friendship with Camus meant, including his collaboration with him in the preceding years? If he had clearly felt such contempt for his work, why did he play-act at respect for so long? In the savagery of his public humiliation of Camus, Sartre betrays his own duplicity. After years of friendship and collaboration this was, in the words of Lévy, 'a model, not just of contempt but of bad faith'.

But Sartre's venom had another cause. Camus was dashingly good-looking and successful with women and had attracted the attentions of Wanda, Olga's sister, with whom Sartre was in love. When Sartre dismissed Camus' philosophy as lacking seriousness (a preposterous accusation), he was in reality fending off a serious threat to his sexual authority within his harem. Sadly, it was only after Camus' tragic death in a motor accident eight years later that Sartre denied the reality of his earlier criticisms and wrote an obituary worthy of a writer of Camus' stature.

Another reason behind the tensions with Camus (and also with Merleau-Ponty, the most serious philosophical colleague and a key figure on the editorial board of Les Temps modernes) concerned the almost inexplicable change in Sartre's attitude to the Soviet Union.

Before 1952 Sartre had been critical of Soviet Communism, both in his play Dirty Hands (Les Mains sales) and through Les Temps modernes (which had criticized the labour camps), and he had sought a modern form of socialism that would distinguish itself from Communism. Then came the change. From 1952 to 1956 he appeared to have become a mouthpiece for Soviet propaganda and highly critical of the USA, at exactly the time when others were becoming aware of the labour camps and other extremes of the Soviet regime. This change of view is seen first in Communists and Peace (Les Communistes et la paix), published in separate parts in Les

Temps modernes, which saw him defending Stalin's USSR and denying the reality of the Gulag. He visited the USSR in 1954 and, in a series of interviews published in the left-wing newspaper *Libération*, notoriously declared that there was total freedom there to criticize the regime. He can be accused of behaving badly (or at least foolishly) in accepting the idea of a Soviet society uncritically and refusing to see evidence to the contrary. In 1956 he even criticized Khrushchev for his denouncing of Stalin and went on to oppose Alexander Solzhenitsyn, the most famous post-war critic of the Soviet regime. As far as Sartre was concerned in those years, Soviet dissidents were simply criminals.

His endorsement of such a totalitarian regime suggests that he had become deeply attracted to power and control – the very things he had formerly rejected in the name of personal, existential freedom. The scale of what he was prepared to accept was amazing. In the light of all the evidence he endorsed some of the most brutal regimes, and he did so while seeing Marxism as in some way the horizon of modern political thought, encompassing everything. His view seems to have become as narrow as the autodidact in his book *Nausea*, who systematically reads his way through a library, taking the books in alphabetical order.

And yet, someone as brilliant and prolific as Sartre could hardly have been fooled if he had not deliberately chosen to be. He had explored the limits of human freedom, had claimed it for himself, and yet, beneath this, there is this fascination with authority and power, a power that can dismiss the Gulag and the dissidents, a power that clearly puts essence (in this case political ideology) before the facts of existence – an approach that is counter to everything he had argued for in his earlier existentialism. Can Sartre's espousal of those Marxist regimes have been other than – to use his own term – *mauvaise foi?*

It was not until the invasion of Hungary in November 1956 that Sartre started to take a more critical stance and a full twenty years later before he was to acknowledge that he had actually lied about the Soviet Union, admitting that he had said things he fundamentally did

not believe, even at the time, but excusing himself on the grounds that he did not want to speak ill of those who had offered him hospitality. It seems a lame excuse, coming from someone who seemed quite willing to denounce anyone who stood against him.

There was also a fundamental divergence between Sartre's existentialism and the brand of Marxism he encountered in the Soviet Union. In the latter, action was related to an ongoing dialectic of class opposition, and the actions of individuals are part of – and may therefore be justified with reference to – that ongoing historical process. The significance of the individual is diminished. It seems incredible that Sartre could support Stalin's political regime after having championed an existentialism that demanded a level of personal freedom which Stalin would have denied anyone who disagreed with him.

It is tempting to speculate on whether Sartre had personal reasons for not acknowledging the reality of the repressive forces within Soviet Communism during those years. Having failed to acknowledge his own super-ego and having denied ever setting himself up as a figure of authority (a ridiculous claim in the light of his treatment of Camus and others), he may have preferred to announce that freedom ruled in the USSR than acknowledge the power of authority – whether in a nation or within his own intellectual circle – to crush the individual. If an idea as central as the in-itself and for-itself of his *Being and Nothingness* was shaped by his problems in relating to women, it is at least conceivable that his view of the Soviet system was coloured by his failure to acknowledge his own exercise of authority or his readiness to censor and banish those who challenged him.

His belated criticism of Soviet Marxism found expression in 1957 with 'The Present Situation of Existentialism' which was published as 'The Question of Method' ('Questions de méthode') in *Les Temps modernes*. Although he acknowledged Marxism as the dominant philosophy of the age, he argued that truth was always unfolding rather than static. The implication of this was that no system could ever claim to have the final truth but should be open to revision.

His *Critique of Dialectical Reason* (*Critique de la raison dialectique*), an exploration of the relationship between Marxism and existential‑ism, published in 1960, was a huge accomplishment in every sense, the major statement of his later philosophy, as *Being and Nothingness* had been of his earlier work. Like that earlier book it was concerned with human freedom. This time, however, he recognized that our freedom is restricted by things outside us that take on values over which we have no control. In other words, he related the externally determined Marxist view of action to a sense of individual freedom. In it he attempted to reconcile his interest in Marxism and left-wing politics with his earlier existentialism, by exploring ways in which the material conditions under which people live together (the starting point for Marxism) relates to the issue of human freedom and choice (the starting point for existentialism). In effect, he explores the way in which human history is shaped by the way people choose to act together in groups. Thus existentialism takes its place within what amounts to an overall Marxist framework. It was one of the works with which he was most satisfied.

In the 1960s Sartre became a political globetrotter, visiting the Soviet Union many times. He went to Belgrade to be received by Tito and Cuba to see Castro. He was even to give his support to Mao, who was responsible for the excesses of the Cultural Revolution. The political decade started with his opposition to the actions of the French government in the Algerian Civil War. He became a symbol for the whole affair. Twice his flat was bombed. He was absolutely opposed to colonialism. Some in authority regarded as treasonable the position of those who had signed a petition supporting those who opposed the actions of the French government in Algeria, but it was clear that no action was going to be taken against Sartre. President Charles de Gaulle's famous comment on this was 'You do not imprison Voltaire.' It was Sartre's most powerful moment.

It became a decade of taking political stances. In 1964 he rejected the Nobel Prize for Literature, insisting that he wanted no honours

(although perhaps he could never have brought himself to accept a prize already awarded to Camus, whom he had tried to dismiss as lacking seriousness). In 1966 he joined the War Crimes Commission started by Bertrand Russell. He visited Egypt and Israel, gave a lecture on Vietnam and in 1968 he supported the student uprising in France, and even condemned the USSR for the invasion Czechoslovakia following the 'Prague Spring' under Alexander Dubček. Sartre had hoped that a new form of Marxism could have developed out of the changes that were taking place in Czechoslovakia, and its repression was a blow. The following year he visited Prague. He was still Marxist but had now turned against the Soviet Union.

For years his massive output of work was maintained by a cocktail of stimulants, cigarettes and red wine, and when the day could no longer be prolonged by coffee and whisky it was time for sleeping-pills. Alcohol and tobacco had always been his recreational drugs of choice. His one experience of mescaline (a hallucinogen) in the 1930s had been an unhappy one that he had no desire to repeat. It produced unpleasant after-effects in which he was affected by changed perceptions and the metamorphosis of familiar objects, an experience which may be reflected in the changes that happen as Roquetin looks at the chestnut tree in his novel *Nausea*.

As a writer, Sartre was driven, and his output was enormous. He would sometimes talk and make notes of his own words at the same time, seemingly unconcerned that by never pausing he gave nobody else a chance to engage him in conversation.

His sexual output was equally daunting, such that one of his biographers includes 'Sartre, mistresses of' as an index entry. Mention has already been made of de Beauvoir, Olga, Wanda and Bianca, but there was also the twenty-year-old singer Juliet Gréco – for whom the 41-year-old Sartre wrote a song for his play *Huis Clos* in 1946 – Dolorès, his great American passion, and, shortly after he had broken off with her, Michelle Léglise-Vian with whom he was to remain on friendly terms, to say nothing of his youthful adventures.

Women were his muses; he always preferred them to male company.

Towards the latter part of his life, Sartre found that the philosophical world was shifting away from the approach that he had taken. Foucault and others rejected his 'modernist' view of the creative subject; their concern was with the structures of thought and language within which all creative activity became possible. For them, Sartre's emphasis on the individual did not do justice to the whole social and intellectual matrix within which language makes sense. Foucault described the *Critique of Dialectical Reason* as the magnificent and pathetic effort of a nineteenth-century thinker to conceive of the twentieth century and considered Sartre to be the last Hegelian and also the last Marxist.

As time went on Sartre became unwilling to confront such criticism and thereby marginalized himself from the ongoing stream of thought. He was still active politically, critical of both the Soviet system and American involvement in Vietnam. Otherwise, as things moved on, he became increasingly disengaged from current intellectual and political issues, focused obsessively on writing his book on Flaubert.

In the 1970s his health deteriorated and he suffered heart attacks in 1971 and 1973. By 1974 he was blind and dependent on the help of others, including de Beauvoir and Arlette Elkaïm, a student who had become deeply attached to him and whom he had legally adopted in 1965. He continued to work, with the help and encouragement of Benny Lévy. Finally he fell ill, was taken to hospital and died on 15 April 1980.

Bad faith? The key ethical principle in Sartre's existentialism is authenticity. To act in a way that reflects your own personal decisions, rejecting any roles that others might impose, is the aim of the existentialist. Clearly, Sartre rejected some traditional roles, for example, by rejecting the symbol of literary achievement, the Nobel Prize. However, his treatment of those with whom he disagreed or who had the temerity to challenge his views displayed the tyranny of one who – with or without prizes or a university post – was all too well

aware of his position in an intellectual hierarchy. To control, manipulate and particularly to speak with authority but without conviction (as he did on the Soviet Union) is to act with an arrogance that smacks of a conception, if not a conceit, concerning one's own position. And that, it would seem, should certainly count as bad faith.

The other major issue concerning the behaviour of both Sartre and de Beauvoir is the extent to which they consciously used their sexual relationships as material for their writing. It is fair enough to follow Husserl in taking particular experienced reality as the basis of philosophy and perhaps inevitable that a novelist will use his or her own experience in compiling a work of fiction, but it seems unnecessarily cruel to do it so obviously at the expense of those with whom one has shared what might normally be considered intimate and private experiences or in holding the feelings of others up to ridicule.

Whatever his personal limitations, however, there is no doubt that Sartre stands as a giant among philosophers. He could also be charming, amusing and engaging – with the ability to make as well as lose friends. He was both hated and loved, despised and revered, to an extraordinary degree. He also had the ability to engage at all levels. For those with little inclination to philosophical speculation, his plays and novels opened up the idea and implications of freedom and choice. For those concerned to know the key features of his philosophy, works such as 'Existentialism Is a Humanism' provided a straightforward introduction. For the devotees of erudite and highly articulate expositions of philosophy his major works provide endless opportunities to become immersed. Above all, he was the philosopher as cultural artefact, relating his reasoned arguments to drama and fiction, addressing the human condition in whatever ways enabled him to explore the issues he saw as essential for human freedom and self-understanding.

WOMEN PHILOSOPHERS BEHAVING BADLY

We have listed no women among the ranks of erring philosophers for very good reasons. While women may have long privately studied philosophy, they had, until recently, a low public profile in the field because of the usual historical and cultural factors: the low status of women in the ancient world, only seriously challenged by the Epicureans, and the endemic sexism of Judaeo-Christian tradition. (Plato accepted women as near equals in his ideal Republic but not in his actual Academy.) Although one of the last pagan philosophers was a woman, the Neoplatonist Hypatia, murdered for her views by a Christian mob in sixth-century Alexandria, philosophy long remained a citadel of phallocratic arrogance, dominated by misogynists such as Aristotle, Rousseau and Schopenhauer. Héloïse, as intellectually brilliant as she was ill-fated, remained a unique figure well beyond the Middle Ages.

Yet if women philosophers in modern times have failed to match the obvious iniquities of their male counterparts, that does not imply that they lived in conventional rectitude. Mary Wollstonecraft, who published *A Vindication of the Rights of Woman* in 1792 during the French Revolution, expressed radical views on education and female emancipation, her work having a tremendous if delayed impact on feminist thought. Yet she shunned social norms by her affairs, by having children outside marriage and by describing that institution as a form of slavery. Politically aware, persuasive and dynamic in her thinking, she was also emotionally vulnerable in her relationships, at times suicidal and always unconventional.

Equally unconventional, Iris Murdoch, although known principally as a novelist, was primarily a philosopher. Her love life, while colourfully peripatetic, harmed no one, and she lacked her male peers' intellectual arrogance.

Perhaps, among twentieth-century women philosophers, the only serious contender for inclusion among the ranks of the sexually voracious, egocentric and exploitative is Simone de Beauvoir, best known for her book *The Second Sex* (*La Deuxième sexe*, 1949) and for being Sartre's lifelong partner. She shared and encouraged Sartre's literary voyeurism in frank exchanges about their many sexual partners and was not above setting up *ménages à trois* by introducing him to her girl-friends (she was bisexual, with a preference for young female students). She rivalled Rousseau in her exhibitionist desire to publish her sexual exploits and for her disregard for those whom she hurt in the process.

Hence we have no reason to believe that women philosophers, were they as numerous as men, would have contributed less to the sum of human folly.

8

MICHEL FOUCAULT (1926–84):
MADNESS, SEX AND PUNISHMENT

'In a sense, I have always wanted my books to be fragments of an autobiography. My books have always been my personal problems with madness, with prisons, with sexuality.' – Michel Foucault, May 1981

Some time after his death in Paris on 25 June 1984, the truth became known. Michel Foucault, Professor of the History of Systems of Thought at the prestigious Collège de France, had died of AIDS. His homosexuality had been no secret, but even his long-term partner Daniel Defert had been unaware of his condition. With hindsight the signs were there in his hacking cough the previous summer, but it had not stopped him from living life to the full while in the USA the previous autumn – lecturing at Berkeley but also frequenting the S&M parlours and bathhouses of San Francisco, where anonymity allowed him the freedom to explore sex at its most impersonal and brutal.

Foucault was in some ways a very private person, writing no auto-biography and unwilling to share, even with those closest to him, all aspects of his life. With a gift for giving complete attention to those with whom he spoke, always hospitable, he was mourned by friends. A meticulous researcher and brilliant multi-disciplinary synthesizer of thought, equally profound in philosophy, psychology and history, he was mourned by the academic world. His shaved head and roll-neck sweaters were as easily recognized on the global intellectual scene as his leather and chains must have been within the more covert circles of the S&M world.

But, as he freely admitted, his writings reflected his life and sexual preferences, simply because as an author he put all of himself into them. They reflect his preoccupations – with madness, power, discipline,

punishment and sex. Certainly, he was a thinker whose lifestyle matched his thought and who probably saw his behaviour as – in a Nietzschean sense – 'beyond good and evil'.

Born on 15 October 1926 in Poitiers, Michel Foucault was brought up in good bourgeois comfort. The family had a country house, Le Piroir, which his mother had inherited, and a holiday villa by the sea at La Baule, as well as their house in Poitiers. His father, a surgeon, appears to have been strict, but otherwise Michel had a average and contented childhood with his older sister Francine and younger brother Denys. As an adolescent, however, he rebelled against the assumption that he would study medicine. Crucially, he had realized that he was homosexual, which was certainly incompatible with the respectable family image in Poitiers. The comfort of his youth was disrupted with the coming of war, and the family found themselves under German occupation. The seaside villa was requisitioned, and they came to value the food that they could grow in the grounds of their country house – indeed, summers spent there were to be a regular feature of Foucault's later life.

Having been born into a bourgeois family in provincial France, Michel Foucault spent much of his adult life rebelling against all things provincial and bourgeois. No surprise there. That he should also rebel against the traditional style and content of philosophy, preferring to describe the significance of madness, sex and power, is also no surprise, given his own extreme proclivities. Short-sighted, brilliant, violent and sexually voracious, his work spanned the disciplines (a word he cherished!) of philosophy, psychology, sociology and history, bringing an entirely new flavour to philosophy, a flavour that may not have been quite to everyone's taste but which blended perfectly with his carefully constructed self-image.

At the age of twenty he secured a place at the École Normale Supérieure (ENS) in Paris, bringing him into contact with the brightest intellects and also freeing him from his provincial background. There he studied under Jean Hippolyte, a noted Hegelian, and

Merleau-Ponty. Fascinated initially by the philosophy of Hegel, Foucault found himself linking historical change to an underlying rationality, and by doing so he was able to combine his first love – history – with philosophy, exploring the structures of thought that underlay changing social attitudes.

Like most philosophers in Paris at that time Foucault was also influenced by Heidegger and Sartre, the latter entering into his period of greatest influence in Parisian café society, an inescapable presence. From Hegel and Heidegger he saw the historical process as a way of exploring the roots of present reality. From the fashionable Sartre – but also from Nietzsche – he came to recognize the degree to which one's reality is created through one's own existence and decisions. For those escaping from the narrowness of bourgeois upbringing, the prospect of self-creation through authentic decision-making, shunning the conventional in acts of self-affirmation, seemed a breath of fresh air.

His student days were marred by depression, probably brought on by guilt over his compulsive sado-masochistic sexual needs and by increasingly frequent psychosomatic illnesses. He once slashed his chest with a razor and in 1948 may have attempted suicide by taking an overdose. Much more given to drink and drugs than was fashionable immediately after the Second World War, he could become violent and had to be restrained. He also seems to have developed an intense and aggressive approach to debate. As a result he was shunned by fellow students. His father organized a consultation with Jean Delat, a senior psychiatrist at Hôpital Sainte-Anne, and as a result Foucault was given his own room in the sanatorium at the ENS, allowing him to escape from unwelcome company and have more time for reading.

One of his teachers was also in the sanatorium. Louis Althusser was suffering from schizophrenia and manic-depressive psychoses. Befriending Foucault, Althusser advised him against hospitalization – having experienced too much of it himself – but also encouraged him to join the French Communist Party. Althusser himself continued to

teach at the ENS for another thirty years, promoting his particular approach to Marxism, until he strangled his wife Hélène in November 1980. He spent the final decade of his life in a secure unit for the mentally ill – on account of the murder, not of his persistent Marxism – another philosopher whose behaviour was sadly dominated by the irrational.

The problem of that period was how one might still do philosophy. For much of the Anglo-American philosophical world – influenced by Wittgenstein, A.J. Ayer, Gilbert Ryle and others – philosophy was rapidly losing out on any sense of its own distinctive content. Rather, it was seen as a process of sorting out linguistic and logical errors in all other disciplines. The major alternative to that approach – what is generally termed 'Continental' philosophy – sprang from the work of Husserl and through him Heidegger and Sartre. This was the tradition that examined the experienced world. Even if the external world as it was in itself might be unknowable, at least our own experience of it might provide a sure basis for our understanding.

Influenced particularly by Heidegger, Foucault sought a way of understanding the interpretation that people of various eras had given to their experience of the human world. He was to produce an amalgam of philosophy, history, psychology and sociology and was generally reluctant to define himself either as a philosopher or a historian, for his work took him beyond the conventional parameters of those disciplines. He took historical documents and scrutinized them in order to reveal the structures of thought that allowed their authors to write as they did. In this way he was able to piece together the various ways in which people have understood themselves and their world – in a process for which he was later to use the term 'archaeology'. Wittgenstein had pointed out that language was always used for a particular purpose – and to understand its meaning one had to consider its use. Foucault followed a similar policy. He examined the structures of thought and how they were used in areas of very human concern – especially in madness, punishment, power and sexuality.

He took a degree in psychology at the ENS in 1949, regularly attended the presentation of psychiatric patients at Hôpital Sainte-Anne and continued working there in an informal capacity after finishing his studies. As a tutor in psychology at the ENS he used psychological tests on his students, and his first teaching post at Lille in 1952 (where he spent only two or three nights a week, preferring life in Paris) involved teaching psychology to philosophy students. At this stage he seems to have been unsure which direction his career should take and might well have moved over towards psychiatry.

In 1953 Foucault saw Samuel Beckett's *Waiting for Godot* and felt that it enabled him to break out of the existing philosophical ethos, dominated by Marxism, phenomenology and existentialism. The tramps on stage, emptied of any metaphysical or moral significance, just wait for something or nothing or death. Later that same year, while on holiday in Italy, he read Nietzsche's *Untimely Meditations*. It was not his first reading of Nietzsche, but at that time it came to him as a revelation. He seems to have been influenced particularly by Nietzsche's sense that we create ourselves, that power is key to human action and that beneath the Apollonian structures of reason there seethes a Dionysian urge. In particular he was struck by Nietzsche's early essay 'Schopenhauer as Educator', with the riddle that the human quest is that one should become what one is and not something else, forging one's own purpose in life. Set against the nihilistic background of Beckett's *Godot* it inspired Foucault's great Nietzschean quest.

Other less profound ideas from Nietzsche might equally have appealed to him. While Nietzsche said that when going to a woman one should not forget the whip, it is most unlikely that Nietzsche himself would ever have brought himself to use one. With Foucault, however, Nietzsche's advice (although reversing gender) was both welcomed and applied! In fact, it would have been entirely in line with Nietzsche's sense that each person is driven forward by a daimon. For those whose daimon is good, happiness lies in store, for those

with a bad daimon, there lies disaster – but one should still follow that daimon; to gain the greatest happiness one must 'live dangerously'. We also know that at this time Foucault became fascinated with suicide, dreaming of death as the fulfilment of existence. He was inspired also by the writing of Georges Bataille, with its fascination with the Dionysian in Nietzsche, with Sade and with pushing beyond the boundaries of social restraint in sexual behaviour. Nietzsche, Bataille and Sade proved a heady concoction that exactly suited Foucault's temperament.

At this time Foucault entered into a very intense sexual relationship with the composer Jean Barraqué, who was heavily into both drink and Nietzsche. Their life was marked by sado-masochistic sex, drinking and intense discussion. It lasted only a couple of years, being ended by Barraqué, who withdrew from what Foucault's biographer, James Miller, describes as his 'erotic theatre of cruelty', and who refused to tolerate what he described as 'degradation' possibly a reference to Foucault's sado-masochism. But by the time the relationship with Barraqué come to an end, Christmas 1954, Foucault had already started teaching in Sweden.

He taught French at Uppsala from 1954 to 1958, but his courses were shaped to suit his very particular interests, including one on 'Love in French Literature; from the Marquis de Sade to Jean Genet'. While in Uppsala he worked on the relationship between society and madness, and there are continuing signs of his fascination with suicide and death, with the sense that the prospect of life slipping away at the end of a noose as being one of unspeakable pleasure. But he was not without flamboyant indulgences. He bought a Jaguar and enjoyed driving at speed, sometimes drunk. He was also seldom short of boyfriends. At this point, however, his academic career was far from established, and his lifestyle was partly funded by an allowance from his family.

Following Uppsala, he worked for a year in Warsaw, in charge of the university's Centre Français, where he taught French language

classes and later acted as a replacement for the cultural attaché. However, one young man to whom he was attracted turned out to be a police informer, and Foucault was advised to leave as quickly as possible. His final overseas posting was at the Institut Français in Hamburg, where he again gave French language classes and lectures while familiarizing himself with the already well-known entertainment possibilities in that city.

Returning to France in 1960, he taught for the next six years in Clermont-Ferrand, where he was Head of the Philosophy Department. However, he visited the university for only one day a week, living for the rest of the time in Paris. It was during this period that his academic reputation grew, aided by the publication in 1961 of his first major book, *Madness and Civilization: A History of Madness in the Age of Reason* (*Folie et déraison: Histoire de la folie à l'age classique*). In it he analysed the way in which society's understanding of madness had changed after about 1500. Before that date the 'mad' were treated with respect and frequently viewed as having spiritual perception, whereas later madness was treated as a sickness that required social control and treatment. In an interview in 1982 he said, 'After having studied philosophy, I wanted to see what madness was: I had been mad enough to study reason; I was now reasonable enough to study madness.'

Madness and Civilization shows his continuing interest in the relationship between reason and the more violent, primitive human urges, which Nietzsche saw as represented by Apollo and Dionysus. He said, 'Through Sade and Goya, the Western world discovered the possibility of surpassing reason through violence.' The distinctive idea for Foucault is that reason is surpassed, revealing his assumption that reality reveals its secrets through violence in a way that it cannot do through reason. And that, of course, is a key psychological feature of the sado-masochistic urge – to get within the other person, breaking through to a deeper personal reality through the experience of pain. Miller's summary of the ethical implication of *Madness and*

Civilization suggests that for Foucault the person who is called 'mad' is innocent; rather, it is society that is guilty, and the wild impulses and fantasies seen in those deemed 'mad' are the result of the repression by society of natural Dionysian impulses.

His work in the 1960s was mainly devoted to a method of historical enquiry to which he gave the term 'archaeology', involving a painstaking examination of historical documents. His work is therefore unlike most twentieth-century philosophy, for Foucault loved facts, and his books are packed with them. He uses facts to build up a general picture of the matrix of thought that every generation uses to interpret its experience. He argues that statements only become meaningful within such a framework of ideas. His archaeologies look at the different levels in the history of understanding – in this first case the different ways in which society has understood madness. The implication is that there is no single or absolute way of describing madness but that everything is related to what he was later to call the 'episteme', or structure of thought, within which it is found. Like a physical archaeologist, who relates each small find to its level and setting, so Foucault related all gathered facts to their intellectual layer and setting. The end product is a study that shows how society and language shape perception – giving it a historical *a priori*.

It is this process that gives his philosophy a very different flavour from that of most other philosophers, for it reads more like a history but with an emphasis on the conceptual frameworks that give a context for each event and statement. Thus, for example, he looks at the role of hospitals in the eighteenth century and the development of clinics for the poor so that they might treat themselves at home. Or he examines the criteria used for deciding which of the poor are considered 'deserving', whether a person is able to work, and so on. In this way he gradually builds up his image of the concepts of health, disease, poverty, work and so on within the context of that particular period. Foucault's way of working – both in the archaeologies and later the genealogies – produces a relativist view. The process of

understanding is not absolute but evolves through time and forms part of an overall artificially constructed set of views. So it is that both science and the overall view of the nature of physical reality can evolve, in just the same was as society's understanding of madness can change.

Foucault's study of the background of thought looks back to the work of two thinkers who influenced him from his student days. Hegel had criticized Kant for constructing a moral philosophy that did not take into account the general background of thought that formed the context of a moral choice. It was Hegel, too, who explored the idea that there was a particular *Geist* or spirit of an age, which provided the context for all social and cultural work. Heidegger, too, emphasized that we are 'thrown' into the world, and therefore all our choices are related to that specific background. Indeed, Heidegger explored the problem of having an infinite number of background facts to be taken into account before anything can be understood completely.

It was in the early 1960s that Foucault met Daniel Defert, who was to become his partner for the rest of his life and with whom he had a close bond but not one that required sexual exclusivity. Younger than Foucault, Defert was a political activist, and this influenced and nourished Foucault's own political commitments.

In 1963 Foucault published *The Birth of the Clinic* (*Naissance de la clinique*), in which he explored issues of suicide, sado-masochism and drugs through a study of the writer Raymond Roussel. Subtitled *An Archaeology of the Medical Gaze*, it explored areas of human experience that had become important features of Foucault's own life. It was followed in 1966 by *The Order of Things: An Archaeology of the Human Sciences* (*Les Mots et les choses: Une archéologie des sciences humaines*), an exploration of the way in which human self-understanding has evolved over time through an analysis of the changes through the eighteenth and nineteenth centuries in science, economics and related disciplines. He developed the idea of an

213

episteme – an overall framework of thought, within which life is interpreted. Such an episteme is developed during a particular period and can then change, giving way to an alternative. This is similar to the work of Thomas Kuhn, who saw science progressing by way of paradigm shifts, where a whole way of understanding is revised, interspersed with periods of normal science, where there is systematic work within the established paradigm.

The book ends on a curious, almost poetic note, with the prophecy that one day man will vanish 'like a face in the sand at the edge of the sea' – the end of a concept that had dominated social thinking during the preceding couple of centuries. There would seem to be interesting parallel here with Nietzsche. For Nietzsche there was a radical distinction to be made between the last man, docile, lacking any sense of himself or his destiny, and the *Übermensch*, whose very essence is to go beyond whatever has been. In *Daybreak* Nietzsche presents this contrast with the question, 'Do we wish humanity to end in fire and light, or to end in the sands?' Clearly, the poetic climax of Foucault's book looks at exactly that Nietzschean challenge. The social thinking that has repressed man in past centuries has produced a Nietzschean last man, whereas Foucault, always preferring the Dionysian to the Apollonian, the frenzied and dangerous to the rational and ordered, longs for the *Übermensch*.

In order to avoid doing two years' national service Daniel Defert opted instead to go to teach in Tunisia. Foucault followed him in 1966 and taught at the University of Tunis, enjoying the relaxed pleasures of North Africa but also increasingly becoming politically aware and active.

Following demonstrations against the government, the student uprising and the dramatic confrontations between students and police during 1968, in an atmosphere intoxicated with radical politics, Foucault returned to Paris and took up a teaching post at the newly created University of Vincennes as Chair of its Philosophy Department. Defert followed and became a lecturer in sociology. The

university was a radical left-wing establishment and very much at the forefront of the new student mood. Foucault was later to claim that it was the uprising of the students in 1968 that jolted him out of his fascination with discourse and led him to become increasing active in political and social issues. As a consequence he became involved in a number of political campaigns, including, notably, prison-reform work. Vincennes was soon to be the scene of demonstrations and confrontations with the police – and here the Chair of the Philosophy Department played his part, hurling down missiles and manning the barricades. However, the demonstrators were no match for the police, and Foucault and Defert found themselves arrested with a couple of hundred others, eyes watering from tear gas.

Foucault clearly had a very different image now – as a radical academic and champion of political causes. He also looked the part: aged forty-two and faced with increasing baldness, he took the initiative and shaved his head. His image and casual clothes set him apart from the average academic. Some would claim that he was consciously constructing his own reality, affirming himself in a very Nietzschean way; others might claim that he was just following fashion and making the most of his new situation.

What distinguishes Foucault from many other philosophers, however, is the way in which he was always reviewing his concrete experience of life, engaging in an ongoing process of reflection. In May 1984, not long before his death, in an interview conducted by Paul Rabinow Foucault described this process:

> Thought is not what inhabits a certain conduct and gives it its meaning; rather it is what allows one to step back from this way of acting or reacting, to present it to oneself as an object of thought and to question it as to its meaning, its conditions and its goals. Thought is freedom in relation to what one does, the motion by which one detaches from it, establishes it as an object and reflects on it as a problem.

And this reflects his earlier assertion that his works are autobiographical, since they are exactly his objective reflections on himself and his actions.

It would be wrong, however, to see Foucault at this period as giving himself entirely to teaching at Vincennes or supporting his various political causes. There remained a conventional academic core to his life, and it was not long before he started to spend less time at Vincennes and more at the Bibliothèque Nationale, carrying out the meticulous research that formed the basis of his publications. *The Archaeology of Knowledge* was published in 1969. This is another major work, in which he unearths layer upon layer of concepts and problematics, disinterring the process by which thought understands action and the elements of power and control that shape it.

A year later the radical philosopher of the barricades was elected to become a professor at the Collège de France, the most prestigious of French academic institutions, choosing the title Professor of the History of Systems of Thought. Freed from the burden of teaching, he was able to develop his own field of work on which to deliver public lectures. It marked his establishment at the heart of French philosophy.

But his new status did not make Foucault less radical. In a debate with that American political philosopher and activist Noam Chomsky, filmed for Dutch television in 1971, he made it clear that he was prepared to dispense with any principle of justice. Chomsky argued that the state sometimes needed to be challenged and opposed but that – in order to do so – one needed one's own principle of justice. Foucault pressed on, insisting that in the class struggle the aim was to win rather than to establish justice and that when the proletariat takes power it might exert its power over those it has vanquished in ways that are violent and bloody – and he could see no objection to that. Chomsky, appalled, felt that he was debating with someone who did not even inhabit the same moral universe. The following year Foucault was to take this further, advocating 'popular justice' rather than the judicial system and apparently citing the September

Massacres of 1792, when, in one of the bloodiest episodes of the French Revolution, more than a thousand people – including priests, aristocrats and those suspected of being traitors – were killed by mobs in Paris. Clearly for Foucault there seemed no limit to the brutality that could be accepted: rather than going through courts he was in favour of giving people information and allowing a popular need for vengeance and retaliation to take place. When pushed, he seemed to delight in shocking people, perhaps fulfilling at the same time his own sexual need to transgress.

He set his sights on things other than academic distinction, however. Establishing himself on the eighth floor of a block of flats, his voyeuristic inclinations were helped by the use of binoculars to spy on young men in other flats. But his sexual inclinations found their match on the other side of the Atlantic, for 1970 found him in San Francisco, where he discovered the sexual freedoms of the bathhouses. Compared with the more restrained possibilities of the Paris scene, the unceasing sexual orgies he found in California were an intoxicating liberation, enabling him to act out things he had previously only dreamed of.

The opening of his *Discipline and Punish* (*Surveiller et punir*, 1975) lingers on the details of torture in the mid eighteenth century and then traces the way in which prisons were devised as an alternative way to deal with the bodies of offenders – restraining rather than destroying them. He sees in this a pattern of social control and restraint. Tracing the development of the modern prison, he showed that what might be taken as kindness and humanity masked an increasing degree of social control; another opportunity for him to examine the nature and use of power in society. In some ways the soul is seen as the prison of the body (to reverse Plato's view) and thus that society is the prison within which human bodies (deprived of their Dionysian mode) are confined. To the innocent philosophical student, much of the violent detail might seem unnecessary to make the argument. To those who shared Foucault's interests, however, his philosophy would have been highly arousing!

In the 1970s his approach changed from an archaeology, where human discourse seems to define reality, to genealogy, a term used by Nietzsche. Foucault was now more concerned with the process by which ideas and concepts change with a changing social structure. Clearly, however, Foucault was concerned with 'systems of thought' (as we see from the title he devised for his Chair at the Collège de France) in both these phases of his work, the principle difference being that the earlier archaeologies were structuralist – where the matrix of ideas and language define reality – whereas the later works show the way in which ideas change along with society, with one concept giving birth to another. And in the later works he homed in again on a particular theme: power. He saw himself as a critical historian rather than a social theorist, and as such he demonstrated the way in which power and social control (whether overt or hidden) is crucial for understanding issues such as punishment, prisons and – later – sexuality. He saw social control, and the branding of people as 'normal' or 'abnormal', as a form of discipline to which he was utterly opposed.

In 1975 he was lecturing in Berkeley, California, and again frequenting the bathhouses and other S&M establishments in San Francisco. From the mid-1970s all sexual acts between consenting adults were deemed lawful in California, and the gay community in San Francisco was growing. Gay bars, gay clubs and even gay communities were being established. Some bathhouses had orgy-rooms for the experience of multiple sexual contacts between strangers. Here Foucault could experience the generation of sexual pleasure with strangers, with the freedom given by anonymity. He was particularly interested in the leather scene and was astounded to find a culture devoted to casual sex and drugs. In what he termed the 'desexualization of pleasure', he was fascinated by the possibility of arousing and giving physical pleasure through the use of the whole body, not just the genitals. Freed from concerns about one's own subjective identity, he also wanted to explore ways in which one could give and receive sexual pleasure simply on a physical level; direct and impersonal. He

also describes having had a profound experience while high on LSD overlooking Death Valley, California. In fact, Foucault was so impressed with the effect of the hallucinogenic drug that he commented, 'The only think I can compare this experience to in my life is sex with a stranger.' Not the sort of comment one might expect from a Professor of the Collège de France!

But there was a very different side to his life. Every summer, following the death of his father in 1959, he would spend time back in the family country home of Le Piroir, working away in the study he had converted from the former servants' quarters, sharing time with his nephews and nieces, gathering produce and helping his mother to water the garden – a task he managed every year until 1983, when prevented by ill health.

His final great work, three volumes of which were published, was his *History of Sexuality* (*Histoire de la sexualité*) – clearly a study close to his heart. The first volume appeared in 1976, entitled *The Will to Know* (*La Volonté de savoir*), with the second and third published only days before his death. In it his focus moved towards understanding ethics in an historical context – how did people in earlier eras understand the ethical implications of their actions? Whereas in the first volume he had looked at sexuality in the modern era, the second and third were to explore sexuality in Ancient Greece and Rome. A fourth volume was near completion when he died but never published. In it he returned again to the study of the use of power in society, since he believed that the constraints placed upon people stopped them expressing their power, which would therefore find an outlet in sexual fantasies. But in this final phase of his work he seemed to give more credit to the role of the individual – both in the *History of Sexuality* and in the Berkeley lectures in his final year. He explores the idea of a Stoic or a Cynic making some gesture, or deliberately flouting convention, in order to make a point.

High on opium, one day in July 1978, crossing the rue de Vaugirard outside his flat, he was struck down by a car. Thinking that

he was dying, he described the experience as one of the happiest of his life! In what is a fairly common experience for those near death he sensed that he was leaving his body, and found it unspeakably pleasurable. Clearly, he wanted intensity of experience, whatever the pain involved – indeed, because of the pain involved. Death was obviously not to be feared; in fact, it confirmed so much that he had explored earlier in his life. His sense of total pleasure was closely related to death.

Throughout the 1970s, along with Daniel Defert, he was active politically, supporting the revolution in Iran against the Shah and going there in 1978. In June 1979 he joined Sartre and others in appealing to the French President to give more help to the Vietnamese 'boat people'. He was now able to campaign on a humanitarian basis for refugees and the rights of political dissidents without his earlier need to promote extreme left-wing views. His attitudes had mellowed, and he was no longer prepared to see every law or principle as in some way oppressive and constricting.

At the end of the 1970s his interests shifted once again. This time he gave his attention more to classical philosophies – and particularly to the Stoics – in a quest for an understanding of the human subject. He even moved his usual place of research from the Bibliothèque Nationale (where he complained about the slowness of book delivery) to the Bibliothèque du Saulchoir, which was run by the Dominicans and in which he could more easily research the early Christian texts, for he had started to read the works of Saints Augustine, Ambrose, Jerome and Benedict – looking at the early church in the context of the political thought of the time and also at its spiritual discipline. He was even thinking of quitting the Collège de France and moving to the countryside.

The second and third volumes of his *History of Sexuality* were delivered to the publishers in early 1984. By that time Foucault had probably been suffering from AIDS for at least a year, if not more. He collapsed in his Paris flat, was hospitalized – and died on the 25 June, aged fifty-seven.

At first the medical bulletins did not suggest AIDS, and newspaper speculation was condemned. AIDS had only been named two years earlier, and any association with it brought suggestions of guilt or divine punishment among significant parts of the population and press. It was to be another two months before Rock Hudson's death made it more possible to speak of AIDS without such overtones. Some were later to regret that Foucault's death could not have been the opportunity to start to overcome such prejudice. In fact, the original death certificate had put the cause of death as AIDS, but the family had insisted that this information should be suppressed. The question remains whether Foucault knew he had AIDS, and he was posthumously criticized by some in the gay community for his silence if he did.

What is clear is that the previous summer some of his friends had opted for safe sex and had advised him to do the same. He had ignored their advice and thus deliberately put the lives of others at risk. He returned unprotected to the bathhouses – places which only a year later would come under close scrutiny or closure. But in 1983 it appears that even a world-class thinker could be unwise enough to gamble with his own life and that of others. He had long been pre-occupied with death and with suicide. Perhaps in the desperate final year of unprotected abandon he was able to experience something that his most morbid thoughts had long contemplated. He went, knowing the risks but still desperate to experience the exquisite trans-formation of pain into erotic pleasure.

And yet there is quite another side to Foucault in that autumn of 1983. He was giving a series of lectures in Berkeley on parrhesia, a Greek term that may broadly be translated as free speech but with overtones of honest or direct speech. They were to be developed into a series for the Collège de France the following spring – his final lectures. In meticulous detail he takes his students through examples of the word in classical Greek literature and in Greek philosophy, exploring how such speaking of the truth related to lifestyle and to the risk that comes with honesty. And then he turns to the Cynics, a much maligned

group of thinkers, who were not above public masturbation (Diogenes) or public suicide (Peregrinus) in order to show their disdain for social norms and their determination to live honestly and naturally. Of them, he says in 'Discourse and Truth: The Problematization of Parrhesia':

> The high value which the Cynics attributed to a person's way of life does not mean that they had no interest in theoretical philosophy, but reflects their view that the manner in which a person lived was a touchstone of his or her relation to truth – as we saw was also the case in the Socratic tradition. The conclusion they drew from this Socratic idea, however, was that in order to proclaim the truths they accepted in a manner that would be accessible to everyone, they thought that their teachings had to consist in a very public, visible, spectacular, provocative, and sometimes scandalous way of life. The Cynics thus taught by way of examples and the explanations associated with them. They wanted their own lives to be a blazon of essential truths which would then serve as a guideline, or as an example for others to follow. But there is nothing in this Cynic emphasis on philosophy as an art of life which is alien to Greek philosophy . . . the Cynic attitude is, in its basic form, just an extremely radical version of the very Greek conception of the relationship between one's way of life and knowledge of the truth. The Cynic idea that a person is nothing else but his relation to truth, and that this relation to truth takes shape or is given form in his own life – that is completely Greek.

And perhaps here, in the academic lecture hall, with all the attention to detail that marked him out as an academic of the first rank, is the key to why he could also explore his own parrhesia in the dance of death that was taking place in the bathhouses – he was deliberately risking all in order to live out the speaking of his own truth.

In exploring Foucault's behaviour in relation to his work, there is a fundamental question to be answered: did he follow fashion or set a trend? When he shaved his head and appeared at the barricades at

the University of Vincennes, was he genuinely acting out of a new conviction or simply following a fashionable new movement and searching for a new audience? In the last decade of his life was he seduced by the background ethos of the gay scene in California or was he acting out of personal conviction as an individual? This is crucial for understanding his philosophy. California may have given him permission to make choices and act in ways that he could only have dreamed of (literally) back in provisional Poitiers.

But are his actions to be understood only within the episteme of the bathhouse culture? Or should individuals be responsible for their actions in any absolute sense? This was not just the issue that caused Hegel to criticize Kant, it was also reflected in Foucault's own work, as – right at the end of his life – he seems to be exploring the ability of the individual to stand out and make a gesture of defiance against the norms of his or her culture. Was he just obeying cultural orders or making a huge, life-risking gesture of defiance in the tradition of the Cynics? Perhaps we ask too much if we expect any life to be either/or on that issue.

He left no formal will, but a note indicated that Defert should have the flat and that there should be no posthumous publication. In fact, he had gone out of his way to make sure that many of his notes and papers would be destroyed. Whatever sad legacy he may have left in the bathhouses of San Francisco, Defert only found out after his death than he had been extremely generous to the Dominicans who ran the Bibliothèque du Saulchoir where he worked during his last years. It is a setting of monastic simplicity, and it now holds his archives. As implied by David Macey's biography *The Lives of Michel Foucault*, Foucault was a man of many lives.

Whatever his inclinations towards monastic discipline, he had always been fascinated by death, by suicide and by risk. In the final year of his life, in discussing the risk of AIDS, he said, 'Besides, to die for the love of boys: what could be more beautiful?'

DEMETRIUS, PHILOSOPHER-KING OF ATHENS

History, repeating itself, notoriously does so as farce. Twenty-five years after Plato was found dead in his study at work on *The Laws*, his last and grimmest meditations on the human predicament, Athenian democracy was finally destroyed by the armies of the Macedonian generals as Alexander the Great's successors carved up the world. In Athens the improbable beneficiary of this overthrow was a rogue-philosopher called Demetrius of Phalerum, a follower of Aristotle rather than Plato, although he presumably knew the works of both.

In 317 BC Cassander, the general who at that time controlled Greece, installed Demetrius as *epimetheletes*, overseer or guardian of Athens, still the greatest of Greek cities. Demetrius has been damned as a collaborator, even a Fascist, as he extinguished Athens' long-standing democracy, but he was a colourful figure, his regime at times showing almost surreal qualities. Few firm facts are known about his guardianship, but plenty of anecdotes survive. During his rule Demetrius had processions led by a mechanical snail that spat out saliva. He accepted flattering epithets such as *heliomorphos* (sun-shaped) and *lampito* (radiant). He may have been blind for a while before being cured by Sarapis, the Graeco-Egyptian god of healing. Demetrius imposed stringent sumptuary laws on Athenian citizenry (it was a hard time economically), while throwing wild parties himself. For these he dyed his hair purple and made up his face with rouge and cream – unusual behaviour for a philosopher or a dictator. But Demetrius was sexually insatiable, strolling down the Street of the Tripods every day after lunch, 'where the prettiest boys would gather, hoping to be noticed by him'. The street is still there, with the same reputation. He also had 1,500 bronze statues erected in his honour. After his overthrow they were melted down into chamber pots, as Athenians expressed their real opinions of him.

Although often seen as a philosopher-king, Demetrius' surviving works in fact deal with almost everything except philosophy: literature, *haute cuisine*, hair-dressing, clothes, etc. When his protector lost power over Greece in 307 BC, Demetrius went on to advise Ptolemy I of Egypt on establishing the vast new library in Alexandria. He fell out of favour in Egypt, too, but the library, with its 600,000 volumes, one of the Seven Wonders of the Ancient World, undoubtedly bore his mark. *Si monumentum requiris, circumspice* (If you require a monument, look around) . . .

POSTSCRIPT

There is, of course, another side to this story. If we have presented our eight badly behaved philosophers in an unflattering light, it is only to illustrate the general point that a life of reason does not necessarily lead to a reasonable life. The philosophical fraternity has never been immune to human frailties, nor should we expect those whose thoughts are exalted to have emotions or sexuality to match. Whatever folly their lives may reveal, their contribution to human thought and self-understanding has been immense.

Rousseau, when not too self-obsessed, set out principles of education and democracy and ideas about our relationship with non-human nature that others were to develop and which have had a profound effect on our modern consciousness.

Schopenhauer, in developing an awareness of the extent to which our own consciousness shapes our experience, and taking into account the philosophies of the East, was able – when not sunk in gloomy pessimism – to present a cogent and influential analysis of the way in which we, as human beings, relate to our world.

As for Nietzsche . . . We can hardly even to start to describe his influence, whether good or bad or beyond both categories, on subsequent thought. Sickly in body and spirit he might have been, but his aphoristic insights have inspired our view of the future of humankind. In a world loosed from the bonds of pre-determined values, his is a challenge to say 'Yes' to a freely chosen future.

Russell, in addition to his brilliant logical analysis, brought

philosophy out of its academic closet and broadcast it far and wide in a journalistic engagement with all the issues of his day. Whatever his patrician background and domestic mayhem, he was a superb publicist for the process of actually thinking.

Of Wittgenstein it is tempting to say that by sheer intellectual weight he was able to take philosophy for a walk as one might a dog, first leading it off in one direction and then bringing it back again. The lead with which he did so was as short as his temper, but philosophy has since found its way out of the rather narrow alley down which he led it, and aspirants to serious thought are no longer required to wear open-necked white shirts!

Heidegger's analysis of the way in which we understand ourselves in terms of past and future has been deeply influential and his later thought on technology and ecology highly relevant to the new century. His thought cannot entirely be separated from his great political folly but can be appreciated in spite of it.

And Sartre, taking philosophy from lecture hall to café, making existentialism (even for those who understood little of it) a fashion to be celebrated after dark and between the sheets, produced literary gems that transcend and illustrate the limitations of the rational – obsessively writing all of himself into his works. Love him or hate him, he stands as a giant.

Finally, Foucault, easily criticized for his excesses, should equally be celebrated for the boldness of his work and his unflinching eye for the truths embodied in the changing patterns of thought and language. Madness, punishment and sex may not be standard fare for philosophers, but their exploration is essential for an understanding of multi-faceted human nature.

And an appreciation of their fallibility may encourage us – however aware we may be of our own follies and limitations – to dare to think beyond ourselves.

FURTHER READING

General
Applebaum, David and Mel Thompson (eds), *World Philosophy*, London: Vega, 2002
Comte-Sponville, André, *A Short Treatise on the Great Virtues*, London: Heinemann, 2002
Honderich, Ted (ed.), *The Oxford Companion to Philosophy*, Oxford: Oxford University Press, 1995
Lilla, Mark, *The Reckless Mind: Intellectuals in Politics*, New York: New York Review of Books, 2001
Magee, Bryan, *Aspects of Wagner*, Oxford: Oxford University Press, 1988
— *The Great Philosophers: An Introduction to Western Philosophy*, Oxford: Oxford University Press, 1988
— *The Story of Philosophy*, London: Dorling Kindersley, 1998
Russell, Bertrand, *A History of Western Philosophy*, London: Routledge, 2004
Steiner, George, *Lessons of the Masters*, Cambridge, Massachusetts, and London: Harvard University Press, 2003

Jean-Jacques Rousseau
Beer, Sir Gavin de, *Jean-Jacques Rousseau and His World*, London: Thames and Hudson, 1972
Cranston, Maurice, *Jean-Jacques: The Early Life and Works of Jean-Jacques Rousseau, 1712–54*, London: Allen Lane, 1983
— *The Noble Savage: Jean-Jacques Rousseau in Exile and Adversity*, London: Allen Lane, 1991
— *The Solitary Self: Jean-Jacques Rousseau, 1754–62*, London: Allen Lane, 1997
Dent, N.J.H., *Rousseau: An Introduction to His Psychological, Social and Political Theory*, Oxford: Blackwell, 1989
— *The Rousseau Dictionary*, Oxford: Blackwell, 1992
Grimsley, Ronald, *Jean-Jacques Rousseau*, Brighton: Harvester, 1983
Orwin, Clifford and Nathan Tarcov (eds), *The Legacy of Rousseau*, Chicago and London: University of Chicago Press, 1997
Schwartz, J., *The Sexual Politics of Jean-Jacques Rousseau*, Chicago and London: University of Chicago Press, 1984

229

Arthur Schopenhauer

Atwell, John E., *Schopenhauer: The Human Character*, Philadelphia: Temple University Press, 1990

Copleston, Frederick, *Arthur Schopenhauer: Philosopher of Pessimism*, London: Continuum International Publishing Group, 1975

Hamlyn, D.W., *Schopenhauer*, London: Routledge, 1980

Jacquette, D. (ed.), *Schopenhauer, Philosophy and the Arts*, Cambridge: Cambridge University Press, 1996

Janaway, Christopher (ed.), *The Cambridge Companion to Schopenhauer*, Cambridge: Cambridge University Press, 1999

Magee, Bryan, *The Philosophy of Schopenhauer*, Oxford: Oxford University Press, 1983

— *Misunderstanding Schopenhauer*, London: Institute of Germanic Studies, 1989

Safranski, Rüdiger, *Schopenhauer and the Wild Years of Philosophy*, Cambridge, Massachusetts: Harvard University Press, 1991

Simmel, Georg, *Schopenhauer and Nietzsche*, Urbana, Illinois: University of Illinois Press, 1986

Young, Julian, *Willing and Unwilling: A Study in the Philosophy of Arthur Schopenhauer*, Dortrecht, Boston and Lancaster: Martinus Nijhoff Publishers, 1987

Friedrich Nietzsche

Chamberlain, Lesley, *Nietzsche in Turin: The End of the Future*, London: Quartet Books, 1996

Diethe, Carol, *Nietzsche's Women: Beyond the Whip*, Berlin: Walter de Gruyter, 1996

Gilman, Sander (ed.), *Conversations with Nietzsche: A Life in the Words of His Contemporaries*, New York and Oxford: Oxford University Press, 1988

Golomb, Jacob and Robert Wistrich (eds), *Nietzsche, Godfather of Fascism? On the Uses and Abuses of a Philosophy*, Princeton and Oxford: Princeton University Press, 2002

Hayman, Ronald, *Nietzsche: A Critical Life*, London, Weidenfeld and Nicolson, 1980

Hollingdale, R.J., *Nietzsche: The Man and His Philosophy*, Cambridge: Cambridge University Press, 1999

Kaufmann, Walter, *Nietzsche: Philosopher, Psychologist, Antichrist*, Princeton and Oxford: Princeton University Press, 1974

Safranski, Rüdiger, *Nietzsche: A Philosophical Biography*, London: Granta Books, 2002

Tanner, Michael, *Nietzsche*, Oxford: Oxford University Press, 1994

Bertrand Russell

Blackwell, Kenneth, *The Spinozistic Ethics of Bertrand Russell*, London: Allen and Unwin, 1985

Carr, Brian, *Bertrand Russell: An Introduction*, London: Allen and Unwin, 1975

Clark, Ronald, *The Life of Bertrand Russell*, London: Thames and Hudson, 1981

Grayling, A.C., *Russell*, Oxford: Oxford University Press, 1996

Ironside, Philip, *The Social and Political Thought of Bertrand Russell: The Development of an Aristocratic Liberalism*, Cambridge: Cambridge University Press, 1995

Monk, Ray, *Bertrand Russell 1872–1920: The Spirit of Solitude*, London: Jonathan Cape 1996

— *Bertrand Russell 1921–70: The Ghost of Madness*, London, Jonathan Cape, 2000

Moorhead, Caroline, *Bertrand Russell*, London: Sinclair-Stevenson, 1992

Ryan, Alan, *Bertrand Russell: A Political Life*, London: Allen Lane, 1988

Seymour, Miranda, *Ottoline Morrell: Life on the Grand Scale*, London: Hodder and Stoughton, 1992

Tait, Katharine, *My Father Bertrand Russell*, London: Gollancz, 1976

Ludwig Wittgenstein

Bartley, William Warren, *Wittgenstein*, London: Quartet Books, 1974

Bernhard, Thomas, *Wittgenstein's Nephew: A Friendship*, London: Quartet Books, 1987

Cornish, Kimberley, *The Jew of Linz: Wittgenstein, Hitler and Their Secret Battle for the Mind*, London: Century, 1998

Edmonds, David and John Eidonow, *Wittgenstein's Poker: The Story of a Ten-Minute Argument Between Two Great Philosophers*, London: Faber and Faber, 2002

Finch, H.L., *Wittgenstein*, Rockport, Massachusetts, and Shaftesbury, Dorset: Element, 1995

McGuinness, Brian, *Wittgenstein: A Life: Young Ludwig 1889–1921*, London: Gerald Duckworth, 1988

Malcolm, Norman, *Ludwig Wittgenstein: A Memoir*, New York and Oxford, Clarendon Press, 2001

— *Wittgenstein: A Religious Point of View?*, London: Routledge, 1993

Monk, Ray, *Ludwig Wittgenstein: The Duty of Genius*, London: Jonathan Cape, 1990

Stroll, Avrum, *Wittgenstein*, Oxford, Oneworld Publications, 2002

Martin Heidegger

Heidegger, Martin, *Being and Time*, Joan Stambaugh(tr.), Chicago and
 London: University of Chicago Press, 2002
Mulhall, Stephen, *Heidegger and Being and Time*, London: Routledge, 1966
Ott, Hugo, *Heidegger: A Political Life*, London: HarperCollins, 1993
Pattison, George, *Routledge Philosophy Guidebook to the Later Heidegger*,
 London: Routledge, 2000
Safranski, Rüdiger, *Martin Heidegger: Between Good and Evil*, Ewald Osers
 (tr.), Cambridge, Massachusetts: Harvard University Press, 1998
Wolin, Richard, *The Heidegger Controversy: A Critical Reader*, Cambridge,
 Massachusetts: Massachusetts Institute of Technology Press, 1993
— *Heidegger's Children*, Princeton, New Jersey: Princeton University Press,
 2001
— *The Politics of Being*, New York: Columbia University Press, 1990

Jean-Paul Sartre

Card, Claudia (ed.), *The Cambridge Companion to Simone de Beauvoir*,
 Cambridge: Cambridge University Press, 2003
Cohen-Solal, Annie, *Sartre: A Life*, London: Heinemann, 1987
Lamblin, Bianca, *A Disgraceful Affair: Simone de Beauvoir, Jean-Paul Sartre,
 and Bianca Lamblin*, Boston: Northeastern University Press, 1993
Lévy, Bernard-Henri, *Sartre: The Philosopher of the Twentieth Century*,
 Andrew Brown (tr.), Cambridge: Polity Press, 2003
Levy, Neil, *Sartre*, Oxford: Oneworld Publications, 2002
Murphy, Julien S., *Feminist Interpretations of Jean-Paul Sartre*, University
 Park, Pennsylvania: Pennsylvania State University Press, 1999
Wicks, Robert, *Modern French Philosophy: From Existentialism to
 Postmodernism*, Oxford: Oneworld Publications, 2003

Michel Foucault

Halperin, David M., *Saint Foucault: Towards a Gay Hagiography*, Oxford:
 Oxford University Press, 1995
Hoy, David Cousins (ed.), *Foucault: A Critical Reader*, Oxford: Blackwell,
 1986
Macey, David, *The Lives of Michel Foucault*, New York: Pantheon Books,
 1993
Miller, James, *The Passion of Michel Foucault*, London: HarperCollins, 1993

INDEX

ABC of Atoms, The
(Bertrand Russell), 112
Abelard, Peter, 27, 128,
179
Abraham a Sancta
Clara, 155
AIDS, 66, 205, 221, 223
Alcibiades, 179
Alembert, Jean d', 21, 26
Alexander the Great,
225
Althusser, Louis, 207–8
Amberley, Lady Kate,
née Stanley (Bertrand
Russell's mother), 96
Amberley, Lord
(Bertrand Russell's
father), 96
Antichrist, The (Friedrich
Nietzsche), 86–7
anti-Semitism, 74, 76,
77, 83, 89, 91, 131,
149, 155, 164–5, 169
Archaeology of
Knowledge, The
(Michel Foucault), 216
Arendt, Hannah, 151,
153, 157–9, 160, 164,
165, 173, 174, 177
Aristotle, 43, 102, 203,
225
art, role of, 47, 48
Auden, W.H., 10
Augustine, St, 35, 146,
220
Autobiography (Bertrand
Russell), 103, 108, 124
Ayer, A.J., 208
Banville, John, 64

Barenboim, Daniel, 10
Barnes, Alfred, 116–17
Barraque, Jean, 210
Barry, Griffin, 114
Bartley, W.W., III, 134,
135
Bataille, Georges, 210
Baudelaire, Charles, 69
Bauhaus, 137
Baümler, Alfred, 91
Bayreuth Festival, 74, 75
Beauvoir, Simone de,
181, 186–8, 192, 201,
202
Beckett, Samuel, 41,
209
Beethoven, Ludwig van,
61, 82
Being and Nothingness
(Jean-Paul Sartre),
188, 190, 192, 198
Being and Time (Martin
Heidegger) 153, 156,
159, 162, 168, 173,
174, 176
Bell, Julian, 139, 148
Berlin, Isaiah, 38, 145
Berenson, Bernard, 98,
102
Berger, Georg, 135
Bergson, Henri, 185
Bernard, St, of
Clairvaux, 128
Bernhard, Thomas, 135
Beyond Good and Evil,
(Friedrich Nietzsche),
65
Birth of the Clinic, The
(Michel Foucault), 213

Birth of Tragedy, The
(Friedrich Nietzsche),
72
Bizet, Georges, 66, 85,
90
'Blue Book, The'
(Ludwig Wittgenstein),
144
Blunt, Anthony, 138
Bodhisattva, 46, 47, 62
Boothby, Brooke, 36–7
Borgia, Cesare, 13, 84,
91
Boswell, James, 34
Brahms, Johannes, 85,
129
Brandes, Georg, 85
Braithwaite, Richard, 143
Broad, Professor C.B.,
143
Brockhaus, Eberhard, 57
'Brown Book, The'
(Ludwig Wittgenstein),
144
Buddha, 46, 51
Buddhism, 13, 41, 45,
51, 61, 64
Bulow, Franz von, 73
Bultmann, Rudolph,
153, 166
Burkhardt, Jacob, 77, 84
Byron, Lord, 10, 98, 117

Caesar, Julius, 82
Campaign for Nuclear
Disarmament (CND),
93, 120
Camus, Albert, 64, 195,
199

Candide (Voltaire), 26
Carnap, Rudolf, 128, 138
Case of Wagner, The (Friedrich Nietzsche), 85
Castro, Fidel, 121, 199
Cérémonie des Adieux, La (Simone de Beauvoir), 181
Cheerful Science, The (Friedrich Nietzsche), 76, 79
Chomsky, Noam, 216
Cohen-Solal, Annie, 187
Committee of 100, 120
Communists and Peace (Jean-Paul Sartre), 196–7
Confessions (St Augustine), 35
Confessions (Jean-Jacques Rousseau), 9, 16, 28, 34, 35–6, 39
Conrad, Joseph, 41
Conti, Prince de, 35, 37
Critique of Dialectical Reason (Sartre), 198, 201
Cynics, 222

Darwin, Charles, 83, 95
Darwin, Erasmus, 34
Daybreak (Friedrich Nietzsche), 78
Daniel, Defert, 205, 213, 214, 223
Demetrius of Phaleron, 10, 225
Derrida, Jacques, 152, 159
Descartes, René, 7, 14, 141, 148, 185, 190
Deussen, Paul, 69

Discourse on Inequality (Second Discourse) (Jean-Jacques Rousseau), 24–5
Discourse on the Sciences and Arts (First Discourse) (Jean-Jacques Rousseau), 21–2
Diderot, Denis, 20, 21, 29
Dionysiac Dithyrambs (Friedrich Nietzsche), 88
Dionysius II of Syracuse, 9, 166
Dirty Hands (Jean-Paul Sartre), 196
Disgraceful Affair, A (Bianca Lamblin), 187
Dolorès V., 200
Donizetti, Gaetano, 69
Dostoevsky, Fyodor, 84, 140
Drury, Maurice, 141
Dudley, Helen, 107–8

Einstein, Albert, 93, 119
Ecce Homo (Friedrich Nietzsche), 87–8
Eliot, George, 60
Eliot, T.S., 107, 109–10, 123
Eliot, Vivien, 109–10
Elkaïm, Arlette, 201
Emile: Concerning Education (Jean-Jacques Rousseau), 29–31, 39
Engelmann, Paul, 134, 137
Epicurus, 10, 47, 54
Epinay, Madame d', 20, 27–8, 29
Encylopédie (Jean-Jacques Rousseau), 20, 23, 26

Eros and Civilization (Herbert Marcuse), 153
Estaing, Valéry Giscard d', 182
Ettinger, Elizabeta, 158
Euclid's axioms, 97
Euripides, 72, 102
existentialism, 63, 153, 154, 168, 188–9, 190, 193–5, 197–9, 201, 209, 228

Fascism, 13, 91
Fichte, Johann Gottlieb, 54, 55
Findlay, J.N., 127
First World War, 108–9, 133–4
Flies, The (Jean-Paul Sartre), 188
Förster, Bernard, 83
Foucault, Michel, 90, 201, 205–23, 228
 and AIDS, 205, 220, 221, 223
 and archaeologies, 212, 216
 and bathhouses, 205, 217, 218, 223
 and Christianity, 220
 and Communist Party, 207
 and Dominicans, 223
 and drugs, 207, 219
 and madness, 205, 211–12, 210
 and popular justice, 216
 and sadomasochism, 205, 207, 210, 213, 217, 218
 and suicide, 207, 210
 and voyeurism, 217
Frederick II of Prussia, 33

Free Man's Worship, A
(Bertrand Russell), 102
Frege, Gottlob, 105, 132, 137
French Revolution, 22, 38, 84, 165, 203
Freud, Sigmund, 41, 59, 77, 81, 90, 124, 128, 184
Fry, Roger, 105

Gast, Peter 78
Gaulle, President Charles de, 199
Genealogy of Morals, The (Nietzsche), 84–5
General Will, 32, 38–9
Genet, Jean, 194, 210
George III, King, 34
German Social Democracy (Bertrand Russell), 93
Gibbon, Edward, 98
Gillard, Paul, 114
Gladstone, William, 98
Gluck, Christoph Willibald, 23
Goethe, Wolfgang von, 52, 54–5, 56, 82, 86
Gray-Lucas, Peter, 127
Gréco, Juliet, 200
Greene, Graham, 110
Grimm brothers, 52
Gulag, 197

Habermas, Jurgens, 91, 115
Hayek, Friedrich, 145
Hegel, Georg Friedrich, 54, 57 58, 60, 99, 100, 101, 117, 213
Heidegger, Elfrida, née Petri (Martin Heidegger's wife), 157, 158, 159, 177

Heidegger, Friedrich (Martin Heidegger's father), 154–5
Heidegger, Johanna (Martin Heidegger's mother), 154
Heidegger, Martin, 9, 11, 91, 151–77, 159, 179, 188, 189, 190, 192, 193, 228
and adultery, 157–8, 174
and anti-Semitism, 152, 158, 159, 164, 165, 173, 174
and *Blut und Boden*, 152
and Christianity, 154–6
and *Dasein*, 160, 162–4
and Denazification Commission, 168
and *Der Spiegel* interview, 167
and enframing, 169, 171
and factory farming, 169, 173
and German nationalism, 165, 170, 171, 176
and Gestapo, 166
and *Gleichschaltun*, 151
and *Heimat*, 173, 177
and Holocaust, 169–71, 173, 174
and industrialization, 173
and *Lebenswelt*, 156
and the Nazi Party, 151–2, 155, 161, 162–7, 172, 173, 175
as Rector of Freiburg University, 152, 161, 167, 168, 172

and suicidal thoughts, 168
and thrownness, 160, 162
and *Volk*, 161–2
and Weimar Republic, 152, 162
Heine, Heinrich, 91
Héloïse, 179, 203
Heraclitus, 90
Hijab, Wasfi, 127
Hinduism, 41, 45, 46
Hippolyte, Jean, 185, 206
Historia Calamitatum (Peter Abelard), 179
History of Western Philosophy (Bertrand Russell), 93, 117
Hitler, Adolf, 39, 89, 91, 121, 149, 161, 163, 165, 176
Hobbes, Thomas, 24, 31
Hofmannsthal, Hugo von, 128
homosexuality, 116–17, 119, 130–1, 134, 138, 186, 194, 203, 205–6
Houdetot, Sophie de, 28–9, 36
Houellebecq, Michel, 41
Human, All Too Human (Friedrich Nietzsche), 76–7
Hume, David, 33–5, 156
Huis Clos (Jean-Paul Sartre), 188, 195, 200
Husserl, Edmund, 151, 156, 165, 172, 174, 187, 188, 190
Huxley, Aldous, 104, 109, 115, 123
Hypatia of Alexandria, 203

Islam, 87

Isle Adam, Villiers de l',
62

Jaspers, Karl, 91, 158,
159, 161, 165, 167,
170
Jonas, Hans, 153

Kant, Immanuel, 10, 11,
45, 49, 53, 54, 65, 76,
91, 117, 143, 213
Kennedy, J.F., 121
Keynes, John Maynard,
99, 123, 124, 125
Kierkegaard, Søren, 159,
190
Klimt, Gustav, 128, 129
Kokoschka, Oskar, 128
Kosakiewicz, Olga, 186,
192
Kosakiewicz, Wanda, 187

La Rochefoucauld,
François, duc de, 76,
77
Lamblin, Bianca, 187,
192
Laforgue, Jules, 62
Lambercier, Mlle, 17
Lawrence, D.H., 90,
104, 124
Leavis, F.R., 149
Léglise-Vian, Michelle,
200
Lenin, Vladimir Ilyich,
101, 111
Letter on Humanism
(Martin Heidegger),
168-9
Levasseur, Thérèse, 20,
24, 27, 29, 34, 35, 39
Lévi-Strauss, Claude,
185
Lévy, Benny (a.k.a.
Pierre Victor), 181,
201

Lévy, Bernard-Henri,
181, 194
Lisbon earthquake, 25-6
Liszt, Franz, 73
Locke, John, 31
Logical Positivism, 11,
125, 128, 138
Loos, Adolf, 137
Louis XV, King, 23
Löwith, Karl, 167
Luxembourg, Duke and
Duchess of, 29, 33, 37

Machiavelli, Niccolò,
84, 98
Mahler, Gustav, 10, 64,
128, 129
Malcolm, Norman,
139-40, 145, 147
Mancy, Joseph (Jean-
Paul Sartre's
stepfather), 183-4
Manet, Edouard, 69
Mann, Thomas, 41, 69
Marcuse, Herbert, 91,
115, 153, 169
Marguet, Caroline, 60
Marie-Antoinette,
Queen, 37
Marx, Karl, 13, 101, 143
masochism, 17
masturbation, 29, 76
Meistersinger, Die
(Richard Wagner), 70
Merleau-Ponty, Maurice,
152, 185, 188, 196,
207
Mill, J.S., 96, 98
Monk, Ray, 95, 134
Montaigne, Michel de,
22, 43, 76
Montessori, Maria, 39
Moore, G.E., 99, 118,
138, 145
Moral Letters (Jean-
Jacques Rousseau), 29

Morrell, Lady Ottoline,
104-6, 107, 108, 111,
123, 133
Morrell, Philip, 104
Mozart, Wolfgang
Amadeus, 61
Murdoch, Iris, 203
Musil, Robert, 128
Mussolini, Benito, 91

Napoleon I, 55, 82, 90,
96
Nazism, 90, 151-5,
161-2, 163-4, 165-7,
169-70, 171-6
Nausea (Jean-Paul
Sartre), 188, 189, 193,
197, 200
Newton, Isaac, 56
Nietzsche, Elisabeth
Förster (Friedrich
Nietzsche's sister), 68,
73, 81, 83, 89
Nietzsche, Franziska
(Friedrich Nietzsche's
mother), 68, 85, 89
Nietzsche, Friedrich, 9,
13, 61, 63-90, 117,
124, 140, 147, 159,
160, 164, 166, 167,
179, 185, 207, 209,
210, 211, 214, 215,
228
attacks anti-Semitism,
77
and Christianity, 13,
67, 68-70, 78, 79,
84, 87, 90
and compositions, 73
and Dionysus, 67, 72,
89, 90
and Francophilia, 76
and Germanophobia,
74, 75, 88, 90
and health problems,
66, 68, 70, 77, 87-9

and masochism, 68, 90
and poverty, 83
resigns university post,
 77
and syphilis, 66, 69,
 80, 87
and Übermensch, 66, 82,
 84, 86, 90
Nietzsche, Karl Ludwig
 (Friedrich Nietzsche's
 father), 68
Nobel Prize, 93, 102,
 199, 200
Nouvelle Héloïse, La
 (Jean-Jacques
 Rousseau), 27–8, 39

Offenbach, Jacques, 91
On Education (Bertrand
 Russell), 112
O'Neil, Colette, 110, 118
On the Fourfold Root of
 the Principal of
 Sufficient Reason
 (Arthur
 Schopenhauer), 45
Order of Things, The
 (Michel Foucault), 213
Oupnekhat, The
 (Friedrich Majer), 45
Overbeck, Franz, 81, 89
Ovid, 179

Parerga and Paralipomena
 (Arthur
 Schopenhauer), 42, 60
Parsifal (Richard
 Wagner), 75, 76
Pascal, Fania, 140
Pavlov, Ivan, 111
Pearsall Smith, Hannah
 (Bertrand Russell's first
 mother-in-law), 98
Pearsall Smith, Logan
 (Bertrand Russell's first
 brother-in-law), 98

Pearsall Smith, Mary
 (Bertrand Russell's first
 sister-in-law), 98, 102
Pearsall Smith, Robert
 (Bertrand Russell's first
 father-in-law), 98
Pestalozzi, Johann, 39
philosopher-king, 9, 166,
 225
Philosophical
 Investigations (Ludwig
 Wittgenstein), 125,
 126, 153
Picasso, Pablo, 10
Pilgrim Fathers, 31
Pinsent, David, 133
Pirandello, Luigi, 91
Plato, 9, 17, 22, 32, 41,
 48, 53, 59, 99, 115,
 131, 143, 145, 158,
 164, 166, 171, 203,
 225
Plotinus, 146
Pompadour, Madame de,
 23
Popper, Karl, 115, 143–4
Porphyry, 146
Pound, Ezra, 91
Powys, John Cowper,
 114
Pre-Socratic
 philosophers, 90, 152
Prime of Life, The
 (Simone de Beauvoir),
 186
Principia Mathematica
 (Bertrand Russell and
 Alfred North
 Whitehead), 101–2,
 106
Principles of Mathematics
 (Bertrand Russell),
 101, 106
Problems of Philosophy
 (Bertrand Russell), 105
Proust, Marcel, 41, 62

Ptolemy I, 225
Pythagoras, 99

Rabinow, Paul, 215
Rameau, Jean-Philippe,
 23
Ree, Paul, 67, 75, 80–8,
 90
Reprieve, The (Jean-Paul
 Sartre), 189
Republic, The (Plato), 9
Revaluation of All Values,
 The (Friedrich
 Nietzsche), 65
Reveries of the Solitary
 Walker (Jean-Jacques
 Rousseau), 37
Richter, Caroline, 58, 60
Rilke, Rainer Maria, 64,
 81
Ring of the Nibelungen,
 The (Richard Wagner),
 61, 75
Ritschl, Professor
 Friedrich, 69, 71
'Roads to Freedom'
 trilogy (Jean-Paul
 Sartre), 188
Robespierre,
 Maximilien, 15, 33, 38
Robinson Crusoe (Daniel
 Defoe), 29–30
Rohde, Erwin, 70, 71,
 74, 77
Romanticism, 15, 16, 38,
 40, 66
Rossini, Gioacchino, 61
Rousseau, Jean-Jacques,
 5–40, 84, 165, 203, 227
 abandons children, 20
 and amour de soi, 15, 22
 and amour-propre, 15,
 22
 and Christianity, 13,
 18, 22, 25, 26, 31,
 33, 35

and democracy, 30–2
and Genevan
citizenship, 27, 33
and masochism, 17
and music notation
system, 19
and theatre, 26, 40
and views on education,
29–30
and women's inferiority,
24, 26, 30
Rotblatt, Joseph, 121
Roussell, Raymond, 213
Russell, Agatha
(Bertrand Russell's
aunt), 97
Russell, Alys, née Logan
Smith (Bertrand
Russell's first wife),
98–9, 100–1, 103, 110
Russell, Bertrand, 11,
93–124, 125–6, 132–3,
227–8
and ancestral pride,
95, 111, 114
and apostles, 99
and appeasement of
Hitler, 116
and his children's
upbringing, 111–14,
115
and Christianity, 96–9,
100, 105, 114, 116
and Communism, 101,
110–11, 121–2
and divorces, 110, 115,
115
and First World War,
108–9
is imprisoned, 109, 121
and fear of madness,
95, 97
and marriages, 100,
110, 115
and Nobel Prize, 93,
102, 119

and Order of Merit,
117
political career, 103,
108–9, 113, 117, 120
is rejected by New
York City University,
116
and Telegraph School,
112–14
and Soviet Union,
110–11, 117–18, 120
Russell, Conrad
(Bertrand Russell's
second son), 116, 118,
123
Russell, Dora, née Black
(Bertrand Russell's
second wife), 110, 113,
114, 118, 119, 122
Russell, Edith, née Finch
(Bertrand Russell's
fourth wife), 122
Russell, Frank (Bertrand
Russell's brother), 97,
112 , 115
Russell, Kate (Bertrand
Russell's daughter),
105, 112, 115, 117,
122, 124
Russell, Lady (Bertrand
Russell's grandmother),
96–7, 100
Russell, Lucy (Bertrand
Russell's
granddaughter), 119,
122–3
Russell, Lord John
(Bertrand Russell's
grandfather), 96
Russell, John (Bertrand
Russell's elder son),
95, 111–12, 113,
116–17, 118–19,
122
Russell, Patricia 'Peter'
(Bertrand Russell's

third wife), 114–15,
116
Russell, Rollo (Bertrand
Russell's uncle), 97, 98
Russell, Sarah
(Bertrand Russell's
granddaughter), 122
Russell, Susan, née
Lindsay (Bertrand
Russell's daughter-in-
law), 119
Russell, Willy (Bertrand
Russell's uncle), 97, 98
'Russell–Einstein
Manifesto', 119
'Russell's Paradox', 101
Ryle, Gilbert, 145–6

Sade, Marquis de, 17, 18,
208, 210, 211
Saint Genet (Jean-Paul
Sartre), 194
Saint-Lambert, Marquis
de, 29
Salis, Meta von, 83, 88
Salomé, Lou, 14, 67,
79–81, 179
Santayana, George, 97
Sartre, Anne-Marie
(Jean-Paul Sartre's
mother), 182–4
Sartre, Jean-Paul, 11,
152, 153, 159, 167,
175, 181–202, 207,
208, 220, 228
and Algerian Civil
War, 199
and authority figures,
183–5
and brutality in sex,
187
and castration fears,
191
and Christianity, 193
and for-itself, 190–2,
198

and funeral, 182
and in-itself, 190–2,
 198
and masochism, 190
and Marxism, 182,
 198–9., 201
and *mauvaise foi*, 181,
 189, 197
and *ménages à trois*,
 186–7, 192
and mescaline, 200
and rejection of Nobel
 Prize for Literature,
 199
and Soviet
 Communism, 196–8
and Soviet invasion of
 Czechoslovakia, 200
and Soviet invasion of
 Hungary, 197
and Vietnam War, 199,
 201
and War Crimes
 Commission, 200
Scaevola, Mucius, 68
Schlick, Moritz, 138
Schoenberg, Arnold, 69,
 128
Schoenman, Ralph, 95,
 120–2
Schopenhauer, Adele
 (Arthur
 Schopenhauer's sister),
 50, 52, 58, 60
Schopenhauer, Arthur,
 41–62, 70, 79, 147,
 159, 203
 and art, 47, 62
 and atheism, 57
 and Buddhism, 45, 46,
 61
 and childhood neglect,
 50
 and grand tour, 51
 lectures in Berlin,
 57–8

and money, 59–60
and music, 48
and paranoia, 42,
 43–4, 49
and political views, 43
and poodles, 49
and routine, 49
and views on sex, 41,
 58, 59, 61
and views on suicide, 52
and views on women,
 44
Schopenhauer as Educator
 (Friedrich Nietzsche),
 70, 209
Schopenhauer, Heinrich
 Floris (Arthur
 Schopenhauer's
 father), 49–51
Schopenhauer, Johanna
 (Arthur
 Schopenhauer's
 mother), 44, 50–6, 57
Schubert, Franz, 52, 69
Schweitzer, Albert, 182
Second Sex, The (Simone
 de Beauvoir), 203
Sex and Character (Otto
 Weininger), 131
Shakespeare, William,
 146
Shaw, George Bernard,
 64, 140
Shelley, P.B., 38, 98
Skinner, Francis, 140–1
Social Contract, The
 (Jean-Jacques
 Rousseau), 29, 31–3
Socrates, 9, 72, 86, 116,
 146, 179
Spalding, Douglas, 96
Spengler, Oswald, 131
Spinoza, Benedict,
 10–11, 31, 90
Stalin, Josef, 71, 140,
 198

Stendhal, 76
Stonborough, Margaret
 (Ludwig Wittgenstein's
 sister), 129
Strachey, Lytton, 99,
 104, 123
Strindberg, August, 64,
 85
Strauss, Richard, 64, 66,
 129

Tagore, Rabindranath,
 138
Temps modernes, Les (ed.
 Jean-Paul Sartre), 182,
 188, 195
Thus Spake Zarathustra
 (Friedrich Nietzsche),
 63, 65, 66
Tillich, Paul, 153, 157,
 166
*Tractatus
 Logico-Philosophicus, The*
 (Ludwig Wittgenstein),
 61, 106–7, 125, 126,
 131, 133, 134, 136,
 137, 138, 141, 142,
 143, 148
Tristan und Isolde
 (Richard Wagner),
 61
Turing, Alan, 144–5
Twilight of the Idols
 (Friedrich Nietzsche),
 63, 86
Tolstoy, Leo, 41, 133,
 140, 146

Untimely Meditations
 (Friedrich Nietzsche),
 76–7
Upanishads, The, 45

Vermeer, Jan, 62
Vienna Circle, 125, 126,
 136–8

Vindication of the Rights of Woman, A (Mary Wollstonecraft), 203
Vinnalot, John, 127
Virgil, 38
Voltaire, 21, 25–6, 36, 38, 95

Wagner, Cosima (Richard Wagner's second wife), 71, 73–4, 77
Wagner, Richard, 10, 60–1, 65, 67, 70–6, 83, 85, 86 131
Waiting for Godot (Samuel Beckett), 209
Walpole, Horace, 34
Walter, Bruno, 129
War Crimes Tribunal, 121
Warens, Madame de, 18, 19
Watson, J.B., 111–12
Webb, Beatrice, 103, 140
Webb, Sidney, 103, 140
Weininger, Otto, 131–2, 133
Weil, Simone, 185, 186
Whitehead, Alfred North, 11, 94, 101–3, 108
Whitehead, Evelyn, 102–3
Wieland, Christoph, 41, 53
Wilde, Oscar, 98
Will to Know, The (Michel Foucault), 219
Wittgenstein, Hans (Ludwig Wittgenstein's brother), 129, 130
Wittgenstein, Hermine (Ludwig Wittgenstein's sister), 106

Wittgenstein, Karl (Ludwig Wittgenstein's father), 128–30, 131, 132
Wittgenstein, Kurt (Ludwig Wittgenstein's brother), 130
Wittgenstein, Ludwig, 12, 57, 61, 94, 106–7, 118, 125–50, 152, 228
 and Christianity, 12, 128, 130–1, 136, 146–8
 as engineer, 132
 and homosexuality, 130, 131 134, 136, 139, 140
 and lifestyle, 135, 150
 and personality cult, 149
 and religious feelings, 128, 131, 136, 147–8, 150
 as schoolteacher, 134–6
 and Soviet Union, 144
 and suicidal thoughts, 130, 132, 133, 134
 and wealth 129, 134–5, 141
Wittgenstein, Rudolf (Ludwig Wittgenstein's brother), 130
Wodehouse, P.G., 139
Wolin, Richard, 152
Wolff, Michael, 144
Wollstonecraft, Mary, 203
Wordsworth, William, 39
World as Will and Representation, The (Arthur Schopenhauer), 42, 56–7, 70

Yeats, W.B., 64, 90

Zamyatin, Yevgeny, 115
Zeno of Citium, 10